POWERLIFTING

Dan Austin ▪ Bryan Mann, PhD

Human Kinetics

Library of Congress Cataloging-in-Publication Data

Austin, Dan, 1958-
  Powerlifting / Dan Austin, Bryan Mann.
    p. cm.
  ISBN 978-0-7360-9464-1 (soft cover) -- ISBN 0-7360-9464-4 (soft cover)
  1. Weight lifting. I. Mann, Bryan, 1979- II. Title.
  GV546.3.A87 2012
  796.41--dc23
                          2011049601

ISBN-10: 0-7360-9464-4 (print)
ISBN-13: 978-0-7360-9464-1 (print)

This publication is written and published to provide accurate and authoritative information relevant to the subject matter presented. It is published and sold with the understanding that the author and publisher are not engaged in rendering legal, medical, or other professional services by reason of their authorship or publication of this work. If medical or other expert assistance is required, the services of a competent professional person should be sought.

Acquisitions Editor: Justin Klug; **Developmental Editor:** Cynthia McEntire; **Assistant Editor:** Elizabeth Evans; **Copyeditor:** Joanna Hatzopoulos Portman; **Permissions Manager:** Martha Gullo; **Graphic Designer:** Bob Reuther; **Graphic Artist:** Francine Hamerski; **Cover Designer:** Keith Blomberg; **Photographer (cover):** Neil Bernstein; **Photographer (interior):** Neil Bernstein; **Visual Production Assistant:** Joyce Brumfield; **Photo Production Manager:** Jason Allen; **Art Manager:** Kelly Hendren; **Associate Art Manager:** Alan L. Wilborn; **Illustrations:** © Human Kinetics; **Printer:** McNaughton & Gunn

We thank the University of Missouri in Columbia, Missouri, for assistance in providing the location for the shoot for this book.

Human Kinetics books are available at special discounts for bulk purchase. Special editions or book excerpts can also be created to specification. For details, contact the Special Sales Manager at Human Kinetics.

Printed in the United States of America.   10   9   8   7   6

The paper in this book is certified under a sustainable forestry program.

Human Kinetics
Web site: www.HumanKinetics.com

United States: Human Kinetics
P.O. Box 5076
Champaign, IL 61825-5076
800-747-4457
e-mail: humank@hkusa.com

Canada: Human Kinetics
475 Devonshire Road, Unit 100
Windsor, ON N8Y 2L5
800-465-7301 (in Canada only)
e-mail: info@hkcanada.com

Europe: Human Kinetics
107 Bradford Road
Stanningley
Leeds LS28 6AT, United Kingdom
+44 (0)113 255 5665
e-mail: hk@hkeurope.com

Australia: Human Kinetics
57A Price Avenue
Lower Mitcham, South Australia 5062
08 8372 0999
e-mail: info@hkaustralia.com

New Zealand: Human Kinetics
P.O. Box 80
Mitcham Shopping Centre, South Australia 5062
0800 222 062
e-mail: info@hknewzealand.com

POWERLIFTING

Contents

Guide to Muscles **vi**

1 **Physiology of Strength and Power** 1

2 **Muscle Fueling** 9

3 **Power Training Preparation** 23

4 **Squat** 47

5 **Bench Press** 69

6 **Deadlift** 99

7 Power Periodization 121

8 Foundational Training 133

9 Experienced Training 151

10 Advanced Training. 159

11 Powerlifting Mindset 173

12 Meet Preparation 185

13 Meet Day 195

About the Authors   **211**

Guide to Muscles

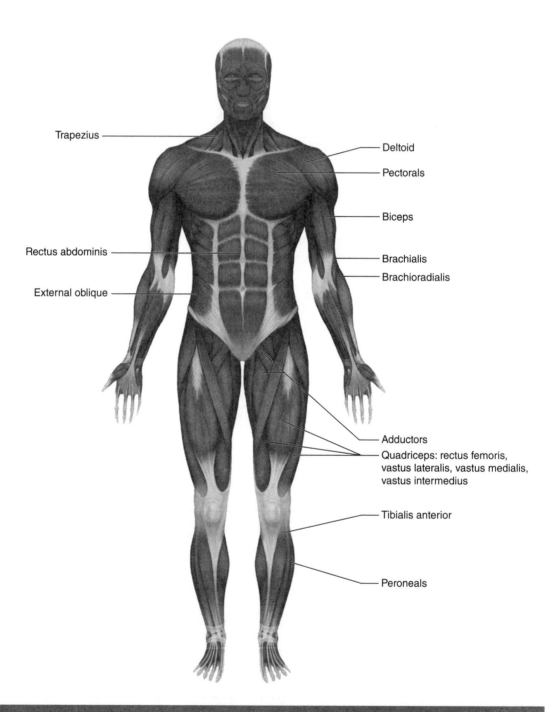

Trapezius

Deltoid

Pectorals

Biceps

Rectus abdominis

Brachialis

Brachioradialis

External oblique

Adductors

Quadriceps: rectus femoris, vastus lateralis, vastus medialis, vastus intermedius

Tibialis anterior

Peroneals

FRONT VIEW

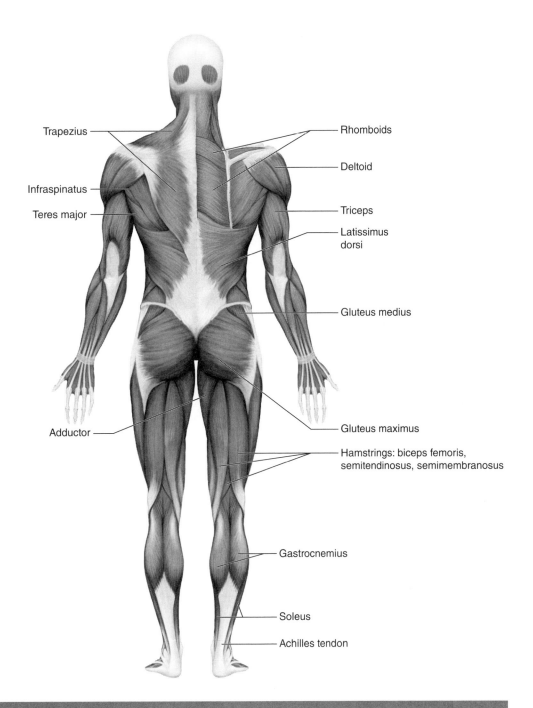

Trapezius

Infraspinatus

Teres major

Adductor

Rhomboids

Deltoid

Triceps

Latissimus dorsi

Gluteus medius

Gluteus maximus

Hamstrings: biceps femoris, semitendinosus, semimembranosus

Gastrocnemius

Soleus

Achilles tendon

BACK VIEW

CHAPTER 1

Physiology of Strength and Power

To understand how the body works in powerlifting, you first must understand some basic physiology. A basic understanding does not include topics such as sliding filament theory, the way the mitochondria work in the cell, or the role of fatty acids in metabolism for a long day at a meet. If those topics interest you, you can read books on exercise physiology or even take courses in human anatomy, physiology, and kinesiology. This chapter covers the level of physiology you need to know to become as strong as possible and perform optimally on competition day.

Motor Learning

Knowing how the body learns can help you understand how and why to use various techniques. For example, think about how an infant learns to walk. He observes people walking and he wants to try it too. After watching and analyzing others, he begins to try to walk. He slowly pulls himself up to a stand, he wobbles, and he falls down. Next he pulls himself up to a stand, he wobbles, and takes a step or two before falling down. Eventually after persistence, practice, and muscle development, he begins to walk naturally.

In their book *Weightlifting: Fitness for All Sports* (International Weightlifting Federation 1988), Tamás Aján and Lazar Baroga said that every movement, no matter how new it may seem, is based on previously learned movement patterns. So the more motor patterns you possess, the more movement patterns you can learn and the more quickly you can learn them. Consider two people who start squatting. Why does one struggle while the other excels? Because one person already possessed the necessary motor patterns and the other did not. The second person may be able to master the technique and excel at the squat but needs more time. A coach or trainer must demonstrate the movement several times so the struggling lifter understands it, then the lifter must get under the bar and do it himself. At first the movements feel funny to him, and he does all sorts of funny things as well, just as a baby does when trying to walk for the first time. The lifter may crash his knees together then do an impression of the worm break dance, but while standing with a weight on his back. He may perform something that looks like a good morning with bent legs. All along, he is attempting to put together movements that resemble the squat. The coach's job is to teach him to be aware of what he's doing wrong and how to fix it. Eventually he will have a squatlike movement down but will still need to refine his technique. Louie Simmons once said that a coach needs to educate each one of his lifters to the point at which the lifter is a coach. That way whenever you're doing a lift, you'll have 10 coaches watching instead of one.

When learning a new technique, it helps if you can watch someone who has great technique, be coached on the technique, and then perform the lift yourself. If anything in this sequence has to be dropped, it should be watching someone with great technique. The coaching is crucial. If you don't know what it's supposed to feel like, you won't realize when you are doing it wrong.

When someone first begins lifting, he experiences humongous gains in strength. It is not uncommon for someone who just begins lifting to put 30 or 40 pounds on his bench in a month or even less. This has a lot to do with increasing the efficiency of the neuromuscular system. Essentially the brain is the CPU that runs the entire body. Nothing happens in the body that the brain has not processed either consciously or subconsciously. When gaining strength at this rate, the lifter does not add any muscle; it takes too long to add any significant muscle to improve strength by this much, this quickly. The body simply learns how to do the movement and recruit more motor units that it already has. Remember the saying, *Use it or lose it.* The body has many high-threshold motor units it has never used. You must learn to use them or you will never be able to recruit them in regard to weight training.

Motor units work as all or nothing. When a motor neuron causes a muscle to contract, all the fibers that the nerve innervates will contract. It is impossible for some of the fibers to contract but others not when the nerve impulse is sent. However realize that one nerve doesn't innervate all of any one major muscle group. Several nerves innervate the muscle, so if it will take more muscle to lift a weight, then more neurons will fire to recruit more muscle.

The entire muscle doesn't work all of the time; only a few units are used at a time. For example, consider the biceps. When raising a 12-ounce can of soda to the lips, the biceps recruits enough motor units to move the can from the table to the mouth. Now, if the biceps used everything it had to lift the 12-ounce can, the speed at which it was moved and the force generated would not allow the can to stop before the mouth. Instead it probably would bust open a lip and knock out some teeth. Conversely, if the biceps had to perform a curl with 40 pounds, which is a load often encountered by the body in everyday life, it would be able to recruit the number of fibers to do that. Say you're moving up to a personal record curl of 85 pounds. The first time you try it, you may not be able to complete it or it may look ugly. However, you try the 85-pound curl again the following week and it goes up smoothly. No muscle was added, but the body learned how to recruit motor units that were previously unused.

When dealing with more complex exercises such as the powerlifts, the motor units from different muscle groups have to work together. These lifts are much more complex than a simple single-joint exercise such as the curl. Think of a single-joint exercise as teaching a task to one 3-year-old child. It's tough at first, but the child catches on and is able to do simple things on his own. A complex exercise is like getting 15 3-year-olds to do one task. When most of them are heading in the right direction, a few decide to take off and do their own thing. When learning the squat, sometimes lifters can't push their hips back appropriately, sometimes their knees crash in, and sometimes their hips rise out of the hole before their shoulders. It takes time to be able to recruit the motor units in the proper muscles at the proper time in the proper sequence. It takes constant coaching from others for someone to be able to do the exercise properly.

Two types of motor recruitment exist—*intra*muscular and *inter*muscular—and thus two types of muscle learning exist too. Intramuscular motor recruitment occurs within the muscle. It is a single muscle group learning how to do something better and work within itself. In intramuscular coordination, muscle fibers of an individual muscle learn to work together more efficiently in order to produce more strength or speed.

In intermuscular coordination, the muscles learn to work with each other to perform gross movements more efficiently. Efficiency is gained when muscles perform the movements over and over again, but while trying to use the best form possible. For instance, think of an uncoordinated kid who just finished a growth spurt and is trying to perform a lunge for the first time. Most likely he will fall over to the side, drop his chest, possibly even fall backward when lunging forward. If he continues with proper coaching, eventually he will be able to lunge with the chest up and body in a straight line, not fall, and look good doing it. At that point of competency, the muscles have learned to perform the task. This phenomenon resembles a worker in a factory. At first a new worker at an auto plant may take 3 hours to put together a transmission. With repetition, however, he learns how to do it efficiently and the time is cut in half. It is simply learning how to do things. Once you have learned how to do something, you can do it more efficiently and more quickly.

While the body gains strength very quickly by learning how to use its motor units more efficiently, gaining muscle is a much slower and more arduous process. You can gain strength more quickly than muscle.

Agonist Versus Antagonist Muscle

The muscle that is actively doing the work and producing the force to move the weight is called the *agonist*. The agonist can be a prime mover, secondary mover, or stabilizer. The *antagonist* is the muscle or muscle group opposite the agonist. When the agonist is working, the antagonist is relaxing.

Typically agonists and antagonists are on opposite sides of the joint. For example, examine the elbow joint. During a biceps curl, the biceps is doing the lifting so it is the agonist. The triceps, the antagonist, is relaxed, allowing the greatest contraction and range of motion for the biceps. If the agonist and antagonist contract at the same time, the muscle is unable to change its length. In the rare event that the muscle length does change, meaning one muscle group is stronger than the other and wins the tug of war, the bar movement is inefficient and the bar moves very slowly. In this situation, the weight isn't the opponent, the body is.

Motor Learning Enhancement

Sport psychology for powerlifting will be discussed in great detail later. Meanwhile, this section covers an intrinsic portion of learning technique that greatly speeds up the process for any exercise: the use of Cook's model (Vernacchia, McGuire, and Cook, 1996, *Coaching Mental Excellence,* Warde Publishers, page 84). This model uses the mental routine "See it, feel it, trust it, believe it, and achieve it." This model works well because the visualization prepares the nerves involved in the movement to fire in the proper sequence. Visualization is a proven method. If you are having a hard time performing an exercise or correcting technique, go back to Cook's model to improve your technique.

The first step is to see it: You have to see yourself doing the technique properly, like a movie in your head. You must see everything—the weight, the crowd, and the judges. You must see yourself perform the exercise successfully with perfect form, with three white lights on the judges' board.

The next step is to feel it: Feel the weight, the gear, the platform, the crowd, the power, and the muscles firing in proper sequence. Taste the air and smell the ammonia and liniment in the air.

Once those two steps are complete, you must believe you can execute the weight with perfect form and trust yourself to be able to act on it. Next is to simply go achieve it.

Muscle Fibers

The body has two main muscle fiber types and an indefinite number of smaller types. The main types are slow-twitch and fast-twitch fibers. Slow-twitch muscle fibers are slow. They are primarily endurance fibers that are set to go all day but can't produce much force per contraction. Slow-twitch fibers are used in everyday walking and standing.

Fast-twitch fibers are fast and produce power. These fibers are used in activities that require more effort such as sprinting, jumping, throwing, and lifting weights. How strong or explosive a person can be greatly depends on muscle fiber type. People are born with predominately one type or the other. This is why some people are naturally good at endurance exercises but can't bench the bar or can sprint a 10-second 100-meter dash but can't run a full lap without getting gassed. Because of their fiber type, some people naturally are able to lift more weight than others who are similarly sized even with no training. Fiber type is a big reason a guy who weighs 165 pounds can bench 405 pounds for multiple repetitions. He has a high predominance of fast-twitch fibers that produce more force and allow him to move more weight with a smaller muscle mass.

Building Muscle

Many people think that muscle is built in the weight room because that is where they see it get big. This assumption is both right and wrong. Muscles get big as a function of what is done in the weight room, but they don't get big in the weight room. They get big in the bedroom.

Hypertrophy

When weights are lifted, microtraumas occur to the muscle fibers. The concentric and eccentric contractions of the muscles as they lift and lower the weights cause some damage, especially if the lifter is using progressive overload and forcing the muscles to adapt to a new stimulus. Along with this damage, additional blood and fluid flow to the muscles, providing that pumped-up feeling familiar to lifters. When the muscle is damaged, the body repairs itself by various means. It doesn't want damaged muscle fibers, so it will rebuild them. The body also recognizes that it needs more muscle to meet the demand imposed on it, so it adds muscle. It breaks down proteins in the damaged muscle and adds more proteins on top to create the additional muscle. These additions are made in small amounts at a time, so it takes time to add any additional muscle. Adding muscle is called *hypertrophy*.

There are two speculated types of hypertrophy. One is functional, or myofibrillar hypertrophy. The other is nonfunctional, or cytoplasmic hypertrophy. Myofibrillar hypertrophy develops from the use of heavy weights. This is typically a much slower means of gaining muscle size, but the increase in the size of the muscle fiber increases the strength of the muscle fiber. This hypertrophy occurs in the myofibril's actin and myosin within the muscle, which increases the strength of contraction.

Cytoplasmic hypertrophy develops from using lighter weight and higher volume. It taxes the muscle, but not in how much it is able to move. The damage to the muscle is different. Therefore, the myofibrils don't increase, but the space in between the sarcomeres does. This type of hypertrophy does not feature consistency between the size of the muscle and the force it can produce, which is why it is called nonfunctional.

The goal of powerlifting is to be able to move the greatest amount of weight on the bar with the lightest bodyweight possible. To do this, you want to ensure that you focus on functional rather than nonfunctional hypertrophy. Bodybuilding relies primarily on high volumes of exercises with short rest periods and light weights to get the greatest amount of volume in the shortest time. This method makes a person bigger, but not stronger. There is an old saying that *big ain't strong, only strong is strong.* Many bodybuilders look as if they could bench press 900 pounds, but they struggle with 315. This is because the type of hypertrophy they have induced. The powerlifter, on the other hand, is often deceptive. Jason Fry, who competes at either the 181- or 198-pound weight class, looks like an in-shape guy. If you saw him in the gym, you'd think he could bench maybe 365 pounds. However, he has benched well over 750 pounds at the 181-pound weight class and 770 pounds at the 198-pound weight class, so obviously his size is very deceptive. His hypertrophy development has all been functional, and all of the muscle he has gained puts out force.

SAID Principle

The improvement of strength is based on the **s**pecific **a**daptations to **i**mposed **d**emands, or SAID, principle. The body adapts to the stimulus placed on it. For instance, consider someone who gets a job in construction. He starts out swinging an 8-pound sledgehammer all day. When he goes home at night, he is so tired and sore he can't do anything except fall down on the couch and go to sleep without showering. Three weeks later, he can swing that 8-pound hammer all day and be fine. He could even go out and play recreation league softball after work without a problem. However, if he breaks his hammer and has to use one a couple of pounds heavier, he is right back on the couch after work until he adapts to the new hammer weight. This is because his body adapted to the stimulus of the 8-pound hammer. The hammer imposed a demand on the body that led to a specific adaptation in muscle. The body wasn't ready for more than the 8-pound hammer, so he became fatigued and sore.

Progressive Overload

The progressive overload principle states that once the body adapts to the imposed demand from the SAID principle, you need a heavier weight. You use progressively heavier weights to impose new demands on the body, thus making another adaptation. The ancient Greek wrestler Milo of Croton is a classic example of progressive overload. Milo decided that to get stronger, he would hoist a calf on his shoulders and walk laps around the arena. He did this every day and as the calf grew in size, Milo gained in strength. He became so strong that he was never pinned by anyone in Greece and finished his wrestling career undefeated.

Progressive overload is how most periodized programs work. They start with a lower weight and, over the course of the training cycle, work up to a higher weight through a preplanned increase each week, causing the adaptation to occur by overloading the muscle. Just like Milo and his calf, you can get stronger by moving up in weight each week.

Valsalva Maneuver

When people train with weights for health, they are taught to breathe in on the eccentric contraction and out on the concentric contraction. In powerlifting, this technique is incorrect. In powerlifting, you use the *Valsalva maneuver*. With this technique, you bring in the air and hold it to create a fluid ball effect. The pressure that usually causes headaches is also the same pressure that protects the spine under maximal loads and allows the force to transfer through the body rather than stop at a soft spot. For instance, on the squat, the lifter attempts to draw in as much air as possible to expand the stomach. This locks the chest into place, preventing the lifter from rounding over to the front. If the athlete did not hold in the air, the chest would crumple forward from the weight and the legs, no matter how strong they were, would not be able to drive the bar up because it was already going down from the weakness.

Force transfers most perfectly through hard surfaces. The lifter who can get tight and create the most pressure possible is able to transfer the most force through the body and lift the most weight. Consider pushing a car in the snow or on concrete. Which is easier? On concrete, the force you apply to the ground is directly applied back to the car. In snow, however, the force applied toward the ground is dispersed by the snow and not transferred.

This principle is true for all exercises. The more tightness and pressure developed for each exercise, the more force can be transferred, even on the bench press. Consider the ageless wonder, Bill Gillespie, as an example on the bench press. Bill turns purple at 135 pounds because he trains the body to put out the pressure to get tight and transfer the force.

Blood Pressure

A powerlifter's blood pressure goes up into the zones of a myocardial infarction (heart attack) during a maximal attempt. Look at nearly any picture of a power- lifter during squat or deadlift maximal attempt; he is purple. All the muscles are contracting maximally, putting pressure on the arteries and veins and making it difficult for blood to flow through the body. This causes the heart to work harder and push the blood harder.

Remember the SAID principle? This is another example of it. Since the heart has to work harder to overcome resistive forces and push the blood through the body, the left ventricle greatly increases in size and density. Essentially this prevents the left ventricle from bursting. The heart is a muscle like any other. When it has to work harder, it grows in size.

When the heart increases in size as a result of pumping blood through the body, it also increases in contractility, which helps push the blood through without much resistance. In powerlifting, the muscle has to push against great pressure, causing it to get stiffer. This effect needs to be balanced through some sort of cardiovascular work, not necessarily high intensity cardio work, but something that makes the heart work. The heart needs to get its good work in, too.

Summary

The specific adaptations to imposed demands (SAID) principle governs all types of training. In powerlifting, the goal of training is to become stronger, so the demand imposed on the body must cause the adaptation of greater strength. If the right demands are not placed on the body, the adaptations will never occur and the lifter will never become stronger and achieve personal records in any of his lifts.

The concept of progressive overload has been around since Milo of Croton. It involves using a heavier weight each week over time to create an overload that gets progressively heavier, causing the body to adapt, again using the SAID principle.

The Valsalva maneuver is key to all competitors. It works by increasing internal pressure, thereby allowing force to be transferred efficiently through the body. If sufficient tightness is not derived by internal pressure, power is not transferred and the amount of weight that can be lifted is decreased.

These basic concepts are true regardless of training philosophy. They are key physiological concepts that every program is built on. A lifter who doesn't lift heavier weights over time won't get stronger. A lifter who doesn't learn how to do the Valsalva maneuver won't be able to get tight enough to lift maximal loads.

CHAPTER 2

Muscle Fueling

Many powerlifters lack general knowledge in nutrition. All powerlifters spend a lot of time researching exercises and routines to make their squat, bench press, and deadlift go up, but few spend time reading about what or how to eat. Proper nutrition helps you recover for the next workout, have more energy during the workout, and be less likely to get injured. While it may not taste as good as eating fast food, good nutrition will make you stronger.

This chapter introduces you to the basics of good nutrition. Hundreds of books are available to provide more in-depth coverage specifically on nutrition. For the powerlifter, knowing the basics may be enough.

First, at the chapter covers the macronutrients protein, carbohydrate, and fat. It explains what they are, what they do, and where to find them. Water is also considered as a macronutrient. These are called *macro*nutrients because they are the big deal of nutrition. If you take care of these things first, most of the smaller things will fall into line.

Protein

Protein is probably the powerlifter's favorite macronutrient. If not the favorite to eat (which may well be ice cream or pizza, but those aren't macronutrients), it is the most well known. Protein assists in building and repairing muscle after trauma occurs. Remember, powerlifting works by causing muscle trauma. If you have no protein, you have no muscle repair. If the muscles aren't repaired after they are broken down in a workout, they will not get stronger and will be more likely to tear in subsequent workouts. Think of pouring a sidewalk. You can dig down, frame, level, and prepare all you want, but if you have no cement, you have no sidewalk. Likewise, you can train all you want—proper percentages, volumes, and hard work—but without protein the muscle will not recover and you will see no results.

In short, protein is muscle. It provides 4 calories per gram. Protein is made up of 24 amino acids for muscle; 8 are essential. The body does not make essential amino acids, so you have to get them from food or supplements. The body does make nonessential amino acids, so you don't need to get them from external sources such as food.

The main sources of protein are animal based. If it was a muscle of something, it is going to be a good source of protein. Beef, chicken, and fish are all good sources of protein. Eggs, dairy products, nuts, seeds, and legumes provide protein, too. Vegetables have some protein, but for the most part they are incomplete proteins, which means they do not contain all of the essential amino acids. For your body to absorb the protein from a vegetable and use it to build muscle, you must get a complementary protein from another food that has the essential amino acids the vegetable does not contain. Together they make a complete protein. For instance, beans and rice are complementary because the rice has what the beans don't.

Protein is often misunderstood. Many people think that you can't get enough protein. This is not true. The body can process only so much in a day, which is said to be 1.5 to 2.0 grams of protein per kilogram of bodyweight. For example, someone who weighs 220 pounds (100 kilograms) can use 150 to 200 grams of protein per day quite efficiently. This is contrary to the popular belief among powerlifters and bodybuilders that they need 2 grams of protein per pound of bodyweight, or that 220-pound individual would get 440 grams of protein per day. This amount of protein intake leads to one thing—expensive urine!

Someone who does take in excessive amounts of protein should make sure he has a high intake of water. Water is required to help the kidneys process all of this excess protein. Not drinking enough water over extended periods of time can lead to kidney damage. It is similar to overuse injuries such as carpal tunnel syndrome. If you type a lot while in poor position for one day, you may be sore the next day but without long-term effects. If you do it day after day for years, you end up with the overuse injury.

Best Sources of Protein

Egg whites: One large egg white has 4 grams of protein.

Boneless, skinless chicken breast: One 4-ounce serving has 24 grams of protein.

Lean beef: One 4-ounce serving has 22 grams of protein.

Water-packed tuna: One 3-ounce serving has 22 grams of protein.

Skim milk: One 8-ounce serving has 8 grams of protein.

Carbohydrate

Carbohydrate is energy. This is the gas that fuels the fire to keep you going through workouts. Carbohydrate provides 4 calories per gram, the same as protein. Carbohydrate can be broken down into simple and complex, or even further through the glycemic index.

Simple carbohydrates are sugars; think of juices, candy, sodas, and other sweets. Use them for quick energy. Their energy enters the bloodstream quickly and is gone quickly either by use or storage as fat. This explains those times you felt great at the start of a workout but felt fatigue before you could finish the workout; the simple carbohydrate energy was used first and zapped your energy quickly.

Complex carbohydrates are sources of extended energy; think of pasta, potatoes, brown rice, sweet potatoes, and bread. The energy from complex carbohydrates takes longer to hit the bloodstream, providing a more sustained source of energy. Complex carbohydrates are the best source of energy. Consume complex carbohydrates prior to workouts and meets. Before meets, try carbohydrate loading, feeding the body complex carbohydrates three days before competition.

Since carbohydrate is the main source of energy, look to it first to provide the energy for working out. If not enough carbohydrate is left, the body does not immediately look to fat. Instead it breaks down muscle for energy. This is why carbohydrate is said to have a muscle-sparing effect when consumed; it spares the muscle from being broken down for energy. In your entire body, you can store only about 250 grams of carbohydrate, but you have unlimited storage space for fat.

The glycemic index breaks down carbohydrate even further. The glycemic index is a scale based on how quickly the energy from a food will hit the bloodstream. The quicker the energy hits the bloodstream, the higher the glycemic index value of that food. When sugar enters the bloodstream, insulin is released to store the sugar in the bloodstream. The higher the glycemic index, the more sugar hits the blood at one time, which stimulates the pancreas to produce insulin. When high amounts of sugar are in the blood, high amounts of insulin are produced to store the sugar as glycogen in the muscle for immediate usage or to store it in fat cells for the long term. When all of the sugar is stored, the brain signals the stomach to be hungry to bring in more energy.

The lower the glycemic index value of a food, the longer it will take for the food's energy to hit the bloodstream. The glycemic index considers the fat and fiber content of a food to determine how long it will take for the sugar to hit the bloodstream. For instance, potatoes and sweet potatoes are both complex carbohydrates. Sweet potatoes have more fiber, so they have a lower glycemic index value since it will take longer for the body to digest the sweet potatoes and longer for the sugar to hit the bloodstream. Which is better, a food that is low on the glycemic index or one that is high? That depends on your goal. If you are in the middle of an intense workout, you need something quick and readily available. You would pick a carbohydrate high on the glycemic index such as

Best Sources of Carbohydrate

Brown rice: One cup has 44 grams of carbohydrate and a glycemic index of 50.

Oatmeal: One cup has 56 grams of carbohydrate and a glycemic index of 61.

Whole-grain pasta: One cup has 37 grams of carbohydrate and a glycemic index of 45.

Sweet potato: One cup has 41 grams of carbohydrate and a glycemic index of 54.

Whole-grain bread: One slice has 11 grams of carbohydrate and an average glycemic index of 71.

a sports drink. However, if you are spending a long day at the office, you want the longest, most sustained energy as possible. A sweet potato or other food low on the glycemic index would be a good choice. Nonstarchy vegetables are also a source of carbohydrate. They are low on the glycemic index because of their low sugar and high fiber content.

Basic sources of carbohydrate include anything made with a grain, tuber, or sugar—bread, pasta, oatmeal, rice, sports drinks, potatoes, corn, tortillas, vegetables, fruits. The source you choose depends on your goal at the time. For instance, if you want to decrease body fat, pick sources of carbohydrate with the lowest glycemic index as possible. This way you will feel less hunger and consume fewer total calories.

Fat

Fat is a source of energy. All types of fat contain 9 calories per gram. Fat has been demonized over the years simply because of the word *fat*. People have said that fat makes you fat or that the fat you eat goes directly to the fat on the body. Despite some popular beliefs, the fat you consume does not transfer unchanged into body fat.

Fat can be broken down into saturated and unsaturated fats. Saturated fats are considered unhealthy and are thought to promote arthrosclerosis, high cholesterol, and abdominal fat. Some examples of sources for saturated fats are fried foods, red meat, chocolate, baked goods, and potato chips.

Unsaturated fats are thought to clear out the arteries and veins. Some sources of unsaturated fats are olive oil, almonds, and fish.

Fat is important for many reasons. It helps the body absorb the fat-soluble vitamins A, D, E, and K. Body fat keeps you warm and cushions your organs. In terms of athletic performance, the fat you want to consume primarily is unsaturated fat. It provides the greatest health benefits and the most bang for your buck. Keep fat to 25 to 30 percent of your daily caloric intake.

Best Sources of Fat

Olive oil: One tablespoon has 14 grams of fat (1.9 grams saturated, 11.2 grams unsaturated).

Almonds: One ounce has 14 grams of fat (1.1 grams saturated, 12.1 grams unsaturated).

Salmon: One 3-ounce serving has 10.5 grams of fat (2.1 grams saturated, 8 grams unsaturated).

Flax (ground): One tablespoon has 3 grams of fat (0.3 grams saturated, 2.5 grams unsaturated).

Water

Water is one of the most important and underconsumed nutrients for powerlifters. The human body is made up of 60 percent water. Muscle is 80 percent water. When you are dehydrated, you have less muscle to push with. Dehydration occurs when you lose 2 or 3 percent of your body weight in water, which creates noticeable decreases in the ability of the muscle to produce maximal force and sustain force. With a 2 to 3 percent loss in body weight, you can't lift as much weight or be able to attempt several repetitions. Every action in the body to make energy, produce force, or repair itself requires water. Without water, you don't feel good because your body is not able to perform. When your body is dehydrated, you are a greater risk of muscle pulls and tears when training at high levels. Water provides muscle elasticity and flexibility to prevent pulls and tears. When the muscle is dehydrated, it doesn't have these characteristics and is inefficient and unable to perform as normal.

Following are some more negative effects of dehydration:

- Increased heart rate
- Decreased cardiac output; the body works harder per stroke to push the blood through
- Decreased muscular endurance
- Increased muscle cramping
- Decreased strength and power
- Decreased balance
- Increased risk of heatstroke or heat exhaustion

If you feel thirsty, you have already lost about 1 percent of your body weight in water. This alone leads to a decrease in performance. Beyond the scale there is a simple way to check your status to make sure you are hydrated properly. Check your urine in the toilet. First make sure you are not peeing into blue water, which obviously affects the color. Next, check the color. Your urine should be as light as possible. It should be the color of lemonade or lighter. If it is darker than that, you are dehydrated and should consume water immediately.

Water is responsible for carrying nutrients to muscles as well as lactic acid and the byproducts of exercise away from the muscle, allowing it to repair. If you do not take in enough water, the muscles are not able to repair and you stay sore longer. Did you ever think that by drinking more water, you would be less sore or sore for shorter periods? This is an amazing result from such a cheap supplement. Since water is in every cell, it also is partly responsible for cushioning organs and lubricating joints. Some of the daily stiffness people experience is a symptom of dehydration. Simply drinking more water can help them feel a lot better.

Water is available from anything you drink. Liquids are split into two categories: hydrating beverages and nonhydrating beverages.

Hydrating beverages are any liquids you drink that increase your current water content. Hydrating beverages quench your thirst and actually pass the water on to the body. Since the goal of drinking is to hydrate, hydrating beverages are the ones you want to consume the most. Some examples of hydrating beverages are water, lemonade, and sports drinks.

Nonhydrating beverages do not increase hydration. These drinks contain one or more diuretics, chemicals that tell the body to expel water instead of hold on to it. Caffeine and alcohol are common diuretics. It is not fully understood if caffeine's diuretic effect translates into an actual dehydration or a simple balancing out of the water that was consumed with it. Alcohol, on the other hand, does dehydrate the body. A good portion of the hangover felt after consuming alcohol is from dehydration plus a lack of B vitamins and a decrease in blood sugar.

Remember, your body does not produce water; you must consume it.

Gaining Weight

Back in the old days, the way to gain weight was to eat everything available and get to goal weight as quickly as possible. That was considered the best way to get strong. Times have changed, and people now know more about the human body. When a person gains weight relatively quickly, the primary weight gained is fat. Muscle is gained slowly and lost quickly since it does not store energy well. Fat, on the other hand, is gained quickly and lost slowly. It should be pretty obvious that when someone gains 15 pounds in a month, the primary weight gained is fat. When someone puts on 15 pounds of fat, he will be stronger. The old adage *mass pushes mass* is quite correct. However, he will not be as strong as possible. Fat has no contractile components, no actin and myosin. Fat does not contract to push the weight. Any strength gains made from gaining fat are simply gains in leverage.

The proper way to gain weight is to do so very slowly. Look to gain no more than 1 or 2 pounds (0.45 or 0.9 kg) per week to ensure that as much of the weight gained as possible is muscle. Consider the caloric composition of a pound of fat versus a pound of muscle. A pound of muscle and a pound of fat are both about 3,500 calories. However, they are not the same size. A pound of fat is much larger than a pound of muscle. Next time you are grocery shopping, compare the size of a pound of lean ground beef to the size of a pound of lard. You will notice a large disparity in the sizes; the lard is much larger. If the goal is to increase muscle by 1 pound per week, the lifter needs to go 3,500 calories over his basal metabolic rate (BMR) per week, which would break down to about 500 extra calories per day. That's not a lot of calories when you think about it. It's about a 20-ounce (0.59-liter) regular soda, a small hamburger, or a small shake. In the old days of the "see food" diet (*you see food, you eat it*), calorie consumption increased by 2,000 to 3,000 calories per day. It's easy to see how they gained weight so quickly. It was mostly stored as fat.

No set calorie standard exists for weight gain such as taking in 3,000 calories a day. Some may lose weight, some may gain, and some may stay the same on 3,000 calories a day. You can determine caloric needs in multiple ways, ranging from the highly specific bomb calorimeter that costs thousands of dollars to much simpler, less costly ways. Following is a simple way to estimate what you need to gain weight: Take your body weight in pounds and multiply it by 18 and 19 to give a target caloric range. This is how many calories you need to consume per day to gain weight. For example, let's say a lifter is 220 pounds and trying to gain weight to get to be a full 242 pounds. Multiply 220 by 18 (220 x 18), which equals 3,960 calories per day. If the lifter stays at this calorie level or higher, he should gain weight. He doesn't want to go too much over this or he'll just end up getting fat.

More accurate means exist to determine caloric intake, but they often require additional testing such as body composition or the amount of expired carbon dioxide. If these tests are available to you, by all means use them. However, if you just need an estimate, the one provided previously is sufficient.

The types of food consumed greatly affect a lifter's ability to gain muscle as weight. For example, he needs to have lean sources of protein, such as chicken, turkey, fish, venison, and steak.

Carbohydrate is a little trickier. Some people are easy gainers and some are hard gainers. Easy gainers should primarily stick to low to moderate glycemic index sources of carbohydrate to control blood sugar and minimize fat gain, especially if they have no problem with the increased food consumption. Make sure blood sugar stays relatively stable and you never get hungry. If you are trying to gain weight and allow yourself to get hungry, you'll end up binge eating. This will go toward the weight gain, but binge eating typically leads to more weight stored as fat instead of turned into muscle.

Hard gainers typically find it difficult to keep up with the required food consumption. This group should stay with carbohydrate of higher glycemic index. This may seem counterintuitive since it means they are consuming foods that are less healthy. The reason lies in what happens to high glycemic index carbohydrate. Blood sugar spikes relatively quickly, and the body signals the pancreas to pump a high amount of insulin into the bloodstream. This causes a sharp drop in blood sugar. At this point, the brain signals the stomach that it is hungry and leads to eating another meal. For those who have a hard time eating, sugary foods may be the way to go because they essentially make you hungrier in a shorter time. This helps the hard gainer gain weight. It's not often that someone is told to eat brownies, donuts, and cake, so enjoy it while you can.

Losing Weight

To avoid losing muscle when you lose weight, you need to lose weight slowly as well. Many people are able to drop weight quickly, but typically they lose water first and then muscle, not fat. Remember, fat is quickly gained and slowly lost. Aim for the slow loss of about 1 pound (0.45 kg) a week. Losing weight more quickly than that typically means losing muscle.

Fat is around 3,500 calories per pound. So to lose 1 pound (0.45 kg) per week, you need to cut out 500 calories per day. To keep up with this loss, choose appropriate foods. For protein, select the leanest sources possible: egg whites, skinless chicken breasts, or protein powder. These sources of protein are much lower in fat, so you get more protein for fewer calories.

For carbohydrate, choose those with the lowest values on the glycemic index. You want to keep your blood sugar as steady as possible. If blood sugar spikes, you'll feel hungry and may binge eat. You may have created a 3,000-calorie deficit throughout the week, but if you get hungry and consume 4,000 calories of ice cream and pie, you have a 1,000-calorie surplus to go toward weight gain, not loss.

How many calories per day should you take in to lose weight? You need 12 to 13 calories per pound of body weight to establish the appropriate target caloric range. For example, if you weigh 210 pounds (95 kg) and want to get down to the 198-pound (89-kg) weight class, multiply your body weight of 210 by 12 calories to get an intake of 2,520 calories per day or by 13 calories to get an intake of 2,730 calories per day. This gives you a calorie range of 2,520 to 2,730 calories per day to lose weight. This is a simple estimate, and there are more accurate ways of determining calories.

In weight loss, a person's body composition greatly impacts the calorie count needed. Fat is not significantly metabolically active, so someone with more body fat burns fewer calories. For instance, two people both weigh 250 pounds (about 113 kg). Person A has a body fat percentage of 16 percent and person B has a body fat percentage of 28 percent. Person A is more metabolically active since he has more muscle and less fat than person B. This means person B will have to take in fewer calories than person A to be able to lose weight since he has less active muscle to burn calories. Which will burn more gas at 50 miles per hour (80 bkph), a four-cylinder or an eight-cylinder engine? Because the eight-cylinder engine is bigger, it requires more fuel to do the same thing. Having greater muscle mass is essentially having a bigger engine. Muscle produces more force, can move more quickly, and needs more gas to be able to operate. Because weight loss is tied to so many aspects of the body and is so individual, you may need a more specific estimate of caloric needs to lose weight. If you are having a hard time losing weight, see a registered dietitian (RD) to help you achieve your goals. An RD is certified in nutritional techniques and can help you find exactly how many calories you need to meet your goal and help you make changes to get there.

Good carbohydrate sources for those trying to lose weight are green leafy vegetables, cruciferous vegetables such as broccoli and cauliflower, grapefruit, apples, oranges, grapes, cantaloupe, watermelon, sweet potatoes, steel-cut oats, quinoa, beans, onions, peppers, and whole grains such as oatmeal. These are all very low glycemic index sources of carbohydrate and help prevent binges better than higher glycemic index foods.

With weight loss, calories aren't just calories. You may have a goal of 3,000 calories per day to lose weight. If you take in high-calorie and high glycemic foods, you are hungry because you haven't eaten much, and what you have eaten causes blood sugar to spike and then drop off quickly, setting you up for a binge. However, if you take in low-calorie and low glycemic index foods, you are not as hungry because you are eating a greater volume of food each day and blood sugar is more stable.

Often when someone is trying to lose weight he experiences a loss of strength. A decrease in strength always occurs with weight loss, but a massive disparity doesn't have to exist. Following are a few things to remember when losing weight.

First, do it slowly. Be sure that you are sticking to a loss of 1 to 2 pounds (0.45 to .9 kg) per week. Your goal may be to lose 15 pounds (6.8 kg), but you want to lose that weight primarily in fat to maintain strength. Remember that fat is gained quickly and lost slowly; this is a survival mechanism. Lose the weight slowly to keep as much muscle and strength as possible.

Second, keep your protein intake high. Try to keep the muscle in repair as much as possible. If you don't take in enough protein because of cutting calories, the muscle cannot repair itself and it will be broken down as energy. Cut out the fat first, then look to carbohydrate, but keep protein intake intact as much as possible. As you lose weight, you can begin to cut down on protein. For instance, if you go from 300 pounds to 240 pounds (136 to 108 kg), your protein needs become lower and thus you don't have to take in as much protein or calories in general.

Third, do cardio but keep it at lower intensities. You should burn extra calories with cardio, but you don't want to break down the muscles and prevent yourself from being able to train hard or recover for the next workout.

The Magic Key

For either weight gain or weight loss, the magic key to success is consistency. This surprises many people. If you are consistent and diligent about your eating plan, you will achieve your goal. Weight loss or weight gain doesn't happen in just a few days. It happens over weeks and months and years. If you need to lose 30 pounds (13.6 kg) and you decrease your calories for three days, then give up because you didn't lose weight, guess what? You'll never achieve your goal. It takes time and effort to be consistent. Consistently follow the guidelines for six weeks. If you aren't seeing progress, it may be time to consult a registered dietitian. Give it a chance and make sure it happens.

An old Japanese proverb, called the butterfly effect, says that a butterfly flapping its wings in Japan will cause a tsunami in India. While this is not an absolute truth, it does show how small things can lead to unpredictable outcomes. For instance, not eating properly for two meals a week could drastically impact your goal. You may be trying to lose weight, and in those two meals a week end up with a 1,000-calorie surplus for the week. Well, during that one week that doesn't translate much on the scale, but 1,000 calories a week over a year is around 15 pounds (6.8 kg) of fat. Little things can make a big difference. Stick with your plan and be consistent.

Finally, for weight training, keep volumes moderate to low. Higher volume leads to an increase of muscle mass. Increased muscle mass leads to an increase in body weight. This is the exact opposite of what you're trying to do. To compensate, try to keep intensity high. Work with 1 to 3 reps on core exercises and work as heavy as possible. Weights will decrease as you lose weight, but the intensity will cause motor recruitment and the low reps will not cause an increase in size or body weight. You should be able to maintain strength and decrease body weight nicely.

Percentage Breakdowns

Most articles on nutrition include the percentages you should get from protein, fat, and carbohydrate. Why does it matter? Isn't a calorie a calorie? Well, it does matter somewhat, and this section explains why.

Remember, 1 gram of carbohydrate contains 4 calories, 1 gram of protein contains 4 calories, and 1 gram of fat contains 9 calories. When looking at the percentage of calories from fat, protein, and carbohydrate, make sure you are looking at the percent of calories and not the grams. For instance, if something has 20 grams of protein, 20 grams of carbohydrate, and 20 grams of fat, realize that it is not 33 percent protein, 33 percent carbohydrate, and 33 percent fat. It in fact is 24 percent protein, 24 percent carbohydrate, and 52 percent fat. Understanding this difference is very important if you are trying to work on percentage breakdowns.

Percentage breakdowns are usually listed as percent carbohydrate/percent protein/percent fat. They vary from 80/10/10 to 0/40/60. The percentage you should use depends on your goal. If you are trying to lose body fat, stick to around 40/30/30 while maintaining the calorie balance described in the section Losing Weight. To do this, select low glycemic index choices of carbohydrate and stay with mostly lean choices of protein. Use snacks such as nuts to consume daily fat. If you are trying to gain weight, look to around a 60/20/20 breakdown and select higher glycemic index carbohydrates. Since you'll be taking in more calories, you'll want the higher glycemic index carbohydrates to help you consume greater amounts of food.

Supplements

Supplements are not magic bullets or keys. In fact, they aren't anything magical. As their name suggests, they are best used to supplement your diet, making up for any deficiency that you may have due to poor nutrition or nutrition you are simply not able to take in.

Before taking a supplement, check a couple of things. First, check with your organization to learn if the organization allows its competitors to use the supplement. For example, some organizations such as the International Olympic Committee (IOC) test for pseudoephedrine, but others do not. Someone competing in a meet sanctioned by this organization and takes a cold medicine that contains pseudoephedrine may test positive. Another thing to check with supplements is the reputability of the company that makes them. In many instances athletes have tested positive for banned substances simply because they took supplements that were contaminated with them. Some supplement companies do independent testing on their supplements to ensure that they will not cause positive drug tests.

Before using supplements, understand that the foundation of performance comes through proper nutrition; supplements just add a little edge. Taking in all of the latest and most effective supplements while having poor nutrition is like putting three skylights in an outhouse. What's the point?

Creatine

Creatine is a naturally occurring substance found in the mitochondria of muscle cells. The human body makes it, and it is also found in food such as red meat. Creatine does several things for strength athletes. First, it provides extra creatine phosphate (CP) for the muscle cell to use in the ATP-PC energy system. What does that mean for a powerlifter? It means you can get more reps in a training session because you have more juice in the muscles. It's essentially like switching a 20-watt light bulb for a 40-watt bulb; you get brighter light from the 40-watt bulb. Creatine does the same thing for the energy production of the muscle. It is also a cell volumizer. Basically it draws more water into the muscle cell, or fiber, and increases its size.

Creatine comes in various delivery modes. The old creatine monohydrate was very effective for many on the side of strength and size gains, but it did have one major side effect—gastrointestinal distress. This was known as the creatine runs. Now there are different ways to get it, such as creatine phosphate and creatine citrate, which still deliver potent strength gains but without all of the gastrointestinal issues.

The old creatine monohydrate required a loading phase during which you would take 25 grams per day for a week during the load and then drop back to 5 grams per day. This would saturate the system to get the creatine levels high so you only needed to take the maintenance dose of 5 grams to maintain the creatine levels in the system. With the other types of creatine, no loading is required, which not only saves the stomach but the pocketbook as well.

Creatine is best absorbed into the cell when taken with something to drive it into the cell. Most creatines that come as a system deliver the creatine with simple sugar. The insulin released to drive the sugar into the cell takes the creatine in with it. Several studies show that simple carbohydrates such as grape juice greatly intensify the results of creatine. However, current research shows that sodium may be just as effective at driving creatine into the muscle cell without the spike of insulin. This is good for those who are trying to cut back on carbohydrate and still want the strength gains of creatine. Besides just the blood sugar spike, the daily caloric intake is also lower. Cutting back everywhere helps you to weigh in as light as possible on meet day. If you are trying to cut weight and love creatine, look for a sodium-based creatine such as Creatine Clear from FSI to use. This is the exact form creatine that researchers at Baylor University used in a study in which they compared sugar-based and sodium-based creatine delivery systems and their effects on strength gains.

Glutamine

Glutamine is the most abundant amino acid in skeletal muscle. It has anticatabolic properties, which means that it doesn't build anything up but it keeps it from being broken down further. It is also a conditionally essential amino acid. Your body makes it on its own, but it also uses it up rather quickly in times of physiological stress such as exercise or illness.

Although it doesn't directly impact strength or muscle, glutamine helps you recover. If you recover more quickly, your body is more ready for the next training session. The more ready you are for the next training session, the harder you can train during it. The more sessions in a row that you can train harder, the better results you get at the end of a training cycle.

Fish Oil

Fish oil contains omega-3 and omega-6 fatty acids, which are high in unsaturated fats. The benefits most relevant to a bodybuilder, beyond the often-reported heart health benefits and better brain function, are less pain and inflammation through regulation of the body's inflammation cycle. Fish oil prevents and relieves conditions ending in *-itis* such as tendinitis and bursitis. Some research shows that fish oil aids in improvements in body composition (decreased body fat) and also delays fatigue. The recommended dose is 1,000 milligrams per day. You can get fish oil by eating fatty fish such as tuna and salmon, but most people like to take it as a supplement. Fish burps have long been a deterrent for those wanting to take fish oil, as they didn't want to have their breath smell or taste the fish whenever they burped. However, many fish oil capsules are enterically coated, which prevents that from happening.

Glucosamine and Chondroitin

Glucosamine is an amino sugar that may help repair and form joint cartilage. Chondroitin is a part of a protein that helps with the elasticity of cartilage. Together they are thought to prevent cartilage breakdown and improve joint function. Possible benefits include the following:

- Less pain, especially in the knees
- More flexibility
- Anti-inflammatory effects
- No destruction of cartilage
- Better joint lubrication
- More synovial fluid
- Rebuilt cartilage
- Relief from osteoarthritis symptoms

Glucosamine and chondroitin also may decrease healing time needed for acute joint injuries such as sprained ankles or fingers. If you don't feel better after 8 to 12 weeks, it isn't likely to help. Glucosamine and chondroitin come from shellfish, so don't take supplements if you have a shellfish allergy. The recommended daily doses are 1,500 to 2,000 milligrams of glucosamine and 1,200 milligrams of chondroitin. The liquid form is best because the body absorbs it more easily, but if the only form you can take is capsule, that is acceptable as well.

Calcium

Calcium is a mineral found naturally in all dairy products as well as some vegetables such as leafy greens and other non-dairy sources. Calcium is necessary for muscles to contract, and a calcium deficiency is a common reason for cramping. In the cell, calcium ions are released to allow a muscle to contract. If the cell has no calcium, no contraction can be achieved. If calcium is low, either not much force is produced at all or cramping occurs. You can take calcium through food, but if you have a lactose intolerance or cannot take in enough calcium through diet, two calcium supplement types—calcium carbonate and calcium citrate—are available. Calcium citrate has the greatest amount of calcium absorbed through the stomach wall and causes less gastrointestinal distress, but it is much more expensive. Calcium carbonate is much cheaper but is not absorbed nearly as well. Some recent studies have shown that taking vitamin D with calcium assists the body in the absorption and utilization of calcium, especially in the formation of bone.

Potassium

Potassium is another mineral used in muscle contraction. Like calcium, a deficiency in potassium results in either weak muscular contraction or muscle cramping. Potassium is found in white and sweet potatoes as well as in bananas and fortified sports drinks.

Sodium

Sodium is a mineral found in simple table salt and in most foods. Sodium is required to maintain the osmotic balance in the body. Sometimes cramping occurs because the muscles or the blood do not have enough water. If cramping occurs on meet day, sodium is a good quick fix to eliminate cramping. Although moist foods contain sodium, if you're cramping try to get it through sports drinks. Sports drinks are formulated with the proper amount of sodium and other electrolytes to eliminate cramping.

Magnesium and Zinc

Both magnesium and zinc are responsible for proper hormonal function. If you are deficient in one of these minerals, you are deficient in the amount of testosterone in your body. If you are unable to get enough through food sources such as nuts or meat, the minerals are contained in most multivitamins.

Summary

Good nutrition is essential for improving performance. It provides you with the fuel to train hard and the building blocks to recover as quickly as possible after a training session to prepare for the next one. Good nutrition is the brick and mortar. To fill in where needed, use supplements. Supplements are a good way to add in what you are not able to take in through nutrition, be it vitamins and minerals or performance enhancers such as creatine.

Fred Hatfield (aka Dr. Squat) notes that no one eats correctly, but some eat better than others. Remember, good nutrition should always be your primary goal. The magic bullet supplement that makes you gain muscle, strength, and lose body fat all at the same time does not exist.

CHAPTER 3

Power Training Preparation

Before preparing for power training, you need to understand the difference between flexibility and mobility. Flexibility is the ability of a muscle to get into a position. Mobility is the ability of a joint to go through a range of motion. Although these functions may sound similar, they are different and specific. Flexibility is static, or stationary, meaning you can get into that position and hold that position statically (without movement), not dynamically. Mobility is the ability to go through the range of motion, a dynamic action, and not hold a position at any given time.

By nature, getting into position and pressing or lifting a weight is dynamic. To improve ability as a powerlifter, you need to improve mobility. While an elementary relationship between flexibility and mobility exists (if someone is so tight he can't touch his knees, he may experience a small improvement in mobility by simply stretching), the attention and energy needs to focus on mobility. Stretching really won't do much to help you achieve depth during a squat.

Two components of muscle deal with the way the fibers run: the series elastic component and the parallel elastic component. In the series elastic component, the muscle fibers go end to end in a straight line. In the parallel elastic component, the muscle fibers run parallel to each other. The parallel elastic component is more relevant to strength and range of motion, so dynamic stretching works best here. The series elastic component is relevant to speed and static position, so static stretching works best. Both dynamic and static stretching have a place in powerlifting but they need to be separate. Before a workout, dynamic stretching is recommended to improve mobility. After a workout, static stretching ensures that the muscle returns to a normal length.

Dynamic Stretching

Dynamic stretching involves warming up and stretching at the same time. Regardless of where you are in your powerlifting career, this chapter provides a convincing argument that this is the proper way to prepare your body for training and competition. Intermediate and advanced powerlifters have the tendency to take warming up and stretching for granted even to the point of doing little or no warm-up at all. This chapter teaches you the importance of dynamic stretching and how it can improve, and possibly increase, your individual lifts as well as your overall total.

Back when you first got involved in sports at either a recreational or organized level, you probably were told to warm up before you started. This still holds true today. Back then, the most popular way to warm up for a training session or a powerlifting meet was through static stretching. Many powerlifters still warm-up this way. Static stretching involves holding each stretch for 10 to 15 seconds before moving to stretch another body part.

Just as equipment and rules have improved, so has the way powerlifters prepare for training. Dynamic stretching is integral for athletes at any level, whether amateur, high school, collegiate, or professional. The movements in warm-up of dynamic stretching usually mimic the sport or activity in which you are about to engage.

Powerlifters who take warming up and stretching for granted should realize that over the years they are losing range of motion, which could contribute to not getting proper depth when squatting or lowering the bar to the chest. A dynamic warm-up warms the muscles you are about to use, breaks up scar tissue, prepares you for readiness, and increases the elasticity in the tendons and ligaments. When you don't warm up, you don't activate necessary muscle groups to perform the lift. Often this is the reason for inability to hit depth or the proper bar path. Skipping a proper warm-up keeps you from achieving proper form in the lifts, and may cause a faulty motor pattern in your form. Unfortunately, bad motor patterns often lead to improperly pulling on a joint line, which over time may cause injury or arthritis. A dynamic warm-up increases your range of motion.

For powerlifters, it is vital that dynamic stretching become part of the training regimen. This is the best and most effective way to prepare your body for the weight you lift.

When performing dynamic stretches, take your time to perform the stretches thoroughly with proper technique. You can perform dynamic stretching with a barbell, dumbbells, medicine balls, kettlebells, or just your body weight. If this is your first time, expect to feel a little winded at the end because you are stretching and warming-up at the same time. Following are all the benefits you can receive through a dynamic warm-up:

■ **Higher body temperature.** Increasing the body temperature allows the synovial fluid of the joint to turn to a liquid and coat the joint. Synovial fluid is a shortening-like substance in the joint that, when cold, is very viscous. Its role is to lubricate the joint and allow it to go through a full range of motion. If it is cold, the fluid stays in place. Once the core temperature increases, the synovial fluid heats up and becomes more liquid, coating the entire joint. If you try to do work before the synovial fluid is warm, the joint can't effectively move through the range of motion. If you wait until after you warm up, you have less pain and are able to go through motions fluidly and efficiently.

■ **Increased respiratory rate.** A higher respiratory rate delivers more oxygenated blood to the body. Oxygen is one of the main ingredients needed to metabolize fats to produce energy for exercise.

■ **New flow of oxygen and stored energy to the muscles.** This is related to an increased respiration rate. A higher level of oxygen in the blood allows the energy in the muscle to activate.

■ **Activation of capillaries in the muscles.** When you begin exercising, the capillaries in the muscles are not being used. The blood is being used by other functions. When warming up, you allow the capillaries to fill with blood and deliver oxygen to the muscles, opening the muscles for the greatest amount of contractions and strength of contractions.

■ **Scar tissue breakup.** Scar tissue is a by-product of heavy lifting. If you can break up the scar tissue, the muscle becomes more pliable and has greater contractile properties, allowing it to be stronger.

■ **Increased elasticity in the tendons and ligaments.** If not trained to be more elastic, tendons and ligaments become more plastic, which can increase the risk of tears. Sometimes the only work on the tendons and ligaments comes as a function of the warm-up. Don't miss this opportunity to get the work in or else you may be sidelined for a while.

■ **Increased arousal, enthusiasm, eagerness, and mental readiness.** Many times lifters show up at the gym with other things on their minds. The warm-up acts as a transition from the stresses of the day to the joys of the iron. If you fail to warm up and use this transition, you may not be able to hang your worries on the coat rack and just train.

■ **Warmer muscles relax easier.** When the agonist contracts, it forces the antagonist to relax. If the muscles haven't been properly activated, the antagonist may try to work at the same time as the agonist. Essentially the body fights itself to lower or lift a weight. This isn't what you want. You want all of the muscles working toward the same goal. A dynamic warm-up creates a favorable agonist–antagonist relationship.

■ **More ability to lift to heavier loads.** Because the body is warmer, it allows the muscles to withstand more force and easily adjust to heavier loads. The additional blood flow and mobility allow muscles to absorb more force for the exercises at hand.

Another great thing about dynamic stretching is that it is painless, fun, simple, and feels good. This type of warm-up helps reduce the risk of injury and increases range of motion.

Dynamic Warm-Up Routines

Whether you are a beginner, intermediate, or advanced powerlifter, this section provides several sample routines to choose from. You can use your own body weight, a barbell, dumbbells, a medicine ball, or kettlebells. Once you have selected your dynamic stretch, stay with it throughout your training cycle. Do not switch from week to week. If the dynamic stretch calls for using weight, use the most desirable weight. Remember, these are low-intensity exercises. Maintain good posture and technique and perform all exercises will a full range of motion. Do not change the order of the exercises.

Using Body Weight

The first dynamic warm-up routine uses your own body weight. If you are training your upper body, use the dynamic upper body routine to prepare the muscles. Use the lower body routine if you are training your legs or back.

For each repetition, try to go through a slightly greater range of motion. Go through each exercise in a controlled manner. The main difference between dynamic and ballistic stretching is the speed of the exercise. During a ballistic stretch, you try to forcibly and rapidly increase the range of motion. With a dynamic stretch, you gracefully go through the range of motion. If you are able to go beyond your usual range, that's fantastic; if not, stay within the same range. Remember, the goal is to increase range of motion, decrease pain, and prepare for the workout ahead.

If you still feel tight at the end of your warm-up, add more exercises or repetitions to improve the range of motion and loosen that muscle or area. If you start a workout thinking, "Man, I'm tight. I don't know if I can hit depth today," then you didn't warm up long enough.

Upper Body Dynamic Warm-Up

1. Arm circle (motion forward) × 20: Stand with your feet shoulder-width apart and your arms stretched out to your sides, forming a T shape. Rotate your arms forward in a circular motion the size of a 25-pound (11-kg) plate. Perform one set of 20 repetitions.

2. Body twist × 20: Stand with your feet shoulder-width apart. Raise your arms to chest level with your elbows bent and your hands interlocked. Twist to your right as far as possible, then to the left to compete 1 repetition. Perform one set of 20 repetitions.

3. Arm circle (motion backward) × 20: Stand with your feet shoulder-width apart and your arms stretched out to your sides, forming a T shape. Rotate your arms backward in a circular motion the size of a 25-pound (11-kg) plate. Perform one set of 20 repetitions.

4. Side bend (left and right) × 15 each side: Stand with your feet shoulder-width apart. Place your left hand behind your head and your right hand against the side of your body. Lean to the right, sliding your right hand to just below the knee. Slide the hand back up to return to the starting position. Complete the repetitions to the right side, then switch sides, placing your right hand behind your head and your left hand to the left side of your body and bend to the left. Perform one set of 15 repetitions.

5. Arm circle (motion straight out in front to overhead and back) × 15: Stand with your feet shoulder-width apart and your arms outstretched in front of you. Make circular motions the size of a 5-pound (2-kg) plate with your arms while moving your arms up until they are directly over your head. Slowly lower your arms while moving them in a circular motion. Perform one set of 15 repetitions.

6. Push-up × 20: Lie down on your abdomen with your hands at shoulder level, palms flat on the floor slightly wider than shoulder width, head looking forward, legs straight, and toes tucked under your feet. Straighten your arms as you push your body off the floor, keeping your body straight as you straighten your arms. Pause for a second, then lower your body by bending your arms until your chest is on the floor. Perform one set of 20 repetitions.

7. Arm cross (crisscross back and forth in front of body) × 20: Stand with your feet shoulder-width apart and your arms outstretched in front of you. Cross your right arm over your left arm and return to the starting position. Cross your left arm over your right arm and return to the starting position. Alternate the arms top and bottom for one set of 20 repetitions.

Lower Body Dynamic Warm-Up

1. Leg swing (backward) × 15 each leg: Stand tall and hold onto a sturdy object. Balance yourself on your left leg. Tighten your core and keep your right leg straight as you swing it back as high as possible. Control the leg on the way down as you return to starting position. Complete repetitions on the right leg then switch to the left leg. Perform one set of 15 repetitions with each leg.

2. Stationary lunge × 10 each leg: Stand with your feet shoulder-width apart. Place your hands behind your head or on your waist. Step forward into a deep lunge. Keep your head up, shoulders back, posture tall, toes pointed straight, and body weight evenly distributed. Return to starting position by pushing off the front foot. Perform 10 repetitions on the right leg then switch legs and perform 10 repetitions on the left leg.

3. Leg swing (forward) × 15 each leg: Stand tall and hold onto a sturdy object. Balance yourself on your left leg. Tighten your core and keep your right leg straight as you swing the right leg forward as high as possible. Control the leg on the way down as you return to starting position. Complete repetitions on the right leg, then switch to the left leg. Perform one set of 15 repetitions with each leg.

4. Body squat × 15: Stand with your feet shoulder-width apart and toes slightly turned out. Place your hands behind your head or on your waist. Flex at the hips and knees, evenly distributing your body weight from the balls of your feet to the heels. Keep your head and back straight. Once you are below parallel, return to starting position by straightening your legs. Perform one set of 15 repetitions.

5. Leg swing (to the side) × 15 each leg: Stand tall and hold onto a sturdy object. Balance yourself on your left leg. Swing the right leg out to the right as high as possible and slowly return to the starting position. Complete repetitions on the right leg, then switch to the left leg. Perform one set of 15 repetitions with each leg.

6. Spider-man × 10 each leg: Start in a push-up position with arms and legs spread comfortably apart. Lift one leg and bend the knee, bringing the shin toward the arm. Bend your arm as you bring the knee up. Return to starting position. Alternate legs until you complete all repetitions. Perform one set of 10 repetitions with each leg.

7. Side lunge × 15 each leg: Stand with your feet shoulder-width apart. Place your hands behind your head or on your waist. Step out to the right as far as possible, flexing the knee. The left leg should be straight. Keep your head, chest, and torso straight and toes pointed straight ahead. Return to starting position by pushing off the right leg and straightening the left leg. Complete repetitions to the right, then switch to the left side. Perform one set of 15 repetitions on each leg.

Using Resistance

The next five dynamic warm-ups require some type of resistance. Use a desirable weight, remembering this is a low-intensity exercise to warm up the body.

Perform five, four, and three repetitions in one continuous, nonstop movement. Complete all the repetitions before placing the weights back on the floor. For example, for the barbell dynamic warm-up, perform five repetitions of the upright row, five of the high-pull snatch grip, five of the bent-over row, five of the power clean into push press, and five of the straight bar front raise. Then complete the sequence again, performing four repetitions of each exercise, then three repetitions of each exercise.

Upper Body With Barbell

1. Upright row: Place your hands 12 to 18 inches (about 30 to 45 cm) apart on the bar. Hold the bar down at arm's length. Slightly bend your knees and keep your head and chest up. Bend your elbows to pull the bar up to your chin, keeping your elbows out and up. Slowly straighten your arms to lower the bar with control. Complete three sets, performing 5 repetitions for set one, 4 repetitions for set two, and 3 repetitions for set three.

2. High-pull snatch grip: Place your hands wider than shoulder-width apart on the bar. Hold the bar down at arm's length with the knees slightly bent and head and chest up. Pull the bar up as high as possible, bending the elbows so they are out and pointed up. Straighten your arms to lower the bar with control. Complete three sets, performing 5 repetitions for set one, 4 repetitions for set two, and 3 repetitions for set three.

3. Bent-over row: Bend over to grip the bar with a flat back, knees slightly bent, and head up (figure 3.1*a*). Your arms are locked as you grip the bar. Bend the elbows to pull the bar up toward the lower part of your chest (figure 3.1*b*). Straighten your arms to lower the bar with control until the bar touches the floor. Complete three sets, performing 5 repetitions for set one, 4 repetitions for set two, and 3 repetitions for set three.

Figure 3.1 Bent-over row: *(a)* starting position; *(b)* pull bar toward chest.

4. Power clean into push press: Squat to grasp the bar. In one motion, pull the bar high enough to catch it on your shoulders with your feet shoulder-width apart. Perform a quarter squat, then drive the bar up. Push the bar toward the ceiling until the arms are locked. Lower the bar with control by bringing it to your chest, then your thighs, and then the floor. Complete three sets, performing 5 repetitions for set one, 4 repetitions for set two, and 3 repetitions for set three.

5. Straight-bar front raise: Stand with your feet shoulder-width apart or closer. Hold the bar at arm's length. Raise the bar straight out in front of you, keeping your arms straight until the bar reaches eye level. Slowly return the bar with control to starting position. Complete three sets, performing 5 repetitions for set one, 4 repetitions for set two, and 3 repetitions for set three.

Lower Body With Barbell

1. Behind-the-head squat push/press: Place the bar on your shoulders. Squat down in a quarter squat, then push back up as you press the bar up toward the ceiling until your arms are locked. Slowly bend the arms with control to return the bar to the shoulders. Complete three sets, performing 5 repetitions for set one, 4 repetitions for set two, and 3 repetitions for set three.

2. Behind-the-head good morning: Place the bar on your shoulders. Stand with your knees slightly bent. Push the hips and glutes back, keeping the back flat and head up. Lean forward until you are horizontal to the floor. Slowly bring the hips and glutes back under you to return to the upright position. Complete three sets, performing 5 repetitions for set one, 4 repetitions for set two, and 3 repetitions for set three.

3. Snatch grip overhead squat: Stand with the bar overhead and your feet shoulder-width apart. Hold the bar with a grip wider than shoulder-width. Flex at the hips and knees to squat as low as possible. Keep your arms, head, and back straight and your heels flat. Straighten your legs to return to starting position. Complete three sets, performing 5 repetitions for set one, 4 repetitions for set two, and 3 repetitions for set three.

4. Step-up: Place the bar on your shoulders. Stand facing a box that is 18 to 24 inches (about 45 to 60 cm) tall. Step on the box with the right foot (figure 3.2a) followed by the left foot (figure 3.2b). Step down with the right foot, then the left. Complete all repetitions starting with the right foot, then switch to starting with the left foot. Complete three sets, performing 5 repetitions for set one, 4 repetitions for set two, and 3 repetitions for set three.

5. Stationary lunge: Place the bar across your shoulders. Stand with your feet shoulder-width apart. Step forward into a deep lunge. Keep your head up, shoulders back, posture tall, toes pointed straight ahead, and body weight evenly distributed. Push off the front foot to return to starting position. Complete three sets, performing 5 repetitions for set one, 4 repetitions for set two, and 3 repetitions for set three.

Figure 3.2 Step-up: *(a)* step on box with right foot; *(b)* bring left foot onto box.

Upper Body With Dumbbells or Smaller Plates

1. Dumbbell upright row: Hold a dumbbell in each hand at arm's length. Slightly bend your knees and keep your head and chest up. Bend your elbows, pulling the dumbbells up to your chin, keeping your elbows out and up. Slowly straighten your arms to lower the dumbbells with control. Complete three sets, performing 5 repetitions for set one, 4 repetitions for set two, and 3 repetitions for set three.

2. Dumbbell high-pull snatch: Hold the dumbbells at arm's length on the outsides of your legs, knees slightly bent, head and chest up (figure 3.3*a*). Pull the dumbbells up as high as possible, bending the elbows so they are out and pointed up (figure 3.3*b*). Straighten your arms to lower the dumbbells with control. Complete three sets, performing 5 repetitions for set one, 4 repetitions for set two, and 3 repetitions for set three.

3. Dumbbell bent-over front raise: Start with your knees bent, back flat, and head up. Hold the dumbbells at arm's length. Raise the dumbbells straight out in front of you as high as possible. Slowly lower the dumbbells with control to the starting position. Complete three sets, performing 5 repetitions for set one, 4 repetitions for set two, and 3 repetitions for set three.

Figure 3.3 Dumbbell high-pull snatch: *(a)* starting position; *(b)* pull dumbbells up.

4. Dumbbell snatch: Start with your knees bent, back flat, head up, right hand hanging down the side and left hand grasping the dumbbell. Extend your knees, hips, and ankles to stand tall. At the same time, pull the dumbbell straight up over your head and lock the arm. Lower the dumbbell by bringing it to your chest, thigh, and then the floor. Complete three sets, performing 5 repetitions for set one, 4 repetitions for set two, and 3 repetitions for set three.

5. Dumbbell bent-over fly: Stand with your knees bent, back parallel to the floor, and head up. Hold a dumbbell in each hand, hanging them downward at arm's length. Lift the dumbbells laterally until they are parallel to your shoulders. Slowly lower the weights with control to the starting position. Complete three sets, performing 5 repetitions for set one, 4 repetitions for set two, and 3 repetitions for set three.

Lower Body With Dumbbells or Smaller Plates

1. Dumbbell lunge: Hold dumbbells in both hands at arm's length, feet shoulder-width apart. Step forward into a deep lunge. Keep your head up, shoulders back, posture tall, toes pointed straight ahead, and body weight evenly distributed. Push off the front foot with control to return to the starting position. Complete all repetitions on one leg, then switch legs. Complete three sets, performing 5 repetitions for set one, 4 repetitions for set two, and 3 repetitions for set three.

2. Dumbbell Romanian deadlift (RDL): Stand with your feet shoulder-width apart, holding a dumbbell in each hand; the dumbbells should hang at arm's length in front of the body. Keep your head and chest up and your back straight. Bend at the waist until your torso is parallel to the floor, knees slightly bent. Lower the dumbbells until they are mid-shin. Straighten the torso with control to return to the starting position. Complete three sets, performing 5 repetitions for set one, 4 repetitions for set two, and 3 repetitions for set three.

3. Dumbbell squat: Stand with your feet shoulder-width apart and toes slightly turned out, holding dumbbells at arm's length at your sides, resting the dumbbells against your outer thighs. Flex at the hips and knees, evenly distributing your body weight from the balls of the feet to the heels. Keep your head and back straight. Once you are below parallel, straighten your legs to return to the starting position. Complete three sets, performing 5 repetitions for set one, 4 repetitions for set two, and 3 repetitions for set three.

4. Dumbbell step-up: Stand in front of a box that is 18 to 24 inches (about 45 to 60 cm) tall. Hold a dumbbell in each hand at your sides, dumbbells resting against your outer thighs. Step onto the box with your right foot followed by your left foot. Step down with the right foot, then the left. Complete all repetitions starting with the right foot and then switch to starting with the left foot. Complete three sets, performing 5 repetitions for set one, 4 repetitions for set two, and 3 repetitions for set three.

5. Dumbbell side lunge: Stand with your feet shoulder-width apart. Hold a dumbbell in each hand in front of your body at arm's length (figure 3.4a). Step to the right side as far as possible, flexing the knee (figure 3.4b). The left leg should stay straight. Keep the head, chest, and torso straight and the toes pointed straight ahead. Push off the right leg and straighten the left leg to return to the starting position. Complete three sets, performing 5 repetitions for set one, 4 repetitions for set two, and 3 repetitions for set three.

Figure 3.4 Dumbbell side lunge: *(a)* starting position; *(b)* step to right.

Upper Body With Kettlebell

1. Kettlebell power clean: Squat down to the kettlebell. Keep your heels flat, back straight, head up, and arms locked. Straighten your legs and pull the kettlebell off the floor into a shrug. Continue pulling by bending the elbows, rotating them under the weight, and catching the kettlebell on your shoulders. Complete three sets, performing 5 repetitions for set one, 4 repetitions for set two, and 3 repetitions for set three.

2. Kettlebell one-arm row: Bend at the waist with your chest slightly raised and head up. Bend the knees and hold the kettlebell in front of you at arm's length in one hand. Brace the other hand on a bench. Flex at the elbow, keeping the arm close to your body, to lift the weight to the side of your body. To lower the kettlebell, extend the arm until the arm is straight. Complete three sets, performing 5 repetitions for set one, 4 repetitions for set two, and 3 repetitions for set three.

3. Kettlebell one-arm swing: Place your feet wider than shoulder width, bend your knees, and keep your back straight. Hold a kettlebell in one hand, hanging between your legs at arm's length. Swing the kettlebell up above your shoulders and control the motion as you lower it back to the starting position. Complete three sets, performing 5 repetitions for set one, 4 repetitions for set two, and 3 repetitions for set three.

4. Kettlebell upright row: Hold a kettlebell in both hands, hanging in front of your body at arm's length (figure 3.5a). Stand with your knees slightly bent and keep your head and chest up. Bend your elbows to pull the kettlebell up to your chin, keeping your elbows out and up (figure 3.5b). Slowly straighten your arms to lower the kettlebell with control. Complete three sets, performing 5 repetitions for set one, 4 repetitions for set two, and 3 repetitions for set three.

5. Kettlebell two-arm swing, alternating hand: Place your feet wider than shoulder width. Stand with your knees bent, back straight, and a kettlebell hanging between your legs at arm's length. Swing the kettlebell up above your shoulders, letting go with your right hand and catching with your left hand. Control the motion as you lower the kettlebell back to the starting position and then back up to your shoulders, switching to the right hand. Complete three sets, performing 5 repetitions for set one, 4 repetitions for set two, and 3 repetitions for set three.

6. Kettlebell military press: Stand with your feet shoulder-width apart and knees slightly bent. Your upper body is vertical and the kettlebell is resting on your shoulders. Press the kettlebell up over your head until the arms are locked. Lower the kettlebell back to the shoulders with control. Complete three sets, performing 5 repetitions for set one, 4 repetitions for set two, and 3 repetitions for set three.

Figure 3.5 Kettlebell upright row: *(a)* starting position; *(b)* lift kettlebell until under chin.

Lower Body With Kettlebell

1. Kettlebell clean and squat: Stand with your feet shoulder-width apart. Squat down to the kettlebell, flexing at the hips and knees until you are below parallel. Keep your heels flat, back straight, head up, and arms locked. Straighten your legs and pull the kettlebell off the floor into a shrug. Continue pulling by bending the elbows, rotating them under the weight, and catching the kettlebell on your shoulders. Stand back up and return to the starting position. Complete three sets, performing 5 repetitions for set one, 4 repetitions for set two, and 3 repetitions for set three.

2. Kettlebell RDL: Stand with your feet shoulder-width apart and the kettlebell in your hands, hanging at arm's length in front of your body. Keep your head and chest up and your back straight. Bend at the waist until you are horizontal to the floor, knees slightly bent. Lower the kettlebell until it is mid-shin. Straighten the torso to return to the starting position. Complete three sets, performing 5 repetitions for set one, 4 repetitions for set two, and 3 repetitions for set three.

3. Kettlebell swing walk: Stand with your feet wider than shoulder width, your knees bent, and your back straight. Hold a kettlebell in both hands, hanging between your legs at arm's length (figure 3.6a). Swing the kettlebell up above your shoulders as you step forward with your right foot (figure 3.6b) then left foot.

Figure 3.6 Kettlebell swing walk: *(a)* starting position; *(b)* swing kettlebell and step with right foot.

Control the motion as you lower the kettlebell back to starting position. Complete three sets, performing 5 repetitions for set one, 4 repetitions for set two, and 3 repetitions for set three.

4. Kettlebell deadlift: Squat down to the kettlebell, gripping it at arm's length. Keep your back and feet flat and your chest up. Push through the floor, raising your hips and lifting the kettlebell until your legs are locked and the kettlebell is at arm's length as you stand. Bend your knees to return to the starting position. Keep your chest up until the kettlebell touches the floor. Complete three sets, performing 5 repetitions for set one, 4 repetitions for set two, and 3 repetitions for set three.

5. Overhead farmer's walk: Hold the kettlebell overhead in your hands at arm's length. Stand tall and tighten your core, looking straight ahead. Walk for a distance while carrying the kettlebell. Complete three sets, performing 5 repetitions for set one, 4 repetitions for set two, and 3 repetitions for set three.

6. Kettlebell squat: Stand with your feet shoulder-width apart and toes slightly turned out. Hold two kettlebells at arm's length to the sides of the body. Flex at the hips and knees, evenly distributing your body weight from the balls of your feet to the heels. Keep your head and back straight. Once you are below parallel, straighten your legs to return to the starting position. Complete three sets, performing 5 repetitions for set one, 4 repetitions for set two, and 3 repetitions for set three.

Upper Body With Medicine Ball

1. Medicine ball front raise: Stand with your feet shoulder-width apart, knees slightly bent, back straight, and a medicine ball in your hands at arm's length. Raise your arms straight out in front of your body until the medicine ball is at eye level. Slowly return the medicine ball back to the starting position. Complete three sets, performing 5 repetitions for set one, 4 repetitions for set two, and 3 repetitions for set three.

2. Medicine ball chest press: Stand with your feet shoulder-width apart, knees slightly bent, back straight, and head up. Hold a medicine ball in your hands at chest level with your elbows bent. Press the medicine ball out in front of your body at arm's length and bring it back to the starting position with control. Complete three sets, performing 5 repetitions for set one, 4 repetitions for set two, and 3 repetitions for set three.

3. Medicine ball standing triceps extension: Stand with your feet shoulder-width apart, knees slightly bent, and back straight. Hold a medicine ball in your hands and bend your arms behind your head (figure 3.7a). Tighten your core and straighten your arms overhead to a locked position (figure 3.7b). Slowly return to the starting position. Complete three sets, performing 5 repetitions for set one, 4 repetitions for set two, and 3 repetitions for set three.

4. Medicine ball giant circle: Stand with your feet shoulder-width apart, knees slightly bent, and back straight. Hold a medicine ball with your arms straight out in front of you. Tighten your core and rotate the medicine ball to your left and right about the circumference of a 45-pound (20-kg) plate. Complete three sets,

Figure 3.7 Medicine ball standing triceps extension: *(a)* starting position; *(b)* lift medicine ball overhead to locked position.

performing 5 repetitions for set one, 4 repetitions for set two, and 3 repetitions for set three.

5. Medicine ball biceps curl: Stand with your feet shoulder-width apart, knees slightly bent, and back straight. Hold a medicine ball at arm's length on the thighs. Tighten your core and bend at the elbows, curling the medicine ball up to the chest. Slowly return to starting position. Complete three sets, performing 5 repetitions for set one, 4 repetitions for set two, and 3 repetitions for set three.

6. Medicine ball diamond push-up: Lie down on your abdomen with your arms at shoulder level, hands on top of the medicine ball forming a diamond shape, head up and looking forward, legs straight, and toes tucked under your feet. Straighten your arms as you push your body off the medicine ball, keeping your body straight. Pause for a second, then bend your elbows to lower your body until your chest touches the floor. Complete three sets, performing 5 repetitions for set one, 4 repetitions for set two, and 3 repetitions for set three.

Lower Body With Medicine Ball

1. Medicine ball overhead split squat: Stand with the legs split; one leg is in front with the knee slightly bent, and the other leg is behind. Toes are pointed straight ahead. Hold the medicine ball overhead with the arms locked. Keep your chest up. Tighten your core and lower the back knee until it touches the floor. Return to starting position. Complete three sets, performing 5 repetitions for set one, 4 repetitions for set two, and 3 repetitions for set three.

2. Medicine ball good morning: Stand with your feet shoulder-width apart. Hold a medicine ball behind your head, resting it on your shoulders. Keep your head and chest up and your back straight. Your knees should remain slightly bent throughout the movement. Bend at the waist until you are horizontal to the floor. Straighten the torso to return to the starting position. Complete three sets, performing 5 repetitions for set one, 4 repetitions for set two, and 3 repetitions for set three.

3. Medicine ball lunge: Stand tall with your feet shoulder-width apart. Hold the medicine ball at chest level. Step out with your right leg as far as possible, bending the knee and touching the floor with your left knee, and your toes pointed straight ahead. Return by pushing off the front foot, bringing it even with the left foot. Complete three sets, performing 5 repetitions for set one, 4 repetitions for set two, and 3 repetitions for set three.

4. Medicine ball squat: Stand with your feet shoulder-width apart and toes slightly turned out. Hold a medicine ball straight out in front of you at arm's length. Flex at the hips and knees, evenly distributing your body weight from the balls of your feet to the heels. Keep your head and back straight. Once you are below parallel, straighten your legs to return to the starting position. Complete three sets, performing 5 repetitions for set one, 4 repetitions for set two, and 3 repetitions for set three.

5. Medicine ball RDL: Stand with your feet shoulder-width apart. Hold a medicine ball at arm's length. Keep your head and chest up and your back straight. Your knees should remain slightly bent throughout the movement. Bend at the waist until you are horizontal to the floor and the medicine ball is at mid-shin. Straighten your torso to return to the starting position. Complete three sets, performing 5 repetitions for set one, 4 repetitions for set two, and 3 repetitions for set three.

6. Medicine ball lunge rotation: Stand tall with your feet shoulder-width apart. Hold the medicine ball at chest level. Step out with your left leg as far as possible, bending at the knee (figure 3.8a), as you rotate the medicine ball to your left (figure 3.8b). Touch the floor with your right knee and keep the toes of your left foot pointed straight ahead. Push off the front foot, bringing it even with the back foot to return to the starting position. Complete three sets, performing 5 repetitions for set one, 4 repetitions for set two, and 3 repetitions for set three.

Exercise bands are excellent tools for increasing dynamic flexibility. The exercises you can use and the angles to stretch muscles are limited only by your creativity and imagination. Dick Hartzell, who is known as the rubber band man and is very flexible for his age, is a big proponent of working with exercise

Figure 3.8   Medicine ball lunge rotation: *(a)* lunge with left leg; *(b)* rotate to left.

bands. He is renowned for his ability to improve flexibility and mobility through the use of the bands. Bands come in a range of colors that reveal their level of resistance:

- yellow (thin)
- red (medium)
- green (average)
- blue (strong)
- black (extra strong)
- silver (super heavy)

Upper Body With Exercise Band

1. Band upright row: Place your feet inside the band and grab the top of the band at arm's length. Keep your body straight and your core tight. Slowly pull the band up toward your chin while bending your elbows, keeping them pointed out and up. Control the band back to the starting position until arms are straight. Perform one set of 10 repetitions.

2. Band bench dip: Sit on the edge of a bench. Place the band across your shoulders and grasp the ends of the band. Put your hands on the edges of the bench next to your hips. Your knees are straight, core is tight, and arms are locked as you lift yourself off the bench (figure 3.9a). Bend at the elbows and lower your

Figure 3.9 Band bench dip: *(a)* lift buttocks off bench; *(b)* lower buttocks toward floor.

buttocks toward the floor (figure 3.9*b*) until your upper arms are parallel to the floor or lower, then straighten your arms to lock to complete a repetition. Perform one set of 10 repetitions.

3. Band lateral raise: Stand tall. Place one end of the band under your right foot and the other end in your right hand. Keep your core tight. Raise your right arm out to the side until it is straight and parallel to the floor. Slowly return to the starting position and repeat. Complete repetitions with the right arm and then switch arms. Perform one set of 10 repetitions.

4. Band biceps curl: Stand tall with your knees slightly bent. Place one end of the band under your feet and the other end in your right hand. Bend your elbow, curling the band to the top of your chest. Slowly return to the starting position to complete a repetition. Complete repetitions with the right arm and then switch arms. Perform one set of 10 repetitions.

5. Band push-up: Place the band around your back with the ends of the band in your hands. Lie down on your abdomen with your arms at shoulder level, head up and looking forward, legs straight, and toes tucked under your feet. Keeping your body straight, straighten your arms as you push your body off the floor. Pause for a second at the top, then bend your elbows to lower your body until your chest touches the floor. Quickly return to the starting position with no pause. Perform one set of 10 repetitions.

Lower Body With Exercise Band

1. Band squat: Stand with your feet shoulder-width apart and feet slightly turned out. Place one end of the band across your shoulders and the other end under your feet. Flex at the hips and knees, evenly distributing your body weight from the balls of your feet to the heels. Keep your head and back straight. Once you are below parallel, straighten your legs to return to the starting position. Perform one set of 10 repetitions.

2. Band lunge: Place one end of the band under your feet and the other end across your shoulders. Stand tall with your feet shoulder-width apart. Step out with your right leg as far as possible, bending at the knees and touching the floor with your left knee, toes pointed straight ahead. Push off the front foot and bring it even with the left foot to return to the starting position. Perform one set of 10 repetitions.

3. Band step-up: Stand with one end of the band on your shoulders and the other end under your feet in front of a box that is 18 to 24 inches (about 45 to 60 cm) tall. (See figure 3.10 to see how the band is looped.) Step on the box with the right foot (figure 3.11a) followed by the left foot (figure 3.11b). Step down with the

Figure 3.10 Band placement for band step-up exercise.

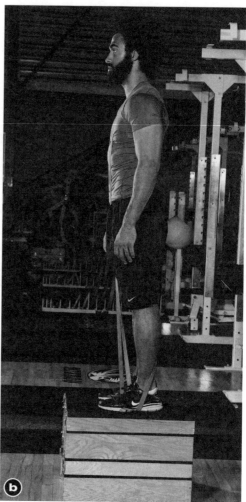

Figure 3.11 Band step-up: *(a)* step onto box with right foot; *(b)* bring left foot to meet right foot on top of box.

right foot, then the left. Complete repetitions starting with the right foot and then switch to starting with the left foot. Perform one set of 10 repetitions.

4. Band good morning: Stand with your feet shoulder-width apart with one end of the band under your feet and the other end across your shoulders. Keep your head and chest up and back straight. The knees remain slightly bent throughout the movement. Bend at the waist until your torso is parallel to the floor. Straighten the torso to return to the starting position. Perform one set of 10 repetitions.

5. Band leg curl: Lie on your abdomen. Place one end of the band around your ankles and the other end around a power rack. Curl your legs up, pulling the band as closely toward your buttocks as possible. Slowly lower the band to the starting position with control. Perform one set of 10 repetitions.

General Exercise Band Stretch

1. Hamstring: Lie on your back. Place one end of the band around your right foot and grasp the other end of the band with your hands. Slowly raise your leg as you pull the band as far as you can. Slowly lower the leg to the starting position and repeat. Complete repetitions with the right leg, then switch to the left leg. Perform one set of 10 repetitions.

2. Popliteus: Lie on your back. Place one end of the band around your right foot and grasp the other end of the band in your hand. Raise and pull the leg to vertical and hold in a static position, stretching the muscles in the back of the knee. Slowly lower the leg to starting position and switch legs. Perform one set of 10 repetitions.

3. Calf: Sit on the edge of a bench with your legs straight. Wrap one end of the band around the ball of your right foot and grasp the other end in your hand. Extend your toes out and in while applying resistance. Switch feet. Perform one set of 10 repetitions.

4. Groin: Lie on your back. Place one end of the band around your right foot and the other end in your right hand. Swing the right leg laterally while pulling with the band, lifting the leg as high as possible. Slowly return the leg to the starting position with control. Switch legs. Perform one set of 10 repetitions.

5. IT band: Lie on your back with your knees bent. Cross the right leg over the left leg. Place the band around the right foot and grasp the band close to your right foot. Pull the right foot toward your chest as you use your left leg to guide your foot. Switch legs. Perform one set of 10 repetitions.

6. Quad and hip flexor: Lie on your abdomen. Place one end of the band around the right ankle and the other end in your hand. Lift the right leg and pull with the band, lifting the leg as high as possible. Your chest will rise slightly off the floor. Return to the starting position and repeat on the left leg. Perform one set of 10 repetitions.

7. Lat and shoulder: Stand with your feet shoulder-width apart, hands grasping the ends of the band at arm's length. Raise the band above your head with both hands and then lower to the buttocks, keeping the arms straight throughout the movement. Pause and bring the band back to the starting position. Perform one set of 10 repetitions.

Regardless of which dynamic routine you choose, you will receive mental and physical benefits from it. Over time, you will develop a better understanding of the dynamic warm-up and the importance of increasing body temperature, which enhances your ability to perform better. You will be able to make the dynamic warm-up more exciting, fun, and challenging by performing all the exercises in a multijoint movement. For example, use a dumbbell, barbell, kettlebell, or medicine ball to do a clean, front squat, and overhead press.

Using Foam Rollers

In addition to a dynamic warm-up, often it is a good idea to use foam rollers to additionally loosen muscles and assist in breaking up scar tissue. If a muscle is tight or in spasm, the pressure from foam rolling can allow the muscle to relax.

When using a foam roller, you may notice an area hurts when you roll over it. This is a *hot spot,* a tight muscle group. Scar tissue has formed in this area, and it needs to be loosened. Instead of avoiding the spot, hold yourself in that spot for a time to let the muscle loosen. Think of a rubber band that is knotted up. If you pull on the ends of the rubber band, the knot gets smaller and tighter; it doesn't disappear. If you mash the knot and twist it, it loosens up until you can untie it and pull it to any length you want. Essentially this describes the relationship between foam rolling and flexibility. If you use the foam roller to break up the knots and static and dynamic stretching to realign the fibers, you have gone a long way to reducing your injury risk. Here is a basic general foam rolling program:

Foam Roller Routine

1. Calf: Sit on the floor with your legs straight. Place the foam roller under both calf muscles. Place your hands behind you for balance and support. Roll your legs forward over the foam roller, from the top of your calf to the bottom of your calf, to complete a repetition. Perform one set of 10 repetitions on each leg.

2. Hamstring: Sit on the floor with your legs straight. Place the foam roller under both hamstring muscles. Place your hands behind you for balance and support. Roll forward over the foam roller, from the top of your hamstrings to the bottom, to complete a repetition. Perform one set of 10 repetitions on each leg.

3. IT band (left and right): Lie on your side on the floor with the roller under your right hip. Roll over the foam roller down to your knee and back up to complete a repetition. Switch sides. Perform one set of 10 repetitions on each leg.

4. Glutes (left and right): Sit on the floor with your right leg bent and right foot flat on the floor. Cross your left leg over your right and place the foam roller under your left glute. Roll from the top to the bottom of your glute. Switch sides. Perform one set of 10 repetitions on each side.

5. Lower back: Lie on your back with your knees bent and feet flat. Place the foam roller under your lower back. Roll up and down over the roller to complete a repetition. Perform one set of 10 repetitions.

6. Thoracic spine: Lie on your back with your knees bent and feet flat. Place the foam roller under your upper back. Roll up and down over the roller to complete a repetition. Perform one set of 10 repetitions.

7. Lat: Lie on your side with your legs stretched out. Place the foam roller under your arm on the lat. Roll to the top and bottom of the lat to complete a repetition. Switch sides. Perform one set of 10 repetitions.

Postworkout Cool-Down Stretch

Once you complete your workout, follow it with a cool-down stretch. At this time, static stretching is more effective because your muscles are warmer and stretched out. Taking no more than 5 minutes for static stretching, stretch only the muscles you trained that day to help speed your recovery, remove lactic acid, and decrease muscles soreness and stiffness from your high-intensity workout. More important, this stretch helps prepare you for your next training session.

A postsession static stretch speeds up recovery, decreases muscle soreness or stiffness, and just makes you feel better. It also gives you time to deactivate from the weight training session and return to the real world. If you show people the same aggression and intensity that you show the weight, it may cause problems. This transition time is necessary to prepare for a reassimilation into society so you can deal with people in a calm and rational manner.

Here is a simple, general stretching routine:

Postworkout Static Stretch Routine

1. Half hurdler (left and right): Sit on the floor with your right leg straight and left leg bent; the left foot touches the right inner thigh. With both hands, reach toward your right ankle. Switch legs. Hold for 20 to 30 seconds on each leg.

2. V-sit (middle, left, and right): Sit on the floor with your legs spread and your upper body vertical. Reach for your right ankle with both hands, then to your left ankle, then down the middle, placing one hand on each ankle. Hold for 20 to 30 seconds for each reach.

3. Pretzel stretch: Sit on the floor with your right leg stretched. Place your left leg over the right with the knee bent. Your upper body is vertical. Twist your upper body to the left, placing your right elbow against your left knee and looking over your left shoulder. Place your left hand on the floor for balance and stability. Switch sides. Hold each stretch for 20 to 30 seconds.

4. Butterfly: Sit on the floor with your legs bent at the knees and your heels touching. Lean forward and use your elbows to push your knees toward the floor. Hold for 20 to 30 seconds.

5. Kneeling quad/hip flexor: Place your right knee behind you and your left leg out in front of you, left foot flat on the floor. Push your hips forward as far as possible. Keep your upper body vertical and hands on your hips. Switch legs. Hold for 20 to 30 seconds.

6. Lying reverse trunk twist: Lie on your back with both legs vertical in the air. Place your shoulders square on the ground and stretch out your hands, palms down. Rotate your legs to the right until your feet touch the floor, hold, then return to starting position. Rotate your legs to the left until your feet touch the floor. Repeat, rotating your legs right and left, for the desired number of repetitions. Hold for 20 to 30 seconds each side.

7. Sleeper stretch for the shoulder: Lie on your right side with your right arm pressed against the floor and bent at the elbow. Use your left hand to grasp your right hand and attempt to pull it toward the floor while keeping your right arm pressed against the floor. Switch sides.

8. 90/90: Sit on the floor on your left hip with your left leg bent at a right angle in front of you and your right leg behind you in the hurdler position. Stretch over the left knee; hold the stretch for 15 seconds. Stretch out diagonally over the left foot. Switch legs and repeat.

9. Overhead triceps stretch: Stand with your feet shoulder-width apart. Straighten your arms over your head and interlock your fingers. Reach up as high as possible. Relax with a little bend of the elbows and repeat.

Summary

Everything has its time and place; it's no different with stretching. Dynamic stretching is most effective to improve mobility before the workout to be able to achieve proper form. Static stretching is best after a workout to return muscles to their proper lengths and decrease soreness. Aggression builds in the mobility work, and relaxation builds in the flexibility work. Make sure you know the time and place necessary to achieve the greatest possible results in mobility and flexibility and you will be ahead of the game in injury prevention and being able to hit depth on meet day.

CHAPTER 4

Squat

In muscle-head gyms around the world, the squat is hailed as the king of the powerlifting lifts, especially when it comes to developing legs. The trickiest thing about the squat is finding the right groove, the correct form and technique that works for you. Many great squatters in the world of powerlifting use a range of forms and techniques, whether it's changing the squat stance or bar placement.

Of the three powerlifting movements, the squat is without question the hardest to master. When squatting, you have to remember so many elements such as bar placement, feet placement, and hip movement. One mishap can throw off your entire lift. Habit is the key here. You have to get in the habit of performing the same squat form and technique, from setup to reracking the weight. Once you get into the habit of performing the squat correctly, your weight will move much faster, easier, and smoother. You will get stronger in your hips and legs because you will be developing the muscles the squat is designed to develop. Also, you will benefit in other areas such as your lower back, abdominals, arms, chest, shoulders, and cardiovascular system.

A beginning powerlifter should set the goal of mastering each lift to eliminate any weaknesses in the three lifts. You do not want to sell yourself short and fall into that *should've, could've, would've* category. Your goal is to be like the great Mike Bridges, Ed Coan, or Bill Kazmaier, who were competitive in all three lifts. Only then will you have given yourself a chance to compete and win every meet you enter.

Because the squat is a difficult exercise to master, a goal of this chapter is to improve your understanding of the squat. This understanding builds confidence. With better form and technique, you can squat a lot of weight. As you begin to pick and choose the elements that go into squatting, you can put together what will become your own personal form and technique for squatting. In doing this, you must consider your genetic makeup; it is what it is. Use table 4.1 to determine your genetic makeup and what stance will feel most comfortable for you. No research has been done to support this theory, however the size of a person's limbs is noticeable to the human eye. Rickey Dale Crain has discovered this by

TABLE 4.1   Squat Stance and Genetic Characteristics

	Short back	**Medium back**	**Long back**
Short legs	Medium/wide	Medium/wide	Narrow/medium
Medium legs	Medium/wide	Medium/wide	Narrow/medium
Long legs	Narrow/medium/wide	Medium	Narrow/medium
Source of strength			
	Hips	Legs	Back
Stance	Wide	Medium/wide	Medium/narrow
Muscles used	Adductors, gluteus, quads	Quads, some adductors	Quads, some glutes

Reprinted, by permission, from R.D. Crain, n.d., Advanced powerlifting techniques. [Online]. Available: http://.crain.ws/advancedtechniques.html [January 3, 2012].

observing hundreds of powerlifters throughout his career. Rarely will you find a powerlifter who goes against these genetic characteristics.

For a closed stance, stand with your feet closer than shoulder-width apart and your toes pointing straight ahead. For a medium stance, stand with your feet shoulder-width apart and your toes pointing out slightly. For a wide stance, stand with your feet wider than shoulder-width apart and your toes pointing out slightly.

As stated earlier, the squat is the most difficult of the three powerlifting movements to master. It also is the one that receives the least amount of attention during training. Most lifters place more emphasis on the other two lifts and just hope for the best when they squat. Many lifters have talked about their training programs and how little they train for the squat.

Mechanics of the Squat

Without question, the squat is the greatest exercise someone can do to develop the legs. Performing the squat correctly with good form and technique will produce the best results.

Addressing the Bar, Backing Out, and Setting Up

1. Facing the bar, place both hands shoulder-width apart on the bar (figure 4.1a). Lifters in bigger weight classes will want to place their hands wider than shoulder-width for comfort.
2. Take one step forward and pull yourself under the bar.
3. Place the bar evenly across your shoulders (figure 4.1b).
4. Place your entire body under the bar.
5. Make sure both feet are under the bar and parallel with each other or that one foot is slightly ahead of the other with your body weight evenly distributed and knees bent.
6. Before lifting the bar out of the rack, inhale to expand the lungs and chest. Hold your breath until you set up.
7. Squeeze your hands, shoulders, and abdominals.

8. Rotate the hips forward slightly and straighten your knees, pushing the hips up as the weight clears the rack (figure 4.1*c*).

9. Stand erect with your chest filled with air.

10. Take one or two steps back to set up.

SQUAT

Figure 4.1 Setup: *(a)* face bar and place hands shoulder-width apart on bar; *(b)* pull yourself under bar and place bar evenly across shoulders; *(c)* lift bar out of rack.

Note: To conserve energy, you can have the spotters help lift the weight out of the racks.

Hand Placement

1. You may grip the bar in your palms (figure 4.2*a*) or with your fingers wrapped (figure 4.2*b*).
2. Use a pronated (overhand) grip and grip the bar tightly.
3. The closer your grip, the better it bunches the muscles in the back, giving a tighter feeling.
4. Your hand placement will vary based on your height and flexibility.

SQUAT

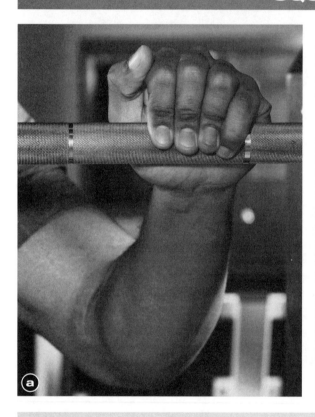 

Figure 4.2 Hand placement: *(a)* grip bar in palms of hands; *(b)* grip bar with fingers wrapped.

Bar Placement

As a powerlifter, you want to gain every advantage you can. Few powerlifters use a high bar placement in competition. Most have found that low-bar squat, in which the bar is 1 or 2 inches (2.5-5 cm) below the trap (figure 4.3), gives them better leverage and involves more of the hip, allowing lifters to generate more power and squat more weight.

SQUAT

Figure 4.3 Most powerlifters perform a low-bar squat in which the bar is 1 or 2 inches (2.5-5 cm) below the trapezius.

Note: To keep the bar from rolling or sliding during the low-bar squat, stay upright and pull the bar into the shoulders as if you were attempting to wrap the bar around your body.

Chalk

Use chalk on your back where the bar rests to help stabilize the bar and keep it from rolling and use it on your hands so prevent them from sliding while you are doing the squat.

Head and Eye Position

It is very important that you know where to place your head and eyes. Once you have walked out with the weight and set up, your head and eyes should be focused straight ahead or slightly up. This is a natural position. Keeping the cervical spine in line with the body maintains proper body weight distribution throughout the squat. Balance is one of the key elements of squatting. If the head is in an improper or unnatural position such as looking up or down, it places unwanted stress on the neck, back, and other areas of the body.

Most novice powerlifters tilt their heads back, causing their weight to shift to their heels, which could lead to them dumping the weight backward. Lifters who tilt their heads down can cause their weight to shift to the balls of their feet, which could lead to them falling forward. Keep your head and eyes straight ahead, just as you see world-class powerlifters and track sprinters do.

Breathing

A beginner or intermediate powerlifter may not put too much thought into breathing pattern when performing the squat. Believe it or not, breathing plays a very important role in whether you make or fail the squat. Never let the weight control you; you control the weight. Through proper breathing, you can and will achieve control.

Once you step under the bar and just before lifting the bar out of the racks, inhale as much air as possible (the Valsalva maneuver; see chapter 1), flexing your abdominals, neck, and back. Hold your breath until you set up, then slowly exhale. This makes your weight feel lighter. Inhale again, tightening every muscle in your body and hold your breath as you descend into the squat. Continue to hold your breath as you break parallel and keep holding until you are nearly finished with the repetition. This keeps your body tight throughout the entire movement. If you exhale too soon, you lose your foundation, causing you to collapse in the squat or miss the lift.

Feet Position

It is very important that you find the proper foot spacing to maximize your full potential. Use table 4.1 (page 48) to select the correct stance. Once you have set up, turn or point your toes out slightly from neutral to 30 degrees for better balance.

Performing the Squat

You have set up and are ready to start your descent (downward movement).

1. Simultaneously flex slightly at the knees and push your hips back and down, as if you were sitting in a chair (figure 4.4*a*).
2. Maintain your torso position. Do not lean too far forward or attempt to keep a straight back.
3. Distribute your body weight evenly over the balls of your feet and your heels.
4. Maintain control of the weight as you descend deeper into the squat (figure 4.4*b*).
5. Do not let your knees extend past the balls of your feet.
6. Keep your shins as vertical as possible.
7. Do not bounce at the bottom of the squat (figure 4.4*c*).

SQUAT

(continued)

Figure 4.4 Squat: *(a)* push hips back as though sitting in chair; *(b)* descend deeper into squat while maintaining torso position and controlling weight; *(c)* at bottom of squat, knees stay at or behind balls of feet, head and eye position are maintained, and there is no bouncing.

Once you break parallel position, you are ready to start your ascent (upward movement).

1. Raise your hips and shoulders at the same time.
2. Drive your feet through the floor.
3. Drive your shoulders and chest back into the bar.
4. Bring your hips under the bar (figure 4.4*d*).
5. Maintain proper head and eye position.
6. Stand tall and erect with knees locked to complete the lift (figure 4.4*e*).

SQUAT

Figure 4.4, *continued* Squat: *(d)* to ascend out of lift, raise hips and shoulders simultaneously and bring hips under bar; *(e)* end lift in tall, erect body position.

Rules and Guidelines

Once you have removed the bar from the rack and have established your starting position, you must become motionless and stand erect with your knees locked. (Some organizations will use a monolift, allowing lifters to set up in the squat without taking a step backward.) Making eye contact with or looking up at the head referee indicates that you are ready, and you will be signaled to start your lift with a downward motion of the arm and on an audible command to squat. You can now squat, and once you stand back up with the weight, the chief referee will signal you to return the bar to the racks with a backward motion of the arm and an audible command to rack it. This completes the lift. There are three judges, the chief referee and one judge on each side of the rack. In order for a squat to be considered good, the lifter must satisfy the judges and receive a minimum of two white lights, indicating the lift is good. Two or more red lights from the judges indicates a bad lift.

Equipment

As a powerlifter, you must become familiar with the equipment and rules for the organization in which you lift. If you are planning to lift in more than one organization, make sure you are familiar with each organization's rules because there is a good chance that there are differences.

The rules you are about to read apply to lifters who lift in the United States of America Powerlifting (USAPL). The following rules meet the guidelines associated with the International Powerlifting Federation (IPF) and International World Games (IWG).

Lifting Suit

- A full-length, one-piece lifting suit must be worn during competition.
- The squat suit must be made of a single-ply stretch material without any patches or padding.
- When attempting a squat, straps must be over the lifter's shoulders at all times.
- The suit can be of any color or colors.
- Squat suit seams and hems cannot exceed 3 centimeters (1.18 in) wide and 0.5 centimeters (0.19 in) thick.
- Seams used for protection or strengthening may be a maximum of 2 centimeters (0.78 in) wide and 0.8 centimeters (0.31 in) thick.
- The leg length of the suit may be cut a maximum of 15 centimeters (5.9 in) and a minimum of 3 centimeters (1.18 in). Measurements are taken from the crotch down the inside leg.

T-Shirt

- You are required to wear a shirt while performing the squat.
- You can wear a T-shirt of any color or colors.
- Your shirt cannot be made of rubberized or stretch material.
- Your shirt cannot have pockets, buttons, zippers, collars, or a V-neck.
- Your shirt cannot have reinforced seams.
- The shirt must be made of cotton or polyester or a combination of the two.
- Shirt sleeves cannot come past the elbows or over the top of the deltoids. Sleeves cannot be rolled up to the deltoids.
- The T-shirt cannot be worn inside out.

Footwear

- When lifting on the platform, you must wear some type of footwear, either in a tennis shoe or boot form.
- Shoes with cleats or spikes are not allowed.
- The bottom of the shoe should be no higher than 5 centimeters (1.9 in).
- The bottom of the shoe must be uniform on both sides.
- You may wear sports shoes, sports boots, weightlifting or powerlifting boots, or deadlifting slippers with a patterned molding.

Socks

- Socks must be clean.
- Socks can be of any color or colors with a manufacturer's logo.
- Socks cannot be so long that they come in contact with your knee wraps or cover your knees.
- You may not wear full-leg stockings, tights, or hose.

Knee Wraps

- Knee wraps keep the ligaments warm and help you out of the bottom of the squat.
- Knee wraps cannot exceed 2 meters (78 in) in length and 8 centimeters (3.14 in) in width.
- Knee wraps cannot extend beyond 15 centimeters (5.78 in) for a total of 30 centimeters (11.81 in) from the center of the knee joint.
- Knee wraps cannot be in contact with your lifting suit or socks.

You can wrap your knees in one of two ways. You can start from the top or the bottom of your knee and work the wraps completely around the knee or you can wrap around your knee once, then crisscross the wrap around once and finish by working the wrap around your knee. Regardless of which option you choose, make sure the wraps are tight and you are comfortable with them. If you like your knees wrapped very tightly, it is better to have your coach or handler wrap them as he will be able to wrap your knees much tighter.

Wrist Wraps

- Wrist wraps help keep the wrists stabilized.
- Wrist wraps cannot exceed 1 meter (39 in) in length and 8 centimeters (3.14 in) in width.
- A loop may be attached to the wraps for securing but cannot be worn over the thumb or fingers when lifting.
- Wrist wraps with hook-and-loop patches or tabs for securing must be no more than 1 meter (39 in) long.
- Wrist wraps cannot extend beyond 10 centimeters (3.9 in) above or 2 centimeters (0.78 in) below the center of your wrist, not totaling over 12 centimeters (4.72 in).
- A standard commercial sweat band can be worn, provided it does not exceed 12 centimeters (4.72 in) in width.

Powerlifting Belt

- A belt helps stabilize the torso and keep you upright during your lift.
- The belt must be made of leather, suede, or other nonstretch material either glued or stitched together.
- The belt cannot have extra padding, braces, or supports either on the surface or laminated in the belt.
- The belt buckle can have one or two prongs or a quick release such as the lever belt.
- On the outside of your belt, you can have your name, nation, state, or club.

The dimensions of your belt must not exceed the following:

- Maximum width of the belt: 10 centimeters (3.9 in)
- Maximum thickness of the belt: 13 centimeters (5.1 in)
- Maximum belt buckle width inside: 11 centimeters (4.3 in)
- Maximum belt buckle width outside: 13 centimeters (5.1 in)
- Maximum width of the tongue loop: 5 centimeters (1.9 in)
- Maximum length between the end of the belt and tongue loop: 15 centimeters (5.9 in)

If you are planning to lift in a USAPL sanctioned meet, expect to have all the lifting gear you will use in competition inspected.

Supplemental Exercises

Supplemental exercises build a strong foundation for the squat. The stabilizing muscles are strengthened to support and prepare the muscles for the heavier weights used during training and competition.

FRONT SQUAT

Powerlifting focus: Improve depth.

Muscle target: Quadriceps femoris, gluteus medius, gluteus maximus, and biceps femoris.

Starting position: Hold the bar in front of the body across the chest (figure 4.5). You can hold the bar in one of two ways: Cross the arms across the bar, holding it in your palms, or use a power clean rack so that the bar rests across the shoulders, elbows in front and palms open with the bar resting near the fingertips.

Execution: Inhale, then squat until the tops of your thighs are below parallel. Straighten your legs to return to the starting position, and exhale at the top.

Coaching points: Keep elbows up, torso upright, and evenly distribute your body weight from the balls of your feet to the heels.

Figure 4.5 Front squat.

OLYMPIC OR HIGH-BAR SQUAT

Powerlifting focus: Strengthen the hips and core.

Muscle target: Quadriceps femoris, gluteus maximus, gluteus medius, and abdominals.

Starting position: Stand with your feet shoulder-width apart or closer and place the bar high on the trapezius.

Execution: Inhale, then descend into the squat until the tops of your thighs are below parallel. Straighten your legs to return to the starting position, keeping your torso upright, and exhale near the top.

Coaching points: Make sure the bar is evenly distributed across the shoulders, and do not exhale at the bottom of the squat.

PAUSE SQUATS

Powerlifting focus: Improve driving power out of the bottom of the squat and stay tight.

Muscle target: Quadriceps femoris and abdominals.

Starting position: Use your competitive squat stance, toes pointed out. Stand tall and fill your chest with air.

Execution: Inhale as you descend into a squat until your thighs are below parallel. At the bottom of the squat, pause for 3 seconds before returning to the starting position. Pausing at the bottom of the squat develops isometric strength and teaches you to stay tight at the bottom. As you ascend and near the top of the squat, slowly exhale. Use no more than 40 to 50 percent of your best competitive squat for 3 to 5 repetitions.

Coaching points: During the pause squat, do not bounce or move until it is time to drive the weight up.

PARTIAL SQUAT

Powerlifting focus: Strengthen your sticking point.

Muscle target: Quadriceps femoris and abdominals.

Starting position: On the bar, load the bar with the weight of your personal best squat then add 100 pounds (45 kg). (For example, if your best squat is 700 pounds, add 100 pounds for a total of 800 pounds on the bar.) Set the safety pins on a power rack just below your sticking point.

Execution: Use your normal squat stance. Squat down until the bar touches the pins and return to the starting position.

Coaching points: Stay tight throughout the movement by filling your chest, lungs, and back with air. Tighten your glutes and abs.

CHAIN SQUAT

Powerlifting focus: Develop explosive power from midrange to lockout of the squat.

Muscle target: Quadriceps femoris, gluteus maximus, gluteus medius, and abdominals.

Starting position: Use your competitive squat stance and about 50 to 60 percent of the weight of your best squat. Chains vary from 10 pounds (4.5 kg) and up. For beginners and advanced lifters, this is a great exercise for developing explosive power.

Execution: From your normal squat stance, descend into the squat until your thighs are below parallel. Return to starting position by straightening your legs. Chain squats force the body to respond to the unloading of the chain at the bottom of the squat and the addition of the chain as you stand up with the weight.

Coaching points: Make sure you stay tight during the entire movement. You control the weight; it does not control you.

BOX SQUAT

Use your competitive squat stance. There are two types of box squats: high-box and low-box. Remember these safety tips:

- Do not touch and go off the box.
- Do not bounce off the box.
- Do not relax or exhale at the bottom while sitting on the box
- Do not lean forward when pushing off the box.

HIGH-BOX SQUAT

Powerlifting focus: Develop the feel of squatting heavy weight and staying tight.

Muscle target: Quadriceps and abdominals.

Starting position: Stand tall and erect using your competition stance. Choose a box high enough so that when you are squatting, your thighs are 2 to 3 inches (about 5-7 cm) above parallel (figure 4.6).

Execution: Descend into the squat and make contact with the box, fully sink into the box, rock your heels slightly, and violently drive your feet into the floor to push the weight back to the starting position. Your goal is to be able to box squat 100 pounds (45 kg) more than your best competition squat for 10 repetitions.

Coaching points: With heavier weight, make sure you stay tight in the squat.

Figure 4.6 High-box squat.

LOW-BOX SQUAT

Powerlifting focus: Improve driving power out of the bottom and stay tight.

Muscle target: Quadriceps femoris, gluteus medius, gluteus maximus, and abdominals.

Starting position: Stand tall using your competition squat stance. Choose a box low enough so that when you are squatting, the tops of your thighs are below parallel (figure 4.7).

Execution: Descend into the squat, fully sinking your hips into the box. Do not bounce or touch and go. Rock slightly on your heels and violently drive your feet into the floor to push the weight back to the starting position. With the low-box squat, use 50 to 60 percent of the weight of your best competition squat for 2 to 5 repetitions.

Figure 4.7 Low-box squat.

GLUTE-HAM

Powerlifting focus: Stabilize and strengthen glutes, hamstrings, spinal erectors, and gastrocnemius.

Muscle focus: Gluteus maximus, hamstrings, spinal erectors, and gastrocnemius.

Starting position: Lie facedown on the machine horizontally with your feet between two pads in the back (figure 4.8a). Your legs are straight and your waist is on the edge of the front pad.

Execution: Bend your knees and press against the pad. At the same time, lift your upper body to a vertical position as if you were sitting on your knees (figure 4.8b). Extend your legs and lower your upper body until you are flexing at the hips to return to the starting position.

Coaching points: Make sure you control your body throughout the entire movement and do not work off momentum.

Figure 4.8 Glute-ham: *(a)* starting position; *(b)* lift upper body.

SAFETY SQUAT BAR

Powerlifting focus: Challenge the body to feel heavy weight.

Muscle target: Quadriceps femoris, gluteus maximus, gluteus medius, and abdominals.

Starting position: Place your neck between the pads resting on your shoulders. Using your competition stance, step back into the rack and grasp the J hook that is set just above the waist.

Execution: Descend into a full squat until the tops of your thighs are below parallel. Straighten your legs to return to the starting position.

Coaching points: Use your legs, not your arms, to rise out of the bottom squat. Practice sitting back and squatting down deep.

WALKOUT

Powerlifting focus: Strengthen the core and challenge the body to feel heavy weight.

Muscle target: Abdominals, gluteus maximus, and quadriceps femoris.

Starting position: Unrack the weight by placing it on your shoulders.

Execution: Step out of the rack and stand there up to 30 seconds. Rack the weight and repeat this process for 3 to 5 repetitions.

Coaching points: Make sure you maintain tightness in the chest, abs, back, glutes, and legs while in an isometric position.

LEG CURL

Powerlifting focus: Strengthen the hamstrings.

Muscle target: Hamstrings.

Starting position: Lie facedown on the leg curl machine. Place the heel of your foot under the pad and rest your knees on the machine.

Execution: Pull the pad up as high as possible or until it touches your buttocks (figure 4.9). Slowly lower the weight until it nearly touches the machine before pulling it up again.

Coaching points: Pause at the bottom and top of the movement, and control the weight during repetitions.

Figure 4.9 Leg curl.

LEG EXTENSION

Powerlifting focus: Strengthen the quadriceps.

Muscle target: Quadriceps.

Starting position: Sit on the leg extension machine and grasp the handles. Bend your knees and place your ankles under the pads.

Execution: Lift your legs until they are parallel to the floor. Slowly lower the weight until it nearly touches the machine and lift it again.

Coaching points: Pause at the top and bottom of the exercise. There should be no fast movement while performing repetitions.

LEG PRESS

Powerlifting focus: Strengthen legs for squatting and deadlifting.

Muscle target: Quadriceps and long head of biceps femoris.

Starting position: Sit on the leg press machine, lying back against the angled back pad. Place your feet about shoulder-width apart on the platform.

Execution: Release the carriage by turning the stop bar out. Bend your knees to lower the weight as your knees travel to the sides of your chest. Press the sled up until your legs are nearly locked to return to the starting position.

Coaching points: Control the weight throughout the movement, and do not lock your knees when pushing the weight to the top.

LUNGE

Powerlifting focus: Improve hip flexibility, balance, and stabilization.

Muscle target: Quadriceps femoris, gluteus maximus, gluteus medius, and abdominals.

Starting position: Stand with your feet shoulder-width apart. Place the bar across your shoulders.

Execution: Step forward with one leg out in front of the body (figure 4.10). Bend the back leg so the knee nearly touches the floor. Keep your chest vertical and your head up. Push off the front foot, bringing it back under the body to return to the starting position.

Coaching points: Control the weight as you step away from the center of the body.

Figure 4.10 Lunge.

STEP-UP

Powerlifting focus: Strengthen the hips.

Muscle target: Quadriceps, gluteus maximus, and gastrocnemius.

Starting position: Stand in front of an 18- to 24-inch (45-60 cm) box with a bar across your shoulders.

Execution: Step up onto the box with your right foot then your left. Step down with your right foot than your left foot to return to the starting position.

Coaching points: Place your feet in the middle of the box. Keeping your torso upright, control the weight up and down.

REVERSE HYPER

Powerlifting focus: Strengthen the spinal erectors, which help with stabilization.

Muscle target: Spinal erectors, gluteus maximus, and hamstrings.

Starting position: Lie with the top half of your body over a flat pad. From the waist down, your legs hang off the machine. Secure a weight strap around your ankles and grasp the handles.

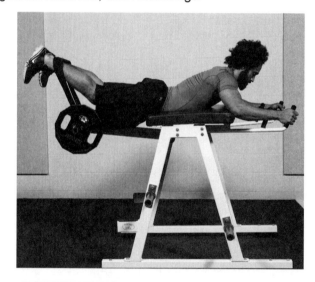

Execution: Squeeze the handles and raise your legs until they are horizontal to the floor or as high as possible (figure 4.11). Lower your legs slowly to return to the starting position with control.

Coaching points: Start with just your body weight and slowly add weights as you get better.

Figure 4.11   Reverse hyper.

CALF RAISE

Powerlifting focus: Develop stabilization during the squat.

Muscle target: Gastrocnemius.

Starting position: Stand with your back straight. Place a weighted bar across your shoulders. Place your toes and the balls of your feet on a block.

Execution: Lower your heels toward the floor (dorsiflexion), then rise as high as possible on your toes (plantarflexion) while keeping your knees locked.

Coaching points: Go through a full range of motion, pausing at the top and bottom.

GOOD MORNING

Powerlifting focus: Strengthen the lower back and hamstrings for squatting.

Muscle target: Erector spinae, gluteus maximus, semitendinosus, long head of biceps femoris, semimembranosus, and short head of biceps femoris.

Starting position: Stand with your feet shoulder-width apart or closer. Rest the barbell across your trapezius or lower on the posterior deltoids.

Execution: With your knees slightly bent, bend forward at the waist and push the hips back until your torso is parallel to the floor. Keep your back straight. Straighten your torso to return to the starting position.

ZERCHER SQUAT

Powerlifting focus: Strengthen the core.

Muscle target: Quadriceps.

Starting position: Squat down to the bar as it rests in the power rack at your knees. Curl your arms under the bar. Place the bar where your forearms and biceps meet. Keep your head and chest up and your back straight.

Execution: Squat the weight up until the legs are locked. Descend into the squat position with control.

Coaching points: Start with a lighter weight, allowing your body and arms to adjust to a new movement.

JEFFERSON LIFT

Powerlifting focus: Develop strength out of the bottom of the squat.

Muscle target: Hamstrings, quadriceps, gluteus maximus, and abdominals.

Starting position: Place the bar on the floor. Straddle the bar so you are standing in the middle of the bar. Squat down to the bar and grasp the bar by placing one hand in front of your body and the other one behind.

Execution: Squat the weight up until the arms and legs are locked. Keep your chest up, back and head straight, and feet flat. Bend your knees as you lower the bar to return to the starting position.

BAND SQUAT

Powerlifting focus: Develop explosive power coming out of the bottom and at the top.

Muscle target: Quadriceps, gluteus maximus, gluteus medius, hamstrings, and abdominals.

Starting position: Attach the bands by looping one end on the inside of the bar where the plates slide on and the other end at the bottom of the power rack or around a heavy object such as a dumbbell. Stand tall in your competition stance.

Execution: Bend your knees to descend into the squat. Squat until the tops of your thighs are below parallel, then straighten your legs to return to the starting position.

Coaching points: Take your time setting up, and control the weight going down and near the top of the squat.

WIDE SQUAT STANCE

Powerlifting Focus: Strengthen the hips and increase flexibility.

Muscle target: Quadriceps, gluteus maximus, gluteus medius, adductor magnus, adductor longus, and pectineus.

Starting position: Place the bar on your shoulders just below the trapezius on the posterior deltoid. Take a stance wider than shoulder-width apart and point the toes out slightly.

Execution: Bend your knees to descend into the squat, evenly distributing your body weight from the balls of your feet to the heels. Go below parallel, bringing the tops of the thighs below the knees. Straighten your legs to return to the starting position.

Coaching points: Make sure your knees stay in line with your feet and your shins stay vertical. Do not bounce at the bottom. Push the knees outward when coming up.

MEDIUM SQUAT STANCE

Powerlifting focus: Increase strength in the hips and legs.

Muscle target: Quadriceps, gluteus maximus, gluteus medius, adductor magnus, and pectineus.

Starting position: Place the bar across your shoulders and space your feet about shoulder-width apart, toes turned out slightly.

Execution: Bend your knees slightly to descend into the squat until the tops of your thighs are below parallel. Straighten your legs to return to the starting position.

Coaching points: Evenly distribute your body weight from the balls of your feet to the heels. Do not exhale at the bottom of the squat.

CLOSED SQUAT STANCE

Powerlifting focus: Develop power in the quadriceps.

Muscle target: Quadriceps and pectineus.

Starting position: Place the bar high on your trapezius and space your feet shoulder-width apart; the toes can point slightly out or straight ahead.

Execution: Bend the knees to descend into the squat until the tops of the thighs are below parallel. Straighten the legs to return to the starting position.

Coaching points: Control the weight throughout the movement, and do not lean forward or round the back. Keep weight on the balls of the feet.

ABDOMINAL WORKOUT

If you compare some of the world's greatest squatters, you will notice they all have one thing in common: a large or thick midsection. A well-developed midsection helps with stabilization and increases your leverage for a great squeeze.

REGULAR CRUNCHES

Lie on your back with your knees bent at 90-degree angles and legs lifted. Place your hands behind your ears. Lift your shoulders 2 or 3 inches (5-7 cm) off the floor. Pause for 2 seconds before returning to the starting position. Complete 30 repetitions.

RIDING THE BIKE

Lie on your back with your bent knees in the air. Place your hands behind your ears. Bring your left knee toward your chest and your right elbow across the body toward the left knee. Return to the starting position then bring the right knee toward the chest and the left elbow across the body toward the right knee. Continue alternating until you have done 30 repetitions.

PLANK

Lie on your abdomen with your elbows bent. Lift your body off the floor so that your body weight is supported by your elbows, forearms, and toes. Keep your back flat in a straight line and hold this position for 30 to 45 seconds. Squeeze your abdominal muscles to prevent injury to your lower back. As you improve, increase your time or get a little creative by holding one leg in the air or lifting the opposite arm and leg off the floor.

UP-UP-DOWN

Lie on your back with your knees bent at 90-degree angles and in the air. Place your hands behind your ears. Lift your shoulders 2 or 3 inches (5-7 cm) off the floor followed by another crunch before returning to the floor.

Summary

Without question, squatting is the king of all leg exercises. It is very important that you find the form and technique that works for you and use the supplemental exercises to build a stronger foundation to help support the heavy squats.

CHAPTER 5

Bench Press

The most frequently asked question of anyone who lifts is "What do you bench?" The bench press is the king of all upper body exercises and is the layperson's mark for how strong someone is. It doesn't matter if someone can squat 1,200 pounds; if he benches only 275 pounds, many will see him as weak.

This chapter describes various techniques for the bench press and ways to develop them. The chapter outlines general principles and also discusses the two most popular current styles: the straight-line bench press and the J-curve bench press.

Principles for All Styles of Bench Press

Some principles carry over from one style of bench press to the next. One similarity is pulling together the shoulder blades and tucking in the lat muscles. The reason for doing this can be traced back to Isaac Newton's third law of motion, *for every action exists an equal and opposite reaction.* When you are pressing a weight, the weight is also pressing back against you. This is obvious as the weight feels heavy in the hands and is hard to press. As a result, your body pushes against the bench, and the bench pushes back against you. The bench is 29 to 32 centimeters (11.41-12.6 inches) wide. To get the maximal amount of force to transfer to the bench and back through the body, you must have the maximal amount of your back on the bench. If you don't get as much of your back as possible on the bench, you are losing valuable force, which translates into weight on the bar. The amount of the back on the bench during the press is comparable to pushing a car on the concrete or in the snow. It doesn't matter how hard you are pushing in the snow, you lose footing and the ground doesn't push back, making it much harder to push the car. On concrete, it's a near perfect force transfer and the car rolls comparatively easily.

Mechanics of the Straight-Line Bench Press

The goal of this style of bench press is to push the bar in a straight line. The bar's path does not arc forward or backward.

Setting Up

1. Set up for this style with a flat back, meaning little to no arcing of the back up toward the ceiling.
2. The feet are flat on the floor and directly under or out in front of the knees (figure 5.1).
3. Draw the shoulder blades together and down, expanding the rib cage and placing more of the lats on the bench.
4. The eyes are directly under the bar with the hands at your preference of hand width. It is recommended to go as wide as possible within the regulations of the chosen federation because it decreases the distance the bar needs to travel.
5. Before taking the barbell out, take a deep breath in to maximize the amount of tightness in the body and thus force transfer from the feet to the hands.
6. Head position is not quite as important as with other lifts; it varies by individual lifter and possibly by individual attempt in setting the shirt. However, some federations do state in their rule books that the head must stay in contact with the bench at all times, so it is best to consult the individual federation's rule book before training for a competition.

STRAIGHT-LINE BENCH PRESS

Figure 5.1 For the setup, place feet flat on floor and under knees and draw shoulder blades together and down to get more of lats on bench.

Performing the Straight-Line Bench Press

1. Position yourself with the bar over your eyes and set your feet.
2. Draw your shoulder blades back and down.
3. Tighten the lats and lower body by squeezing the glutes and legs.
4. When you are ready, the bar is handed to you where you want to descend and press from (figure 5.2a).
5. The bar path has no J-curve, so the handoff will be brought out farther than normal.
6. Try to pull the bar apart in an attempt to maintain the tightness of the upper back and lats and tuck your elbows. After touching the bar to the chest (figure 5.2b) and pausing until the "press" command, drive your heels into the floor and press the bar up as forcefully as possible (figure 5.2c).

STRAIGHT-LINE BENCH PRESS

Figure 5.2 Straight-line bench press: (a) take bar; (b) lower bar to chest; (c) press bar up forcefully.

Mechanics of the J-Curve Technique

It's best to wear a bench shirt when performing this technique. The J-curve technique includes a transition of elbow position from out to in on the descent, and in to out on the ascent to maximize the chest plate of the shirt.

Setting Up

1. The setup for the J-curve technique requires that you arch your back.
2. Your goal is to bring the head and glutes as close together as possible and drive the abdomen as high toward the ceiling as possible (figure 5.3).
3. Draw the lats together and down.
4. The feet are back behind the knees with the balls of the feet in contact with the floor.
5. The area from the ball of the foot to the heel should make somewhere around a 30-degree angle with the floor.
6. The eyes should be directly underneath the bar.
7. The hands are your preference of hand width. It is recommended to go as wide as possible within the regulations of the chosen federation because it decreases the distance the bar needs to travel.
8. Before pulling the barbell out, inhale deeply to maximize the amount of tightness in the body and thus force transfer from the feet to the hands.
9. The head position is not quite as important; it varies by individual and possibly individual attempt in setting the shirt. However, some federations do state in their rule books that the head must stay in contact with the bench at all times, so it is best to consult the individual federation's rule book before training for a competition.

J-CURVE TECHNIQUE BENCH PRESS

Figure 5.3 For the setup, lift abdomen toward ceiling and bring head and glutes as close together as possible. Feet are behind knees, balls of feet in contact with floor. Eyes are directly under bar.

Performing the Bench Press Using the J-Curve Technique

This technique features a J-shaped motion, or arc, during the pressing motion. You have the high arch with the butt and shoulders in contact with the bench before the handoff. The handoff should be where it is comfortable for you (figure 5.4a). This is the position at which you begin the lift. For the initial descent, the elbows are flared out (figure 5.4b), locking the chest plate into position. After a couple inches on the descent, the elbows are tucked in toward the lats until the bar touches the chest (figure 5.4c). During the descent, the bar may drift slightly down toward your waist. This is OK as long as the bar is under your control and not moving toward a dump. When the "press" command is given, begin the press by driving your heels toward the floor while simultaneously pressing the bar up, leaving the elbows in (figure 5.4d). The elbows are flared near the top or at the sticking point to drive through this point.

J-CURVE TECHNIQUE BENCH PRESS

Figure 5.4 Bench press using J-curve technique: *(a)* take handoff; *(b)* initially flare out elbows on descent; *(c)* into descent, tuck elbows until bar touches; *(d)* on "press" command, drive heels into floor and press bar up with elbows in.

Rules and Guidelines

Under the IPF rules and guidelines for the bench press, the lifter must lie on his back with his head, shoulders, and buttocks in contact with the flat bench surface. The hands must grip the bar with the thumbs around, thus locking the bar safely in the palms of the hand. Shoes must be flat on the floor. This position must be maintained throughout the performance of the lift. Any deviation from this position constitutes a disqualification of that attempt.

Hand spacing may not exceed 81 centimeters (31.8 in) measured between the forefingers. The use of a reverse grip is forbidden.

After removing the bar from the racks or receiving it from the spotters or loaders, the lifter must wait with the elbows in a locked position for the chief referee's signal. The signal is given as soon as the bar is motionless and the bar is properly positioned above the chest. The signal consists of a downward motion of the arm along with the audible command "start." Beginning the barbell's descent prior to the start command results in a disqualification of that attempt.

After receiving the signal to start, the lifter must lower the bar to the chest and hold it motionless with a definite and visible pause. The lifter is then required to wait until the chief referee gives the signal to begin the press. The signal consists of the audible command "press." Beginning the barbell's ascent prior to the press command results in a disqualification of that attempt.

After receiving the signal to press, the lifter must press the barbell up with even extension of both arms to a fully extended position. When the bar is held motionless in the full arm extension position, the chief referee gives the signal to rack the weight. The signal consists of the audible command "rack." Racking the barbell prior to the rack command results in a disqualification of that attempt.

In the event of an unsuccessful attempt, the lifter may attempt the same weight or a greater weight. Reduction of the amount of weight is not allowed.

Equipment

Regarding bench shirts, a beginning competitor may hear, "If you're not bleeding, it's not tight enough." This is not a fair representation of how a bench shirt should fit. For a beginning lifter, the shirt should be snug so that he receives some support but not so tight that it takes an exorbitant amount of weight to touch. The beginner needs to learn how to use the bench shirt and how to feel the groove of the shirt. If a shirt is too tight, he will not get the feel for the shirt. All he will feel is chaos. The shirt should be loose enough so that the lifter is able to go at least halfway down with the bar only.

Also it is best to how to bench with a stock shirt, meaning the shirt doesn't have any alterations or only very minor alterations. An individual who is just starting out typically is not strong enough to handle alterations, such as a grid stitched, 3-inch scoop with a supercollar and round stitching on the sleeves. At this point in his career, the beginner needs to focus on getting strong and learning his shirt. After about a year of training and competing, introduce shirt alterations. At this point, strength levels should be on par with where he needs to be for a more advanced shirt.

Bench shirts and beginners can be related to cars and teenagers. A teenager may lust after a Ferrari. He sees the speed and handling and may know all of the specs but has very little driving experience. He is best off driving an old Chevy Cavalier or a car from the 1970s that won't go so fast he will endanger himself. However, after years of driving experience, the middle-aged driver can go and get the Ferrari with fewer risks to his own life. He has built up his driving ability over 20 to 30 years. If he had begun with the Ferrari when he had no experience, he could have killed himself. Although no one is going to kill himself on the bench press, he does risk injury from trying a shirt he is not ready for yet. Due to tightness or adjustments, some shirts may give the lifter a false sense of strength or encouragement because the shirt helps the lifter beat his previous PR (personal record) by 50 pounds (22.6 kg). However, he has not developed his musculature to this point yet, so in fact he is risking injury.

There are two main types of bench shirts: polyesters (poly) and denims. Poly shirts are more forgiving. The proverbial sweet spot on the shirt is bigger. If the shirt goes slightly one direction or the other or touches slightly higher or lower, there is still plenty of pop in the shirt. Poly shirts also are rumored to give more support throughout the entire range of motion during the bench press.

Denim shirts are less forgiving. If the shirt goes slightly out of groove, a lot of pop is gone from the shirt. Also, it is harder to recover when something goes slightly wrong with a denim shirt. Denim gives a lot more pop out of the hole, or bottom, of the bench but much less at the top. Denim shirts seem to do well for those with a higher percentage of adipose tissue, possibly due to the compression of the denim on the body. The denim squeezes the body so the body has some give and rebounds. Leaner athletes don't seem to do as well with denim shirts. Also, using a denim shirt is something of an art form. Not only is there a lot of practice to learning the groove of the shirt, there is a science to the adjusting, or *jacking,* of the shirt—adjusting the shoulders onto the triceps, pulling down the collar, exacerbating the scoop. Some lifters who use denim shirts can touch every rep from 500 pounds (226 kg) all the way to over 800 pounds (362kg) by simply adjusting their shirts.

Poly shirts seem to work best for leaner individuals. With poly shirts especially, you need to maintain your form during the bench and not adjust yourself to the shirt. For instance, it is quite common for a lifter's head and shoulders to be moved due to the tightness of the shirt during the descent. This may make it easier to touch, but is improper form; the lifter loses much of the strength of the shirt. Instead, the lifter should make the shirt conform to him. Jay Fry, the great 181-pound (82-kg) bench presser, often has said, "I try to rip my shirt apart on the bench. I push everything so hard, and I make the shirt conform to me. I don't conform to my shirt. I am in control." This is a great statement. Too many lifters adjust their bodies to get a weight to touch. At issue here may be the fact that their shirts are too tight or have too many alterations, and they are not yet ready for that kind of weight. Getting lifters to focus on making themselves stronger and preparing for the better gear instead of trying to jump right in could greatly reduce the number of forearm fractures.

Guide to Shirt Alterations

Single ply: Only one layer of material for the shirt.

Double ply: Two layers of material for the shirt.

Scooped neck: Alters the stress point, allowing the lifter to get a greater surface area of the collar involved in support.

Grid stitch: Stitching in a grid pattern across the chest plate. This prevents the layers from moving across one another, which provides more support. Also the chest plate is tightened due to the shirt not being able to move as much.

Round stitch: Stitching around the circumference of the arm on the sleeves.

Reinforced collar: Reinforcement through stitching to add strength and support to the collar.

Supercollar: Reinforcement through stitching and additional material to add strength and support to the collar.

Closed back: The shirt is completely together for the full length of the back.

Partially open back: The shirt is completely together at the collar and a few inches down, but at that point is separated on the back of the shirt.

Open back or full open back: The shirt is cut for the entire length up the back of the shirt.

Building the Bench

To build the bench, you must do several things. First, train the bench to perfect its technique and build strength in it. If you do not have great technique that is reproducible (every rep looks the same with the bar landing in the same spot every time), then any development done will not be as effective. This is best done under loads over 80 percent of the raw maximum when training raw, and 85 percent of the geared maximum. (The difference is due to the difficulty touching.) Sets of 6 or fewer repetitions at intensities over 75 percent are best to build strength. Anything lighter does not recruit the largest amount of available motor units, thereby leaving some units untapped and undeveloped.

After training the bench, the next step is to build the bench. First build the muscles of the triceps and lats. Think of all the big benchers—Ryan Kennelly, Rob Luyando, Tony Balonognone, and Tiny Meeker. They all have exceptional lat development and exceptional triceps. A chain is only as strong as its weakest link, so someone with pecs, triceps, and shoulders capable of a 700-pound bench but lats capable of only a 500-pound bench will attain only a 500-pound bench.

Build the bench with special exercises that develop the proper muscles. The triceps are made up of three muscles: the lateral, medial, and long heads. Each muscle head serves a different function, so exercises must train the proper function. For instance, pressing is most directly related to the long head, the not pretty looking part of the triceps that is most visible from the bottom of the horseshoe in the center to the elbow. By understanding this, we can see that to develop the bench press, simply selecting a triceps exercise is not sufficient. The exercise must develop the long head of the triceps. The exercises listed here most directly affect and strengthen the long head of the triceps. An exercise such as a kickback may be an excellent triceps exercise for form, bringing out the shape of the horseshoe, creating a sweep on the outer arm by developing the lateral head of the triceps, but is a poor choice for developing the triceps for the bench press, as the long head is neglected.

The latissimus dorsi, or lats, is another muscle group that must be trained. The latissimus dorsi is a tremendously large muscle group that runs nearly the full size of the back. It must be trained at many angles to train the entire muscle. Training the lats is slightly different than training the triceps in that it doesn't really matter the exercise, as long as you go heavy with high volume and the lat development that occurs increases the bench press. Some exercises, such as pull-ups, in which multiple joints and body stabilization are involved, are better than simple machine rows, but any back exercise is good. In fact, Bill Gillespie swears by the magic of pull-ups and notices when his pull-ups drop off that his bench does as well. For him it is imperative to keep his pull-up strength high.

Upper back development is key for two things: increasing stability of the shoulders and improving the arch. The bigger the upper back, the larger the launching pad for the bench press, because the upper back is the part of the body that remains in contact with the weight bench at all times. For equipped bench pressing, the upper back also must be strong enough to maintain form. With many bench shirts, you have to force the shirt around your body in order to press the bar properly, and you get much more out of your shirt this way. If the upper back is not strong enough to keep the shoulder blades pulled together, the shoulder blades open and take the stress away from the shirt and make the lifter have to do more of the pressing than the shirt. This may be considered cheating by some, but it is the way to get the most out of a shirt. Notice all big bench pressers have a quite large and well-developed upper back.

The shoulders must be built up in both the pressing heads (anterior) and supportive heads (posterior) to increase strength and longevity in the sport. Although increasing only the muscles responsible for pressing (the anterior heads of the deltoids) ensures that the bench press goes up, if you do not strengthen the opposite side (the posterior heads of the deltoids), the shoulders are thrown out of balance and injuries are likely to occur. In this case, a weakness in the chain doesn't equate to a lower bench press, it relates to an injury. Look at the exercises that make your bench press go up. Overhead pressing has long been a staple of bench pressers, as it is a great exercise to strengthen the supporting musculature. Other exercises such as lateral raises, plate raises, rear raises, and bent-over lateral raises are good as they build the individual heads of the shoulders, which helps to enforce balance.

The biceps should be trained as well to help with elbow issues that may occur. You can hold biceps training to a minimum due to the function of the biceps in back exercises. Also, the biceps are not being worked to increase strength in the bench press but to prevent injury. Training the biceps is most important to the three-lift competitor due to the astounding prevalence of torn biceps on the deadlift on the underhand of the over under grip technique.

Supplemental Exercises

The best way to develop the bench press is to do whatever exercises make your bench press go up. No exercises are universally the best. The best exercises for you will help you develop your bench press and get past your sticking point.

Using Boards

The use of boards on the bench press is controversial. Some argue that this is the best way to overload the body. Some argue that all it does is teach lifters how to press to various boards and not to actually bench. Some argue that all it does is teach the body to press for an exact distance. For example, you learn to press for 8 of the full 12 inches, so while the bar may blast off the chest, it falls short at lockout since the body hasn't learned to produce force for 12 inches, only 8.

The key is to realize what happens to your competition bench press, or full-range bench press. This is what matters. If doing board work in a bench shirt makes your bench go up, by all means do it. If doing board work in your bench shirt makes no difference to your competition bench, then do not waste the energy. Above all, do not get caught up in what you can board press; this is not what you perform in competition. If a board press goes up 100 pounds but the competition press remains unchanged, the board presses are a waste of time.

PRESSING

BOARD PRESS

Powerlifting focus: Improve lockout.

Muscle target: Pectorals, triceps, anterior deltoids.

Starting position: Begin in a normal bench press starting position.

Execution: The board press (figure 5.5) is simply a partial range of motion exercise in which you go down and touch the board. Boards are made by joining one to five 2 × 4s. The key to the board press is coming down and pressing up in the same manner as in the bench press. If you come down and bounce the bar off the boards, it essentially becomes a movement of momentum instead of strength. Board presses are great because of their versatility. They allow you to work different ranges and raise various weak points. Within the board press itself, there are three subcategories: the soft touch and press, the sink and heave, and the bounce:

■ **Soft touch and press:** To perform this exercise, bring the bar down to the board very gently, barely touching the board, and then press. Bill Gillespie is a big advocate of this style of board pressing.

Figure 5.5   Board press: *(a)* starting position; *(b)* partial range of motion.

▪ **Sink and heave:** To perform this exercise, bring the bar down in a rapid but controlled manner, allowing the board and weight to sink into the chest, and then heave the bar during the press.

▪ **Bounce:** Perform this exercise like a bad bench press. Let the bar go down at full speed, bounce it off the board, and try to catch and press it on the way up.

There are no wrong or right ways for the board press. Just make sure that the bench press increases congruently with it. If the bench press isn't moving up, try changing variations such as going from a bounce to a sink and heave or a sink and heave to a soft touch and press. The most weight can be achieved on the bounce, followed by the sink and heave. The least weight can be done on the soft touch and press.

Coaching Points: Perform the exercise with as similar technique to bench press as possible. Reinforce technique.

TOWEL PRESS

Powerlifting focus: Increase bench press and refine form.

Muscle target: Pectorals, triceps, lats, deltoids, and rotator cuff.

Starting position: Set up exactly as in the normal bench press. Hold the bar at arm's length and have someone place a rolled-up towel on your chest.

Execution: From the starting position, lower the bar to the towel. In a controlled manner, allow the bar to sink into the towel. Once the bar has ceased to sink into the towel, press the bar to full extension.

Coaching points: Be sure to mimic the form of the regular bench press. Try different-sized towels to suit the needs of training your sticking point.

BAND RESISTED PRESS

Powerlifting focus: Improve the lockout of the bench press.

Muscle targeted: Pectorals, triceps, deltoids, rotator cuff, and lats.

Starting position: Attach bands as described in chapter 10 (page 167). Lie on the bench with the same setup as the normal bench press. Hold the bar at arm's length.

Execution: Lower the bar in a controlled manner to the chest. After touching the chest, press the bar until lockout.

Coaching points: The bands overload the lockout, thus the weight is harder at the top than the bottom. The bands also accelerate the bar down to the chest, so proper setup is essential. Make small jumps when getting close to maximal weights.

FLOOR PRESS

Powerlifting focus: Develop upper body pressing strength.

Muscle target: Pectorals, triceps, deltoids, rotator cuff, and lats.

Starting position: Lie down on the floor with a setup as close to a normal bench press as possible. Hold the bar at arm's length.

Execution: Lower the bar as you would in a bench press until the elbows make contact with the floor (figure 5.6) and then press the bar back to lockout. This is done without leg drive.

Coaching points: Be sure to control the bar slowly on the descent. Hitting the floor too swiftly may not only hurt, it may cause a loss of control with the bar.

Figure 5.6 Floor press.

REVERSE BAND BENCH PRESS

Powerlifting focus: Improve lockout strength.

Muscle target: Pectorals, triceps, deltoids, rotator cuff, and lats.

Starting position: Attach bands to the bar from the top of the power rack. The bands cause the weight to feel much lighter at the chest then at lockout. Start the exercise in a full bench press setup, holding the bar at full extension.

Execution: In a controlled manner, lower the bar to the chest (figure 5.7). When the bar touches the chest, press the bar back to full extension.

Coaching points: Use form as close to bench press as possible. It is common to try to alter the form to lift more weight. It's very important to maintain form.

Figure 5.7 Reverse band bench press.

RACK PRESS

Powerlifting focus: Improve lockout strength.

Muscle target: Pectorals, triceps, lats, deltoids, and rotator cuff.

Starting position: In a powerlifting rack, set the safety rails to match your sticking point. Begin in the same setup as the bench press. The exercise execution begins with the bar at arm's length.

Execution: In a controlled manner, lower the bar until the bar makes contact with the safety rails, which are set to your sticking point. When the bar makes contact with the safety rails, pause momentarily and then press the bar back to the starting position.

Coaching points: Don't allow the bar to crash onto the rails. That will push the bar out of groove.

CLOSE GRIP BENCH PRESS

Powerlifting focus: Improve lockout.

Muscle target: Pectorals, triceps, lats, deltoids, and rotator cuff.

Starting position: Set up as you would for a normal bench press but place your hands closer than you would for a normal bench.

Execution: Lower the bar to the chest in a controlled manner. When the bar makes contact with the chest, press the bar until the arms are fully extended.

Coaching points: Try to keep the elbows in tight to the body. Be sure to not move so close that the wrists must bend laterally as well. This creates undue stress and potential wrist injury.

CLOSE GRIP INCLINE PRESS

Powerlifting focus: Improve maximal strength.

Muscle target: Pectorals, triceps, deltoids, rotator cuff, and lats.

Starting position: Lie on an incline bench. Hold the bar with hands closer than shoulder-width apart and the bar at arm's length.

Execution: In a controlled manner, lower the bar to the chest. When the bar touches the chest, press the bar back to full extension.

Coaching points: Be sure to keep the hips in contact with the bench. It's common for lifters to try to push more weight by allowing the hips to rise. This changes the angles and emphasis of the exercise.

OVERHEAD PIN PRESS

Powerlifting focus: Improve lockout.

Muscle target: Deltoids, triceps.

Starting position: Sit with the bar directly over your head and the bar resting on the safety rails.

Execution: Drive the bar directly overhead until your elbows are locked. After the lockout, return the bar to the starting position.

CARPET PRESS

Powerlifting focus: Increase bench press and refine form.

Muscle target: Pectorals, triceps, lats, deltoids, and rotator cuff.

Starting position: Set up exactly as in the normal bench press. Hold the bar at arm's length and have someone place a rolled up carpet on your chest.

Execution: From the starting position, lower the bar to the towel. In a controlled manner, allow the bar to sink into the carpet. Once the bar has ceased to sink into the carpet, press the bar to full extension.

Coaching points: Be sure to mimic the form of the regular bench press. Try different-sized carpets to suit your sticking point.

FOAM PRESS

Powerlifting focus: Improve lockout strength.

Muscle target: Pectorals, triceps, lats, deltoids, rotator cuff.

Starting position: In a powerlifting rack, place the foam to match your sticking point. Begin in the same setup as a normal bench press. Hold the bar at arm's length.

Execution: In a controlled manner, lower the bar until the plates make contact with the foam, which is set to your sticking point. When the bar makes contact with the foam, allow the weight to sink in. After the weight has ceased to sink, press the bar back to the starting position.

Coaching points: Don't allow the bar to crash onto the foam or the hips to come up.

OVERHEAD PRESS

Powerlifting focus: Improve lockout strength.

Muscle target: Deltoids and triceps.

Starting position: Stand with the bar resting on the clavicles.

Execution: In a controlled manner, press the bar directly overhead until the elbows are locked. Lower the bar to the starting position in a controlled manner.

Coaching points: Don't use the legs, which would turn the exercise into a push press. Eliminate excessive backbend as well. The exercise should look like an overhead press and not an incline press.

TRICEPS

JM PRESS

Powerlifting focus: Improve lockout strength.

Muscle target: Triceps.

Starting position: Lie with your back on the weight bench and arms extended. Grip the bar in a close grip.

Execution: Bring the bar down in a straight path to the collarbone. When it begins to feel difficult to descend any further, press the bar through the hands to full extension.

Coaching points: The elbows should go straight down toward the body, bringing the forearms to parallel with the floor.

ROLLING TRICEPS EXTENSION

Powerlifting focus: Improve lockout strength.

Muscle target: Triceps.

Starting position: Lie with your back on the weight bench. Hold two dumbbells at full extension with the palms turned in.

Execution: Bring the dumbbells down to the heads of the shoulders. Roll the dumbbells back toward your head until the elbows are perpendicular to the floor (figure 5.8a). Rock the elbows back toward your waist and extend (figure 5.8b). The extension should occur before the elbows are even with the rib cage.

Coaching points: Most people tend to roll the elbows all the way down and do a dumbbell bench press. Have someone hold his or her hands at your rib cage or slightly above. When your elbows make contact with your partner's hands, extend the weights.

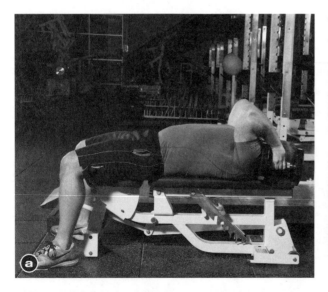 

Figure 5.8 Rolling triceps extension: *(a)* lower dumbbells to shoulders until elbows are perpendicular to floor; *(b)* extend elbows to return weights to starting position.

SKULL CRUSHER

Powerlifting focus: Improve lockout strength.

Muscle target: Triceps.

Starting position: Lie on your back on the weight bench. Hold the bar in a close grip.

Execution: Keeping the elbows pointed directly at the ceiling, slowly bring the bar to your forehead (figure 5.9a). When the bar gets 1 to 2 inches (2.5-5 cm) from your forehead, use the triceps to return the bar to full extension (figure 5.9b).

Coaching points: This exercise tends to be hard on the elbows. Play around with grips and compare EZ curl versus straight bar. One may feel better to you.

Figure 5.9 Skull crusher: *(a)* bring bar to forehead; *(b)* use triceps to extend elbows and return to starting position.

TATE PRESS

Powerlifting focus: Improve lockout strength.

Muscle target: Triceps.

Starting position: Lie flat on a weight bench with the dumbbell heads in contact and your palms turned down as they would be in a normal dumbbell bench press (figure 5.10a).

Execution: Keeping the dumbbells in contact, flare the elbows directly out to the sides and bring the dumbbells down to the chest (figure 5.10b). The dumbbells must remain in contact at all times. Once the dumbbells touch the chest, return them to starting position by performing an extension, keeping the elbows out and the dumbbells in contact at all times. At the top, the dumbbells will have the flat portions touching. At the chest, the sides of the dumbbells will be touching.

Coaching points: The elbows will want to drift back in toward the body. Make them stay out throughout the exercise. For variation, play around with different inclines.

Figure 5.10 Tate press: *(a)* starting position; *(b)* lower dumbbells to chest.

FLARE-OUT

Powerlifting focus: Improve lockout strength.

Muscle target: Triceps.

Starting position: Lie flat on a weight bench with the dumbbell heads in contact and your palms turned down as in a normal dumbbell bench press.

Execution: Lower the dumbbells as you would for the rolling triceps extension (page 84). Rock forward and begin the extension. At the halfway point, turn the dumbbells and complete the exercise as if you were doing a tate press with the dumbbells apart.

BAND PUSHDOWN

Powerlifting focus: Improve lockout strength.

Muscle target: Triceps.

Starting position: Hold a band that has been choked overhead. Both hands grasp the band.

Execution: Keeping the elbows in tight to the body, take the band from the chin and press it down to full lockout. Hold for 1 second, then return to the top position.

Coaching points: The greater the stretch of the band, the more resistance. If a burnout is desired, begin the set on the knees and perform repetitions until failure. Once failure is achieved, stand on your feet and keep performing repetitions.

PANORA PUSHDOWN

Powerlifting focus: Improve lockout strength.

Muscle target: Triceps.

Starting position: On a triceps pushdown machine, hold the rope at a half extension.

Execution: Perform a pushdown and spread the rope at the same time. Return to starting position at the halfway point. Do not allow your hands to come up higher than this.

Coaching points: You should perform this exercise for high repetitions. Don't be concerned with the weight, just the movement and getting in quality repetitions.

PISTON PUSHDOWN

Powerlifting focus: Improve lockout strength.

Muscle target: Triceps.

Starting position: With two bands choked overhead, kneel or stand with one band in each hand. The palms may either be turned in toward each other or turned down toward the floor.

Execution: Alternating hands, press the bands down to full extension. It should look like two alternating pistons firing.

Coaching points: This exercise is another one performed for high volume. If possible, start out on your knees and go until fatigue, then stand up and continue performing repetitions to get a great burn. The repetitions should be super high. Try doing sets of 1 minute.

BACK

PULL-UP

Powerlifting focus: Increase stability.

Muscle target: Lats.

Starting position: Grasp a pull-up bar with hands shoulder-width apart. Extend the arms and make sure your feet are not touching the floor.

Execution: Pull yourself up until your chin goes over the bar. Return to the starting position with control. If you cannot perform pull-ups on your own, bend your knees and have a partner grasp your feet to help you up. Your partner will let go of your feet and you will perform an eccentric exercise for 5 seconds until you get to the bottom.

Coaching points: There is a tendency to do a lot of swinging to get up. If you can eliminate that, you can work the muscles more intensely. Look to variations of the pull-up to eliminate boredom. Chin-ups, alternating grip, wide grip—the variations are endless and they all strengthen your lats.

PULL-DOWN

Powerlifting focus: Increase stability.

Muscle target: Lats.

Starting position: Sit in a pull-down machine with your thighs under the roller pad Your arms are at full extension, holding the bar in a slightly wider than shoulder-width grip.

Execution: In a controlled manner and while remaining upright, pull the bar down to your upper chest. Control the bar as you return to the starting position.

Coaching points: Eliminate the tendency to swing with the lower back on this exercise. It is OK to lean slightly, but eliminate the back extension swing that some lifters tend to do. Like pull-ups, the variations are endless. Close grip, wide grip, reverse grip, V-handles, ropes—try them all for variety.

BARBELL ROW

Powerlifting focus: Increase stability.

Muscle target: Lats.

Starting position: With knees slightly bent and back parallel to the floor, grasp the bar in a shoulder-width grip at arm's length (figure 5.11a).

Execution: Using the lats, row the bar to your mid-abdomen (figure 5.11b) until it makes contact with the body. Hold for 1 count and lower the bar back to starting position in a controlled manner.

Coaching points: Eliminate the swing. Make sure to use muscle and not momentum to perform this exercise. Again, there are many variations of this exercise—wide grip, close grip, reverse grip wide, reverse grip close, reverse grip normal, and alternating grip. Try them all for variety and see what works best for you. This exercise puts a significant amount of stress on the lower back. If you have preexisting lower back issues, find an alternative exercise such as the chest supported row (page 90).

Figure 5.11   Barbell row: *(a)* grasp bar with hands shoulder-width apart; *(b)* row bar to abdomen.

SEATED CABLE ROW

Powerlifting focus: Increase stability.

Muscle target: Lats.

Starting position: On a seated cable machine with the legs out straight, grasp a V-handle at arm's length with the chest erect and lower back tight.

Execution: Using the lats, row the V-handle to the navel. Return to the starting position in a controlled manner.

Coaching points: This is the one exercise during which it is OK to have a little movement. When lowering the weight, most people feel a better stretch if they lean forward a little bit. Just make sure not to go into a back extension during the concentric portion of the exercise. For variety, change the handles from the V to the wide grip that is used for pull-downs (and all the varieties of grips that can be done on that bar) or the ropes.

CHEST SUPPORTED ROW

Powerlifting focus: Increase stability.

Muscle target: Lats.

Starting position: With your chest against the pad of the cable machine, grasp the handles at arms' length.

Execution: With the lats, row the apparatus until the lats are fully contracted. In a controlled manner, lower the apparatus to the starting position.

Coaching points: Make sure that the chest never loses contact with the pad and that the lats, not the spinal erectors, are doing the lifting. Change the grip for variety and to see what feels best.

T-BAR ROW

Powerlifting focus: Increase stability.

Muscle target: Lats.

Starting position: Stand with your knees slightly bent and your back straight, the T-bar running between your knees (figure 5.12a). Either grasp the handle attached to the bar or, if no handle is available, use a hand-over-hand grip as if rope climbing.

Execution: While staying strict with the lower back (no movement), row the bar up as high as possible (figure 5.12b) and return the bar to the starting position in a controlled manner.

Coaching points: Make sure to use the lats and not the spinal erectors when performing the exercise by eliminating any swing in the movement. If different handles are available, use them for variety. This exercise puts significant stress on the lower back. If lower back issues are preexisting, look to use a different exercise such as the chest supported row.

Figure 5.12 T-bar row: *(a)* starting position; *(b)* row bar.

DUMBBELL ROW

Powerlifting focus: Increase stability.

Muscle target: Lats.

Starting position: Start with one knee on the bench and the other foot flat on the floor. The hand on the same side as the raised knee is on the bench as a brace. The hand on the same side as the foot on the floor grasps a dumbbell, which hangs directly under the shoulder at arm's length with the palm turned in.

Execution: Row the dumbbell up to the outside of the hip and lower it in a controlled manner.

Coaching points: Make sure to not swing, a common mistake on all back exercises.

INVERTED ROW

Powerlifting focus: Increase stability.

Muscle target: Lats.

Starting position: Lie faceup on the floor. With an overhand grip, grasp a bar that is 4 feet (1.21 m) off the ground. Hands are shoulder-width apart. Start out with the body rigid and in a straight line from the back of the head to the heels.

Execution: Keeping the body rigid, pull until the midline of the chest is in contact with the bar. Hold for 3 counts and then lower the body back to the starting position.

Coaching points: Make sure that the midline of the chest stays in contact with the bar for 3 counts. Watch for any slack in the body, especially at the hips. Remember to stay rigid. If this exercise is too easy, make it more difficult by lowering the bar or elevating the feet. This is a good supplemental exercise for the back.

UPPER BACK

CUBAN PRESS

Powerlifting focus: Develop upper back strength and stability.

Muscle target: Trapezius and rotator cuff.

Starting position: Lie facedown on an incline bench with your palms turned back and grasping weight plates or dumbbells that are hanging down but not quite touching the floor.

Execution: Raise the elbows so they are flared directly out to the sides of the body at a 90-degree angle (figure 5.13a). Leaving the elbows in place, rotate the weights back

until the upper arm is parallel to the floor (figure 5.13b) and forming a letter L that can be seen from above. Press the dumbbells horizontally from the body (figure 5.13c). Reverse the entire motion in a slow, controlled manner until you reach the starting position.

Coaching points: Go slowly through the motion and perform for more repetitions (10 and up).

Figure 5.13 Cuban press: *(a)* raise elbows; *(b)* rotate weights; *(c)* press dumbbells.

FACE PULL

Powerlifting focus: Develop upper back strength and stability.

Muscle target: Trapezius and rhomboids.

Starting position: Hold a rope attachment at arm's length with the cable set at or above eye level.

Execution: Drawing the elbows back, pull the rope to the forehead in an overhead rowing manner.

Coaching points: This is a lighter volume exercise to develop the muscles. Too much weight changes the muscles used to do the exercise. Try performing the exercise with the ball at the end of the rope by the pinkie or by the thumb. The change in hand position changes the angle at which the muscles work. Perform 2 to 4 sets of 20 to 30 repetitions.

UPRIGHT ROW

Powerlifting focus: Develop upper back strength and stability.

Muscle target: Trapezius.

Starting position: Stand erect, holding a barbell in front of you at arms' length in an overhand grip with the thumbs 6 to 12 inches (15-30 cm) apart.

Execution: Row the bar up to your chin with your elbows pointed toward the ceiling. Hold at the top for 1 count and then lower the bar in a controlled manner.

Coaching points: Make sure the elbows are pointing up and not back. Try some variations with dumbbells, cables, and an EZ curl bar, both standing and seated. Perform this exercise for 3 to 6 sets of 8 to 12 repetitions.

SEATED SNATCH

Powerlifting focus: Develop upper back strength and stability.

Muscle target: Trapezius and rhomboids.

Starting position: Sit on a weight bench with the back erect and the dumbbells hanging at your sides.

Execution: Start the exercise like an upright row. When near the top of the upright row, bring the dumbbells over your head until your arms are straight.

Coaching points: The dumbbells should stay fairly close to the body and go in a near straight line on the way up. This is another exercise performed for high repetitions with a low weight. Perform 2 to 4 sets of 20 to 30 repetitions.

SEATED CLEAN

Powerlifting focus: Develop upper back strength and stability.

Muscle target: Trapezius, rhomboids.

Starting position: Sit on a weight bench with the back erect and the dumbbells hanging at your sides (figure 5.14a).

Execution: Start the exercise like an upright row. When near the top of the row, flip the dumbbells so they are directly above the elbows. The upper arms and forearms should create 90-degree angles with the dumbbells pointing toward the ceiling (figure 5.14b).

Coaching points: Be sure to keep the dumbbells close to the body instead of doing a front raise and curl. This is another exercise performed for high repetitions with low weight. Perform 2 to 4 sets of 20 to 30 repetitions.

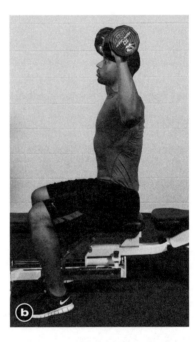

Figure 5.14 Seated clean: (a) starting position; (b) dumbbells point toward ceiling, elbows bent 90 degrees.

MUSCLE CLEAN

Powerlifting focus: Develop strength in the upper back and shoulder girdle.

Muscle target: Trapezius, rhomboids, and deltoids.

Starting position: Stand erect, holding a barbell in an overhand grip.

Execution: Pull the elbows up as you would for an upright row. When near the top of the upright row, shoot the elbows down, under, and through the bar to catch the bar as you would for a hang clean. The elbows point in the same direction as the eyes.

Coaching points: Watch out for trying to use the legs. The knees can bend slightly to take pressure off the back, but this is a muscle exercise and not a momentum exercise. Do 2 to 4 sets of 8 to 12 repetitions.

MUSCLE SNATCH

Powerlifting focus: Develop the upper back.

Muscle target: Trapezius, rhomboids, and deltoids.

Starting position: Stand erect, holding a barbell in an overhand snatch grip.

Execution: Pull the elbows up as you would for an upright row. When near the top of the upright row, simply continue the movement until the bar is locked out overhead.

Coaching points: Watch out for trying to use the legs. The knees can bend slightly to take pressure off the back, but this is a muscle exercise and not a momentum exercise. Do 2 to 4 sets of 8 to 12 repetitions.

SHOULDERS

MILITARY PRESS

Powerlifting focus: Increase shoulder strength.

Muscle target: Deltoids.

Starting position: Stand or sit with the barbell resting on the clavicles.

Execution: Press the barbell directly overhead until the elbows are locked. You may need to pull your head back slightly to avoid hitting your chin with the bar on the way up or hitting your head on the way down. After the bar clears the face, the head should be pushed back through the bar.

Coaching points: The main thing to watch out for is that there is not an excessive backward lean during this exercise. This is a very common way to try to gain additional stability by involving additional muscle groups such as the pectorals. This exercise is very versatile and can be performed for strength or for volume with any set and repetition range desired.

BRADFORD PRESS

Powerlifting focus: Increase shoulder strength.

Muscle target: Deltoids.

Starting position: With an overhand grip, hold the barbell at chin level in front of the body. Elbows are directly in front of the shoulders.

Execution: Press the barbell up slightly to the top of the head (figure 5.15a). Take the barbell over the top of the head, turning the elbows out slightly to help take the bar behind the head to the base of the skull (figure 5.15b). Slowly return to the starting position.

Coaching points: Be sure to go slightly over the top of the head and not perform a full overhead press. A good thought is to give yourself a haircut (a trim, not a buzz cut) with the barbell.

Figure 5.15 Bradford press: *(a)* press barbell to top of head; *(b)* move barbell overhead to base of skull.

LATERAL RAISE

Powerlifting focus: Improve lateral shoulder strength.

Muscle target: Deltoids.

Starting position: Stand or sit erect with the dumbbells directly at the sides, holding the dumbbells in a neutral grip, and turning your palms toward the body.

Execution: Keeping the arms nearly straight (slight bend in the elbows), raise the dumbbells straight out laterally until they reach at or just below shoulder level so the arms and body make a 90-degree angle on each side. Return to the starting position in a controlled manner.

Coaching points: Be sure not to use the legs during this exercise. Stay strict and use just the shoulders. If you have a history of shoulder injuries or pain, try going up to only about 75 degrees. The impingement zone of the shoulder is 90 to 105 degrees. If you have preexisting impingement, simply avoid this zone.

FRONT RAISE/PLATE RAISE

Powerlifting focus: Improve lateral shoulder strength.

Muscle target: Deltoids.

Starting position: Stand or sit erect with the dumbbells directly in front. Hold the dumbbells in an overhand grip and turn the palms toward the body.

Execution: Keeping the arms nearly straight (slight bend in the elbows), raise the dumbbells straight up in front of the body until they reach at or just below shoulder level to where the arms and body make a 90-degree angle. Return to the starting position in a controlled manner.

Coaching points: Be sure not to use the legs during this exercise. Stay strict and use just the shoulders. If you have a history of shoulder injuries or pain, try going up to only about 75 degrees. The impingement zone of the shoulder is 90 to 105 degrees. If you have preexisting impingement, simply avoid this zone.

REAR DELT RAISE

Powerlifting focus: Improve upper back strength.

Muscle target: Rear deltoids, scapulae.

Starting position: Bend over with a flat back until your back is parallel to the floor. Hold the dumbbells at arms' length directly under the shoulders and turn the palms toward the body.

Execution: Keeping the arms straight, push the dumbbells toward the rear of the body. When the palms are even with or slightly past the glutes, return to the starting position in a controlled manner.

Coaching points: Be sure not to use the legs on this exercise. This is a good overall shoulder health exercise to be performed for high repetitions.

BENT-OVER LATERAL RAISE

Powerlifting focus: Develop the upper back.

Muscle target: Rear deltoids, scapulae.

Starting position: Bend over with the back flat and parallel to the ground. Hold the dumbbells at arm's length directly under the shoulders with the palms turned in toward each other.

Execution: Keeping the arms fairly straight (a slight bend is recommended), raise the dumbbells directly out to the sides and slightly forward. Once the dumbbells are even with the back, return to the starting position in a controlled manner.

Coaching points: There are three common mistakes people make when performing this exercise:

1. The back is too high. Put the head on something stable such as an incline bench to make it stay at that point with the hips high.
2. The lower back, not the shoulders, is used to perform the exercise, making it much like a bent-over snatch. Fix this by placing the head on something stable to keep it still.
3. The dumbbells are brought too far back. Try to see the dumbbells in your peripheral vision. If you can't see the dumbbells, you need to bring the dumbbells forward more.

Summary

The bench press is the exercise most often performed incorrectly. Most lifters take the time to learn to squat and deadlift properly but consider bench press to be simple and natural.

Developing a big bench press takes time and patience. Unfortunately, it is easy to alter form with bench press in an attempt to increase weight. This stalls progress on the competition platform. The bench press must be developed, with time spent on exercises that improve weak links. Those who use training gear must spend a significant amount of time learning to use the gear as well.

When training the bench press, remember this: This exercise is the one most commonly overtaken by machismo. When a lifter tries to lift the heaviest weight without using correct form, results are lost. Many lifters push up the board press or floor press to huge personal records without improving their competition lift. Often they don't perform the exercise properly, and sacrifice form for weight on the bar.

Take the time to do everything right. This will help build your bench press to the greatest heights possible.

Deadlift

Former world champion and deadlift world-record holder Don Blue coined the saying *The meet don't start until the bar hits the floor.* Without question the deadlift is the ultimate test of overall body strength as it involves every major and minor muscle in the body. In competition, the deadlift is the last of the three lifts to take place. When the bar hits the floor, you want your deadlift to be considered a lethal weapon. Powerlifting greats Bill Kazmaier, Brad Gillingham, Lamar Gant (considered the greatest deadlifter of all time), and Ricky Dale Crain could pull a winning deadlift if called for during competition.

To create your weapon, you must be aware of proper form and technique and create good habits. Remember that once you develop bad habits, they are hard to break and could possibly lead to serious injury as well as missed attempts during competition. Another problem with bad habits is that when you attempt to change to the correct form and technique, initially it does not feel right and is uncomfortable. However, once your body adapts to the correct form and technique, the weights move much easier and you can work the muscles that the deadlift is designed to work. Beginner powerlifters may not have an experienced coach to critique them and help them with form and technique on the deadlift. This chapter is designed to guide you through the deadlift, especially if you are a beginner.

Whether training or lifting in a powerlifting meet, when performing the squat and bench press, you get an opportunity to start each of these lifts with momentum, thus increasing your chance for a successful lift. Also you have the help of the power suit, knee wraps, belt, and bench shirt. When it comes time to deadlift, it is just you and a loaded bar resting on the floor. You can wear a power suit, belt, and knee wraps if you wish. This equipment may help you execute the lift, but does not help with the initial pull.

Many powerlifters do what is considered a *dive technique,* in which a lifter drops down quickly to the bar, grabs it, and attempts to gain momentum by pulling the weight off the floor. Another technique is called the hurkey-jerky move, in which a lifter eases down to the bar then suddenly grabs the bar and attempts to jerk the weight off the floor. Both of these techniques are wrong and could lead to back injury or a missed attempt. These techniques can cause the hips to rise quickly ahead of the chest, arms, and head, forcing the lifter to perform a stiff-legged or a rounded-back deadlift.

Two styles of deadlift are used in competition: conventional style, in which the feet are shoulder-width apart or closer and the hands are outside the legs, and sumo, in which the feet and legs are spread wide and the hands are inside the legs. In a third style of deadlifting, semi-sumo, the feet and legs are spread shoulder-width apart and the hands are inside the legs. Powerlifters seldom use this technique; however, Ed Coan, one the greatest powerlifters of all time, uses this form. For beginners, it is probably smarter and wiser to use the conventional style because it is easier to master. As you compete more, you can slowly convert to the sumo style based on your squatting stance. For example, if you squat with a wide stance, the sumo deadlift is what you want to use because you have strong hips, adductors, and glutes. If you squat with a shoulder-width stance, you want to use the conventional deadlift. Anything between the wide and close squat stance, you are looking at semi-sumo style or conventional deadlift, whichever one feels comfortable to you.

Grips

Competitors use four types of grips: the double overhand, the alternated grip, the hook grip, and the double underhand grip.

The *double overhand grip* (figure 6.1a) is a carryover from Olympic lifting. In this grip, you take both hands in an overhand position so that the knuckles face away from the body and the palms face the body. This grip creates a nice balance and prevents a lot of the rotation that some competitors perform when they deadlift, which is sometimes referred to as a *helicopter* (one end of the bar swings out wide and then the other to compensate). This is a weaker grip, but sometimes preferred by those who have very large hands and long fingers that can completely wrap around the bar.

The *alternated grip* (figure 6.1b) is the one that powerlifters most commonly use. It allows for the greatest possible grip strength. Usually the dominant hand is in the overhand position and the nondominant hand is in the underhand position. Gripping the bar from different directions means no major gap in the pull. You must be sure to have acceptable upper-body flexibility, which isn't much, or else you pull in a helicopter fashion. Again, the improvement in grip strength is the reason for its use.

The *hook grip* (figure 6.1c) is another grip brought in from Olympic lifting. Competitors with large hands have used this grip and claim it is much stronger. The hook grip is essentially a change in thumb placement. For the hook grip, the thumb is placed on the bar and then covered by the fingers as they wrap around the bar instead of fingers first and thumbs covering. Olympic lifters swear by its use, and those who come to powerlifting from Olympic lifting commonly use it. However, do not use this grip if you have thumb problems.

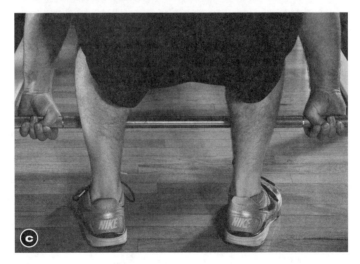

Figure 6.1 Deadlift grips: *(a)* double overhand; *(b)* alternated; *(c)* hook.

The fourth grip, the *double underhand grip,* is never really seen in competition. Some people started using the double underhand grip, in which both palms face away with the knuckles facing the body, as it would theoretically keep the bar closer to the body and not let it swing away. However, the grip causes a lot of strain on the biceps, and people tended to tear biceps fairly easily using only moderate weight. This grip is definitely not recommended.

Mechanics of the Conventional Deadlift

The conventional deadlift is a popular technique that many powerlifters use. The keys to the conventional deadlift are to keep the bar close and straighten your legs last. Do not attempt to jerk the bar off the floor. For a sure grip, make sure the bar is clean of powder.

Setting Up

1. Position yourself in front of the bar by placing the balls of your feet under the bar (figure 6.2*a*).
2. Your toes should be pointed straight ahead or slightly out.
3. Your shins should be close to the bar or touching it. Stand with your feet shoulder-width apart or closer. Stand with your legs shoulder-width apart or place the outside of your leg at the edge of the smooth part of the bar and knurling meet.
4. Get into the downward position. Your head should be straight, chest is up with a flat back, and arms are stretched down and reaching for the bar.
5. At the initial pull, the hips should be higher than the knees.
6. Grab the bar just outside your legs or grab where the knurling begins and the smooth part of the bar ends (figure 6.2*b*).
7. Use an alternate grip in which one palm faces toward the body and the other faces away. This stabilizes the bar, keeping it close to the body and preventing it from rolling out of your hands.

CONVENTIONAL DEADLIFT

Figure 6.2 Setup: *(a)* get in position in front of bar; *(b)* grab bar.

Beginning the Pull

1. Keep your arms straight. Before starting the pull, take the slack out of the bar by pulling on it through your arms, chest, and shoulders (figure 6.3a). Remember that the legs and hips, not the arms, are doing the pulling.
2. Inhale. Squeeze the bar and push your feet and legs against the floor.
3. Raise your hips, shoulders, and chest at the same time as the bar leaves the floor (figure 6.3b).
4. The bar should travel in a straight line. The closer the bar is to the body, the easier the lift.
5. Once the bar passes over the knees, push the thighs forward and pull the shoulders up and back until the legs are straight; knees are locked (figure 6.3c). Arms are straight and the shoulders are slightly back. You are standing erect.

CONVENTIONAL DEADLIFT

Figure 6.3 Pull: *(a)* pull on bar to take out slack; *(b)* lift hips, shoulders, and chest as bar leaves floor; *(c)* push thighs forward and pull shoulders up and back.

Lowering the Weight

1. Lower the weight in a controlled manner.
2. Flex at the knees and hips, letting the bar travel down the same path it came up.
3. Keep the bar close to your body.
4. Keep your back flat and tight and keep your head up.

Mechanics of the Sumo Deadlift

The sumo deadlift is designed for lifters who have great hip flexibility that allows them to use a wide stance. Two things about the sumo deadlift are important to keep in mind: You have to be able to generate power off the floor and you cannot let your legs straighten out too fast.

Setting Up

1. Position yourself in front of the bar. Spread both legs out (figure 6.4*a*), using the ring of the bar as a landmark.
2. Point your toes out at about a 30-degree angle in order to line up your toes with your knees.
3. Stand with feet wider than shoulder-width apart. Shins are close to or touching the bar.
4. In the downward position, hold your chest up with your back flat. Flex at the hips and knees as you lower your body down to the weight (figure 6.4*b*). Your arms are inside your legs and pointed straight down to the bar.
5. At the initial pull, the hips should be higher than the knees.
6. You can grab the bar in one of three ways: grip the bar between the knurling and smooth part of the bar, grab all knurling, or grab the smooth part of the bar. (This last grip is not recommended if you do have strong grips.)
7. Use an alternated grip with one palm facing the body and the other palm facing away (figure 6.4*c*). This will stabilize the bar, keeping it close to the body and preventing it from rolling out of your hands.

Figure 6.4 Setup: *(a)* get in position in front of bar; *(b)* lower body to weight; *(c)* grip bar.

Beginning the Pull

1. Keep your arms straight before starting the pull. Take the slack out of the bar by pulling on it through your arms, chest, and shoulders (figure 6.5a).

2. Pull your chest up, inhaling to fill it with air, and sit back slightly.

3. Squeeze the bar and push through the floor with your feet and legs as if you were trying to separate the floor.

4. Keep the bar close to the body and in a straight line (figure 6.5b). This makes the lift easier.

5. Maintain a flat back with your chest up and slightly over the bar as it moves up.

6. Once the bar passes the knees, push the thighs forward and pull the shoulders up and back until the legs are straight; knees are locked (figure 6.5c). The arms are straight with the shoulders slightly back. You are standing erect.

SUMO DEADLIFT

Figure 6.5 Pull: *(a)* remove slack from bar by pulling with arms, chest, and shoulders; *(b)* lift bar close to body and in straight line; *(c)* push thighs forward and pull shoulders up and back.

Lowering the Weight

1. Lower the weight in a controlled manner.
2. Flex at the knees and hips while letting the bar travel down the same path it traveled up.
3. Keep the bar close to the body.
4. Keep your back flat and tight with your head up. Exhale as the bar touches the floor.

Conventional Versus Sumo

This section is not a discussion of which method is more true powerlifting; it is a discussion of the advantages of the sumo style over the conventional style and vice versa.

The conventional style is much easier to learn. The deadlift may look like a simple exercise, but a lot of technique is involved in learning it. When getting ready for your first meet, go with conventional. The lifter who uses the conventional lift has the advantage of being able to blast off the floor more easily since the quads are more involved due to the foot and leg position. If you can get the bar to your knees, you should be able to lock it out. If you can't, it's back to the drawing board and heavy rack pulls from this position are employed.

The sumo style deadlift is more complex and takes more time to learn. Not only this, but more muscles need to be developed for both strength and mobility. Some individuals were not made to sumo style deadlift due to various mobility issues and lever lengths. The advantage of the sumo style deadlift is the much shortened distance that the barbell must travel. Using the sumo style deadlift, it is very difficult to develop drive off the floor, and once the floor has been broken, the weight is most assuredly locked out.

Rules and Guidelines

In competition, the rules are very simple and are pretty much the standard for all organizations in the sport of powerlifting.

- The lifter must face the front of the platform with the bar laid horizontally in front of his feet.
- At completion of the lift, the knees must be locked and shoulders back.
- The chief referee's signal consists of a downward movement of the arm and the audible command "down." This signal is given only when the bar is motionless and the lifter has apparently completed the lift.
- An attempt is considered valid if the bar is raised or if there is any deliberate attempt to raise the bar. Once the lifter has started the attempt, there is no downward movement of the bar until the lifter is standing erect and the knees are locked.

Any of the following reasons are causes for disqualification:

- Any downward movement of the bar before lockout.
- Not standing erect with shoulders back.
- Knees not locked at completion of the lift.
- Bar resting on the thighs.
- Any stepping forward or backward.
- Bar lowered before the chief referee's signal.
- Not maintaining control of the bar with both hands returning to the platform.

Equipment

Your power suit should meet all regulations. You will prefer a suit that is semitight in the shoulder straps, tight in the hips, and loose in the legs.

Whether you use a weight belt or not is your choice. A weight belt does give the abdomen something to push against. However, a belt that is too tight may be uncomfortable and hurt your performance.

Wear long socks out of consideration for other lifters, especially if you bleed a lot. If you do not like wearing socks, use tape in the area over which the bar will travel.

Besides keeping the bar close to the body, the type of shoe you wear is another way to gain an advantage. Wrestling shoes, slippers, or gymnastics shoes are the best choice for conventional style. Due to the forces put on the foot laterally, cross-training shoes may be better for foot support on the sumo or semi-sumo style deadlift.

As you get into your heavy deadlift, you should use chalk. Chalk your palms and fingers, including the backs of your pointed fingers.

To help cut down on friction, apply powder to the areas over which the bar will travel. A sumo style deadlifter should put powder on the front of the forearm of the palm that faces him and the back of the forearm of the palm that faces away. If you are applying powder, do not use your hands. Use the butt of the bottle to spread the powder. Also, shaving your legs the night before the meet helps lessen friction.

Developing Grip Strength

You can do several things to strengthen your grip for deadlifting. If you are a beginner, stay away from straps, or at least do not get in the habit of using them regardless of how much weight you can pull with them. You are not allowed to use them in competition, so don't train with them.

Use these variations to develop your grip strength:

- Deadlift with both hands over the bar
- Towel pull-ups

- Plate grips for time
- Baseball pull-ups (tie two baseballs on a power rack so they are hanging, grasp the baseballs and pull yourself up)
- Farmer's walk with a 45-pound (20.4 kg) plate

Note: When performing the deadlift, whether using conventional or sumo style, your legs should be the last to straighten out. The best rule of thumb for keeping the bar close to your body is to treat the bar like it is your girlfriend, wife, husband, or boyfriend.

Supplemental Exercises

Whether you need to work on the initial pull, middle position, or the final lockout, these exercises will help improve your weakest points.

INITIAL PULL

STIFF-LEGGED DEADLIFT

Powerlifting focus: Strengthen the initial pull of the deadlift.

Muscle target: Spinal erectors, gluteus maximus, and hamstrings.

Starting position: Stand with your feet shoulder-width apart. Hold the barbell in an overhand grip. Hold the barbell at arms' length.

Execution: Inhale, bending forward at the waist and pushing the hips back. Keep your back flat and rigid, your chest up, and your legs straight, if possible. Keeping the bar close to the body, lower the bar until it is mid-shin or close to the floor. Return to the starting position, exhaling at the top.

Coaching points: Do not round your back. Keep the bar close to the body.

STIFF-LEGGED DEADLIFT OFF A FOUR-INCH BLOCK

Powerlifting focus: Strengthen the initial pull of the deadlift.

Muscle target: Spinal erectors, gluteus maximus, and hamstrings.

Starting position: Stand with your feet shoulder-width apart on a block or bench that is 4 inches (10 cm) high. Hold a barbell in an overhand grip and hang it at arms' length.

Execution: Inhale and bend forward at the waist, pushing your hips back. Keep your back flat and rigid, your chest up, and your legs straight, if possible. Keeping the bar close to the body, lower the bar until it is at your toes or lower. Return to the starting position, exhaling at the top.

Coaching points: Make sure you keep your legs straight and get a full range of motion.

SNATCH GRIP DEADLIFT

Powerlifting focus: Strengthen the muscles used during the initial pull of the deadlift.

Muscle target: Trapezius, spinal erectors, and rhomboids.

Starting position: Stand with your feet shoulder-width apart or slightly wider. Knees are inside the arms, feet are flat, and toes are slightly pointed out. Use a pronated close grip, arms stretched out to the rings.

Execution: Inhale and extend the knees. Move the hips forward and raise the shoulders at the same time. Keep the bar close to the body, elbows fully extended. Drive the hips forward and shoulders back until you are standing erect with your legs locked. Exhale at the top and return the weight to starting position.

Coaching points: Keep your arms straight and do not bend your elbows. Keep your chest up and back flat.

SNATCH GRIP DEADLIFT OFF A FOUR-INCH BLOCK

Powerlifting focus: Strengthen the muscles used during the initial pull of the deadlift.

Muscle target: Trapezius, spinal erectors, and rhomboids.

Starting position: Stand on a block, mat, bench, or weight plates so you are elevated 4 inches (10 cm) off the floor. Stand with feet shoulder-width apart or slightly wider, knees inside your arms. Feet are flat and toes are slightly pointed out. Use a pronated grip, arms stretched out to the rings.

Execution: Inhale and extend the knees. Move the hips forward and raise the shoulders at the same time. Keep the bar close to the body, elbows fully extended. Drive the hips forward, shoulders back until you are standing erect with your legs locked. Exhale as you return the weight to starting position.

Coaching points: Balance your weight. Stay off your toes and breathe properly.

STIFF-LEGGED DEADLIFT WITH BANDS

Powerlifting focus: Develop explosive power at the bottom of the lift.

Muscle target: Gluteus maximus, hamstrings, and spinal erectors.

Starting position: Stand with your feet shoulder-width apart or closer. Hold the barbell in an overhand grip, barbell hanging at arms' length. The bands, which are attached to the bar, are fully stretched.

Execution: Inhale and bend forward at the waist while pushing your hips back. Keep your back flat and rigid, your chest up, and your legs as straight as possible. Keep the bar close to the body, lowering it until the bar is mid-shin or close to the floor and the bands are settled. Return to the starting position, letting the bar travel the same path back up and keeping it close to the body as the bands lengthen, providing resistance as you complete the lift. Exhale as you get to the top of the lift.

Coaching points: Stay tight. Relaxing the bands could pull you forward. Keep the weight off your toes.

STIFF-LEGGED DEADLIFT WITH CHAINS

Powerlifting focus: Develop explosive power.

Muscle target: Gluteus maximus, hamstrings, and spinal erectors.

Starting position: Stand with your feet shoulder-width apart or closer. Hold the barbell in an overhand grip, barbell hanging at arms' length. The chains, which are attached to the bar, are fully stretched.

Execution: Inhale and bend forward at the waist while pushing your hips back. Keep your back flat and rigid, your chest up, and your legs as straight as possible. Keep the bar close to the body, lowering it until the bar is mid-shin or close to the floor and the chains are settled. Return to the starting position, letting the bar travel the same path back up and keeping it close to the body as the chains lengthen, providing resistance as you complete the lift. Exhale as you get to the top of the lift.

Coaching points: Control the weight throughout the movement. Keep your weight evenly distributed between the balls and heels of your feet.

GOOD MORNING

Powerlifting focus: Strengthen the muscles used in the initial pull of the deadlift.

Muscle target: Spinal erectors, gluteus maximus, and hamstrings.

Starting position: Stand erect with your feet shoulder-width apart or closer and a barbell positioned across your shoulders (figure 6.6a).

Execution: Inhale and bend at the waist, pushing the hips back. Keep your head and chest up and your back straight until your torso is parallel to the floor (figure 6.6b) and your lower and upper body are at a 90-degree angle. Return to the starting position, exhaling at the top.

Coaching points: Make sure to bend your knees slightly. Distribute your weight evenly between the balls of your feet and the heels.

Figure 6.6   Good morning: *(a)* starting position; *(b)* torso parallel to floor.

CLEAN PULL

Powerlifting focus: Develop speed on the initial pull.

Muscle target: Trapezius, spinal erectors, rhomboids, and teres major.

Starting position: Squat down to the bar, feet shoulder-width apart and heels flat (figure 6.7*a*). The knees are inside the arms, and the arms are straight. The shoulders are slightly over the bar, and the back is flat. The head and eyes are straight.

Execution: Exhale. Extend the knees and raise the hips and shoulders at the same time (figure 6.7*b*). Lift the bar straight up, keeping it close to the body. As the bar passes the knees, push the hips forward and shrug the weight, coming up on your toes (figure 6.7*c*). Your torso is vertical and erect. To lower the bar, bend the knees and keep the bar close to the body, back flat. Exhale as the bar returns to the starting position.

Coaching points: Keep the bar close to the body and the arms straight. If you are bending your arms, you are trying to lift too much weight.

Figure 6.7 Clean pull: *(a)* squat down to bar for starting position; *(b)* raise hips and shoulders; *(c)* shrug weight and rise on toes.

GLUTE-HAM RAISE

Powerlifting focus: Strengthen stabilization muscles.

Muscle target: Spinal erectors, gluteus maximus, hamstrings, and gastrocnemius.

Starting position: Lie facedown on the glute-ham machine and place your ankles between the support pads and your thighs across the front pad. Your body should be at 90 degrees, your lower body horizontal and your legs straight. Place your hands either across your chest or behind your hand.

Execution: Inhale, flex at the knees, and pull your torso upright until it is vertical and your knees are against the thigh pad. Return to the starting position by straightening your legs as you push your torso out and away from the machine until your upper body is parallel to the floor. Exhale as you lower your torso.

Coaching points: Control your body throughout the entire movement.

RACK PULL BELOW THE KNEES

Powerlifting focus: Develop the initial pull from the bottom.

Muscle target: Trapezius, gluteus maximus, hamstrings, latissimus dorsi, rhomboids, rectus femoris, and quadriceps.

Starting position: In a power rack, place safety pins below the knees near the middle of your shins. Use an alternate grip. Stand with feet shoulder-width apart and squat down to the bar, chest up, arms straight, back flat, and head and eyes straight ahead.

Execution: Inhale and begin pulling the weight straight up close to the body, pushing your thighs forward as the bar passes the knees. Keep your chest up, straightening your legs as you pull the weight to the completion. To lower the weight, bend the knees, retracing the path the bar travelled up. Exhale at the top of the lift.

Coaching points: Keep your hips down. Pull the weight; do not jerk it. Keep a flat back; do not round your back. You can add bands or chains to this movement.

MIDDLE POSITION

WIDE-GRIP CHIN-UP

Powerlifting focus: Add thickness to the back.

Muscle target: Latissimus dorsi, rhomboids, teres major, biceps brachii, and brachioradialis.

Starting position: Using an overhand wide grip with hands wider than shoulder-width apart, hang from the chin-up bar as low as possible (figure 6.8a). Stretch your lats, shoulders, and arms.

Execution: Inhale and pull yourself up until your eyes are above the level of the chin-up bar (figure 6.8b). Return to the starting position, exhaling on the way down.

Coaching points: Make sure you go through a full range of motion. You can use a variety of grips, from medium to close.

Figure 6.8 Wide-grip chin-up: *(a)* starting position; *(b)* eyes above bar.

REVERSE-GRIP CHIN-UP

Powerlifting focus: Develop and strengthen the muscles used as the bar passes the knees.

Muscle target: Latissimus dorsi, teres major, biceps brachii, and brachioradialis.

Starting position: Using an underhand grip with your hands shoulder-width apart, hang from the chin-up bar.

Execution: Inhale. Lean back slightly to pull yourself up until your chin is at the level of the bar. Exhale as you lower yourself down.

Coaching points: Make sure your arms are fully extended while working through a full range of motion.

LAT PULLDOWN

Powerlifting focus: Add thickness to the back and work the center of the lats.

Muscle target: Latissimus dorsi, teres major, and biceps brachii.

Starting position: Use a wide, overhand grip. Sit facing the cable machine with the tops of your thighs under a roller pad. Lean back slightly.

Execution: Inhale and pull the bar down until it touches the top of the chest, arching the back and bringing the elbows back. Return the bar to the starting position while exhaling slowly.

Coaching points: Do not lean back too far or stay too upright. Do not jerk the weight. Use a variety of hand placements from medium to close as well as different bars.

SEATED LOW-CABLE ROW

Powerlifting focus: Build the back and isolate the stabilizing muscles.

Muscle target: Trapezius, rhomboid major, latissimus dorsi, teres major, erector spinae, and posterior deltoid.

Starting position: Sit facing the cable machine. Place your feet on the foot rest and grab the pulley bar (figure 6.9a).

Execution: Inhale and pull the handle until it touches your rib cage (figure 6.9b). As the handle comes close to the body, your legs are slightly bent. Arch your back and attempt to wrap your elbows around your body. Lower the weight stack under control while exhaling slowly.

Coaching points: Do not round your back or straighten your legs.

Figure 6.9 Seated low-cable row: *(a)* place feet on foot rest and grab pulley bar; *(b)* pull handle to rib cage.

BARBELL BENT-OVER ROW

Powerlifting focus: Work the major and minor muscles in the back that help complete the lift.

Muscle target: Trapezius, rhomboids, infraspinatus, teres major, latissimus dorsi, posterior deltoid, and biceps brachii.

Starting position: Stand with your knees slightly bent. Flex at the hips so your back is flat. Using an overhand grip, hang the bar at arms' length.

Execution: Inhale and pull the weight up until it touches your torso. Exhale as you slowly return the bar to the starting position.

Coaching points: Do not jerk the weight up. Keep your back flat and knees bent. Use a variety of grips from wide to close and from overhand to underhand.

ONE-ARM DUMBBELL ROW

Powerlifting focus: Work to help contract the muscles at the end.

Muscle target: Rhomboid major, latissimus dorsi, trapezius, teres major, posterior deltoid, biceps brachii, and brachioradialis.

Starting position: Grab the dumbbell with your palm facing in. Place your opposite knee and hand on the bench with your back flat and straight (figure 6.10a).

Execution: Inhale and pull the dumbbell up as high as possible with your elbow pointing toward the ceiling (figure 6.10b). Exhale as you lower the weight to the starting position.

Coaching points: Do not handle too much weight. Too much weight may alter your form or technique.

Figure 6.10 One-arm dumbbell row: *(a)* grab dumbbell; *(b)* raise dumbbell.

RACK LOCKOUT AT THE KNEES

Powerlifting focus: Develop thickness in the middle of the back.

Muscle target: Trapezius and latissimus dorsi.

Starting position: In a power rack, place the safety pins at your knees. Stand with your feet shoulder-width apart or closer. Using an alternate grip, grab the bar outside your legs. Slightly bend your knees until your arms are straight as you grab the bar. Keep your chest up, back flat, and head and eyes straight ahead.

Execution: Inhale and begin pulling the weight up your thighs, pushing your thighs into the bar and straightening your legs to complete the lift. Stand erect with your arms straight. Lower the weight by bending the knees and keeping the back straight. Exhale at the top of the lift.

Coaching points: For this short movement, you should be able to handle more weight than you can deadlift. For variety, add chains or bands during this movement.

LOCKOUT TOP POSITION

SHRUGS IN FRONT

Powerlifting focus: Helps with lockout at the completion of the lift.

Muscle target: Trapezius.

Starting position: Face a bar resting on a power rack. Stand with your feet shoulder-width apart or closer. Use an alternate grip with your hands shoulder-width apart.

Execution: Remove the weight from the rack. Bend your knees slightly. Keep your arms and back straight. Inhale as you contract your abdominals and shrug your shoulders up toward the ears as high as possible. Hold for 2 seconds and slowly return the bar to the starting position, exhaling slowly.

Coaching points: Keep the arms straight and the feet flat. Too much weight causes you to bend the arms and come up on your toes.

DUMBBELL SHRUG

Powerlifting focus: Isolate the muscles used in the lockout position.

Muscle target: Trapezius and rhomboids.

Starting position: Stand with your feet shoulder-width apart or closer, knees slightly bent, torso erect, and head straight or slightly forward. Hold the dumbbells in your hands at arms' length.

Execution: Inhale and shrug your shoulders as high as possible. Hold for 2 seconds before lowering the dumbbells to the starting position. Exhale slowly as you lower the weights.

Coaching points: Use a weight that is comfortable. Keep your feet flat.

LOCKOUT ABOVE THE KNEES

Powerlifting focus: Help complete the deadlift, pulling the shoulders back.

Muscle target: Trapezius.

Starting position: In a power rack, place safety pins above the knees. Stand with your feet shoulder-width apart, chest up, back flat, and knees bent. Using an alternate grip, grab the bar at arms' length outside the legs. The head and eyes are straight ahead.

Execution: Inhale and pull the weight up against the thighs. Keep your chest up. Straighten your legs to complete the lift. When standing erect, your arms should be straight. To lower the weight, bend the knees, keeping your chest up and exhaling as the weight returns to the rack.

Coaching points: This movement is short, so your load should be heavier than your deadlift but not to the point at which you cannot lift the weight for repetitions. You can add bands or chains to add spice to your deadlift.

UPRIGHT ROW

Powerlifting focus: Strengthen the trapezius and help with lockout.

Muscle target: Trapezius, deltoids, and brachialis.

Starting position: Stand with your feet shoulder-width apart, knees slightly bent, and back straight. Use an overhand grip with your hands 12 to 18 inches (30-45 cm) apart, the bar resting on your thighs at arms' length.

Execution: Inhale and lift the bar straight up until it touches your chin. Keep your elbows high and your body and head straight. In a controlled manner, lower the bar to starting position as you exhale slowly.

Coaching points: Keep the back straight. Avoid rocking or swinging the weight and do not use your legs.

TRAP BAR SHRUG

Powerlifting focus: Strengthen the muscles used in the lockout position.

Muscle target: Trapezius, rhomboids, and teres major.

Starting position: The trap bar requires you to use an overhand grip with the palms facing the body, which allows you to handle more weight than normal and go through a greater range of motion. Stand inside the bar with your feet shoulder-width apart or closer. The bar hangs at arms' length with the palms facing the body. Knees are slightly bent, torso is straight, and the head and eyes look straight ahead.

Execution: Inhale as you contract your abdominals and shrug your shoulders up toward your ears as high as possible. Hold for 2 seconds and return the bar to the starting position, exhaling slowly.

Coaching points: Use a weight you can handle. Control the weight throughout the movement.

T-BAR ROW

Powerlifting focus: Strengthen the muscles used to help with the lockout.

Muscle target: Trapezius, rhomboids, and posterior deltoid.

Starting position: Straddle the T-bar by spreading your legs shoulder-width apart. Flex at the knees and hips, positioning your back in a flat, straight line. Keep your head and eyes up as you grab the crossbar at arms' length.

Execution: Inhale and pull the bar toward your chest until it touches. Lower the bar to the starting position in a controlled manner, exhaling slowly.

Coaching points: Work through a full range of motion. Do not jerk the weight when pulling it up.

Dan Austin's Deadlift Routine

Dan Austin was the first lightweight powerlifter to deadlift more than 700 pounds. His best is 725 pounds. This is the routine Dan used to prepare for the 700-pound deadlift (table 6.1).

TABLE 6.1   Dan Austin's 9-Week Deadlift Training Program

Goal: 700-pound (317.5 kg) deadlift

Week	Pounds and repetitions
1	135 × 8, 225 × 5, 315 × 5, 405 × 3, 505 × 1, 560 × 2 × 4
2	225 × 5, 315 × 5, 405 × 3, 505 × 1 545 × 1, 580 × 2 × 4
3	225 × 5, 315 × 5, 405 × 3, 525 × 1, 565 × 1, 600 × 2 × 4
4	225 × 5, 315 × 5, 405 × 3, 525 × 1, 575 × 1, 620 × 2 × 4
5	225 × 5, 315 × 5, 405 × 3, 525 × 1, 585 × 1, 640 × 2 × 2
6	225 × 5, 315 × 5, 405 × 3, 525 × 1 585 × 1, 635 × 1 660 × 2 × 2
7	225 × 5, 315 × 5, 405 × 3; 525 × 1, 585 × 1, 635 × 1,680 × 2 × 2
8	De-load week at 70%: 225 × 5, 315 × 5, 405 × 3, 490 × 2 × 8
9	Meet week: first attempt 633; second attempt 672; third attempt 705

Dan does deadlifts on Thursdays with a light leg workout. To help warm the hips, legs, and back, he does five sets of box squats based on the weight he used Monday, his heavy squat day. He uses an eight-week training cycle with the meet in the ninth week. During the offseason, Dan trains the deadlift in a conventional stance performing 10 repetitions for five sets. Three weeks prior to starting his training cycle, Dan switches his stance to sumo style. The weight Dan uses the first week is based off his goal weight (700 pounds) multiplied by 80 percent (700 x 80 = 560) for two sets of 4 repetitions.

In supplemental exercises, Dan's goal is to strengthen stabilizers and strengthen weaker muscles as much as possible. He achieves this by going as heavy as possible while maintaining good form and technique with each exercise. Dan trains his back from the bottom to the top in the order of the exercises listed in table 6.2. On his light leg day, he supersets leg curls with reverse hypers.

TABLE 6.2   Supplemental Exercises in Dan Austin's Deadlift Program

Exercise	Weeks 1 and 2	Weeks 3 to 5	Weeks 6 to 8
Romanian deadlift (RDL)	3 × 10	3 × 8	3 × 5
Good morning	3 × 10	3 × 8	3 × 5
Lat pulldown (reverse grip)	3 × 10	3 × 8	3 × 5
One-arm dumbbell row	3 × 10	3 × 8	3 × 5
Chin-up (weighted)	3 × 10	3 × 8	3 × 5
Barbell or dumbbell shrug	3 × 10	3 × 8	3 × 5

Summary

Without question, the deadlift is the one exercise that tests a lifter's true strength. The lifter uses no momentum to start the lift, so it is very important to use good form and technique to get the most from the deadlift. Since it is the last lift in a meet, you never know when you will need it to pull out a win or set a record.

CHAPTER 7

Power Periodization

Periodization is simply a means of planning and organizing training. Several methods of periodization exist, including undulating, conjugate, linear, and block. All of these methods are ways to try to reach the same goal—getting stronger. It's like two friends who live in Washington D.C. and are trying to get from point A to point B. One may like taking the beltway, and the other may prefer to stay on the smaller roads. They'll both get to the same point; it's just a matter of personal preference how they get there.

This chapter is an overview of undulating and conjugate periodization. Each type of periodization is worth a book in itself; in fact, each type has more than one book written on it. Each type has its own nuances, so it is a good idea to learn these nuances before you attempt to do the program. Many people claim a type of periodization doesn't work at all, when in fact they weren't applying it appropriately.

Undulating Periodization

In undulating periodization, you are always working up to a repetition maximum (RM). In each workout, the RM varies, so you never perform the same RM from week to week or often within several weeks. The body adapts to repetitions before it adapts to exercises or weights, so the constant altering of repetitions does not allow the body to adapt to one stimulus. This keeps the body fresh and responsive for a longer period of time.

The undulations in training allow the lifter to train multiple traits concurrently, much like the conjugate method. In undulating periodization, though, the lifter uses the same exercises instead of changing exercises every session or every few sessions.

The RM should be varied enough to not work on the exact same thing in subsequent workouts. For instance, doing a 3RM in week 1 and a 4RM in week 2 may not be enough of a variance. A rule of thumb is to vary workouts by at least 2RM. For instance, in week 1 work up to a 6RM, in week 2 work up to a 4RM, in week 3 work up to a 2 RM, in week 4 work up to a 5RM, in week 5 work up to a 3RM, and in week 6 work up to a 1RM.

In undulating periodization, on days when you want to back off, you can still work up to a RM. Simply work on a higher RM. For instance, instead of working up to a 5RM, work up to a 15RM or 20RM.

You need to understand what each repetition range is trying to accomplish. For instance, a 15RM has little to no impact on strength but significant impact on hypertrophy. Conversely, working up to a 3RM has little or no impact on hypertrophy but significant impact on strength. This all relates back to time under tension. The greater the time under tension, the greater the impact on hypertrophy; the shorter the time under tension, the greater the impact on strength and power.

You want to focus the majority of your training on the main trait you are trying to develop. For instance, if it is off-season and you are trying to gain weight, you want more of your training to focus on 10RM to 20RM, as that RM builds the greatest amount of hypertrophy. If you are trying to gain base strength, you want to stay more in the 4RM to 8RM range as these ranges seem to affect base strength more. If you want to improve absolute strength and power, focus workouts on 1 to 3 rep ranges as this is the range that seems to most effectively develop absolute strength. This is not to say to never do a RM out of those ranges. Absolutely include workouts with a RM out of each range. However, when you look at how many workouts are in each rep range, the trait you desire to train should have the most sessions.

The frequency of the exercise being used should be at least once a week. Many people have seen great results from twice per week, and there have even been reports of people doing well on three times per week. It depends on how much you want to do per week and how you have been training in the past. If you drastically increase volume, for instance go from benching once per week to benching three times a week, you likely will either overtrain or become injured. If you want to increase your sessions per week, start the second session small and build it over time. It may be a good idea to start with only a few exercises and do them light. Once you adapt to that, increase the number of exercises and then the intensity. This will allow the body to adapt properly so you can increase overall training load while reducing the chance of burnout and injury.

Some think it is hard to stay focused on training using the undulating periodization method because the reps are always changing. This is not true. You must always track the RM and try to break it every time you train. When using undulating periodization you can track strength gains in two ways. The first and most obvious method is simply to record the individual RM and try to break it every time you train. If you perform a 5RM 2 weeks later and you can perform it with 10 pounds (4.53 kg) more, you know you have increased strength. The second way is to use an estimated 1RM from either a chart or an equation. According to the National Strength and Conditioning Association (NSCA) guidelines, anything at a 10RM or below will be fairly accurate at predicting or estimating a 1RM. The further you get above 10, the less accurate you are. Likewise, the further you get below 10, the more accurate you are. Understand that estimations are not always going to be completely accurate. For instance, some people are able to do 3 repetitions with 5 pounds (2.26 kg) under their 1RM, but if they add 10 pounds (4.53 kg) they cannot perform a single repetition. Some people can't do repetitions, so they may be 80 pounds off from their 8RM to their 1RM.

A key to undulating periodization is to keep training to maximal levels every session. You must sufficiently fatigue the muscle cells and motor neurons to force an adaptation. The beauty of undulating periodization is that you are always changing repetition schemes and trying to set new personal records. The beast of undulating periodization is that you are always on, and every session you push yourself to the limit. The muscle needs to be broken down to build itself back up and increase the number of myofibrils (the contractile proteins, essentially the engine that drives the muscle car) and increase the size of the muscle (hypertrophy).

Undulating periodization is great for the person who likes consistency on the exercises of each session and consistently trying to set personal records. The lack of core exercise variety does lead some lifters to wish to change the workout.

Tables 7.1, 7.2, and 7.3 show sample workouts for one session, two sessions, or three sessions a week, respectively.

Now that we see how the workouts would be set up for one individual lift, let's examine what occurs with multiple lifts and the supplemental exercises.

Someone who is not a one-lift specialist will want to train more than one lift at a time. There are two setup options for this type of programming, and it really depends on the lifter's personal preferences for his own workouts. The two variations are to perform the same RM for every main lift or to rotate through the RM for the main lift over the course of the week.

Option one, performing the same RM for every main lift, means doing the same RM for your chosen lifts. For example, let's say the bench press and the squat were the main exercises, you were doing two lifts per week, and you were in week 1 of the sample workout shown in table 7.2 (absolute strength emphasis). During session 1, you would perform a 5RM on both the squat and bench

TABLE 7.1 Sample Workouts Using Undulating Periodization: One Session Per Week

BASE STRENGTH EMPHASIS		ABSOLUTE STRENGTH EMPHASIS	
Week	Session 1	Week	Session 1
1	6RM	1	1RM
2	8RM	2	5RM
3	3RM	3	3RM
4	5RM	4	5RM
5	10RM	5	10RM
6	7RM	6	5RM
7	2RM	7	3RM
8	5RM	8	1RM

TABLE 7.2   Sample Workouts Using Undulating Periodization: Two Sessions Per Week

BASE STRENGTH EMPHASIS			ABSOLUTE STRENGTH EMPHASIS		
Week	Session 1	Session 2	Week	Session 1	Session 2
1	5RM	10RM	1	5RM	1RM
2	7RM	2RM	2	3RM	6RM
3	6RM	12RM	3	10RM	2RM
4	8RM	3RM	4	5RM	1RM
5	5RM	12RM	5	7RM	3RM
6	4RM	1RM	6	6RM	10RM
7	8RM	15RM	7	1RM	5RM
8	5RM	1RM	8	8RM	1RM

TABLE 7.3   Sample Workouts Using Undulating Periodization: Three Sessions Per Week

BASE STRENGTH EMPHASIS				ABSOLUTE STRENGTH EMPHASIS			
Week	Session 1	Session 2	Session 3	Week	Session 1	Session 2	Session 3
1	5RM	10RM	8RM	1	1RM	5RM	10RM
2	3RM	6RM	12RM	2	2RM	6RM	3RM
3	4RM	10RM	8RM	3	12RM	1RM	4RM
4	12RM	6RM	3RM	4	2RM	6RM	1RM
5	5RM	10RM	8RM	5	5RM	10RM	3RM
6	4RM	15RM	6RM	6	5RM	15RM	1RM
7	2RM	6RM	10RM	7	3RM	6RM	2RM
8	5RM	3RM	6RM	8	5RM	7RM	1RM

press before moving on to the supplemental exercises. During session 2, you would perform a 1RM on both the squat and bench press before moving on to the supplemental exercises.

Option two is rotating through the exercises. Again, consider the bench press and the squat in a two-session routine. Start with the squat. You worked up to the 5RM for the squat for session 1. Since you are rotating, the next session would feature the bench press workout, which is a 1RM for that day. The second workout for the week would start with squat, working up to a 1RM, followed by bench press, working up to a 5RM.

Now look at using the three lifts in undulating periodization. Again, you can either rotate through the workouts by lifts or keep all lifts in the same workout. You can do whatever exercises you wish as the main exercises, but most people choose to save the deadlift for the third exercise as it is the last competitive exercise. Lifters tend to do the deadlift one of two ways. First, some use the deadlift like any other exercise, performing the exercise in every workout. If doing the deadlift three times a week bothers their backs too much, they do the deadlift on the heaviest days. On the other days, they use supplemental exercises such as rack pulls or good mornings. This is up to you. The best recommendation is to try each one and see what works best for you in terms of developing your lift and preserving your health.

To perform three lifts three times a week using the first option, the first session of the first week begins with the squat followed by the bench press and deadlift performed at a 1RM (table 7.3, absolute strength emphasis.) The second session of the first week features the squat, bench press, and deadlift performed at a 5RM. On the third session of the first week, the squat, bench press, and deadlift are performed at a 10RM.

If you choose to rotate the repetition max, on the first day of the first week perform a 1RM squat, a 5RM bench press, and a 10RM deadlift. On the second day of the first week, perform a 10RM squat, a 1RM bench press, and a 5RM deadlift. On the third day of the first week, perform a 5RM squat, a 10RM bench press, and a 1RM deadlift.

The order of the exercises when using the undulating periodization method is very interesting. Two basic options exist: performing the exercises in the priority in which you need to develop them or in the order of competition. Either way, people have seen excellent results.

If exercises are positioned by priority, lifters are able to devote their energy to that exercise when they have the most energy. They can press on through repetitions more easily and are able to get the greatest amount of weight on that exercise. People often have this exercise see incredible increases in the ability to move weight.

The second variation, performing the exercises in order of meet day, has been found to have great results on meet day. The body is already used to performing bench after squat and deadlift after squat and bench press. When meet day arrives, lifters are better able to judge what weights they are going to be able to lift and they have seen great increases in achieving their attempts successfully because they know how the body is going to feel. This often leads to a bigger total because you are more likely going to go 9 for 9.

When choosing supplemental exercises, go with exercises that give the most bang for your buck. The more main lifts you undulate, the more effective and efficient you need to be with your supplemental exercises because you are using energy toward those main lifts. When training, focus on no more than six exercises in a single workout. If you have three lifts that you are undulating, that leaves room for three supplemental exercises. Understand your weak points and how to bring them up. For instance, if you are having problems maintaining an upright chest during the squat, your best supplemental exercise is a reverse hyper (page 64). If this happens to take care of the issue of driving your hips through on a deadlift as well, great! You can use one exercise to develop two lifts. For the bench press, notice where the bar gets stuck so you can make the best choices. For overall progress on the bench press, it's best to work on complex back movement and pressing. Some have great results from combining pull-ups and overhead presses. Some people have seen great results from close-grip bench press and T-bar rows. Find what makes your bench go up and do it.

Conjugate Periodization

Sport scientist and weightlifting coach Leonid Matveyev designed the original periodization model. Later, the conjugate method was designed in an effort to keep strength levels high and continually push levels higher. The conjugate method is broken down into three main traits: absolute strength, dynamic strength, and hypertrophy. Two or three traits are trained at the same time.

Developing Absolute Strength

Absolute strength is developed through the use of the maximum effort method. The maximum effort method uses special exercises designed to build the main lift, but are not the main lift. Exercises change every few weeks to prevent adaptation and allow the body to continually use over 90 percent of a 1RM. This recruits the most motor units. This also strengthens muscle groups outside of the norm that may be recruited when chaos occurs. For instance, if a lifter is squatting during a meet and the hips rise too quickly, and if he hasn't done a sufficient number of good mornings to increase the strength of the spinal erectors to do a good morning with that weight, the spinal erectors are strong enough. If a lifter is able to maintain perfect technique, then no other muscles are needed, but we all know that things happen on meet day. You get only three attempts, so be ready for anything.

The body seems to work on three-week cycles. After three weeks of performing an exercise, you no longer see any further positive adaptations to that exercise when performed at maximal levels. All of the neuromuscular adaptations that can occur from that exercise have occurred and further training of them may in fact cause a decrease in performance. At this point, the exercise is changed and this allows the new stimulus to take hold and cause more neuromuscular adaptations to occur. This allows the lifter to stay at high levels of intensity. By changing the stimulus, you can maintain more than three consecutive weeks at a high intensity, at or greater than 90 percent of 1RM.

The maximal effort method requires you to go up and find a maximum for that day. You want to push the greatest amount of weight possible on a given exercise and maintain good form. Whatever you get for that day is what you get. It is a good idea to track your personal records so you have a goal to shoot for. As with undulating periodization, you will know you're getting stronger if you continually beat your old personal records.

As you can see from figure 7.1, a marked difference exists in the gain of strength through neural factors and an increase in muscle size. You can also see that there is a peak and a valley from the stimulus from the neural factors and then it begins to increase again. By changing the exercise, you eliminate the valley and allow the strength and power improvements to maintain their increase at a high level.

There is an individual variance for how often you need to change the exercise. When you perform an exercise for three consecutive weeks and for the first two weeks achieve personal records but during the third week you are significantly lower, typically it means you are becoming more advanced in your training and need to change the exercises every two weeks. Of course, if you were out partying until 4:00 in the morning and tried to train at 7:00, you are actually just fatigued and it has nothing to do with your training level. A good rule of thumb is that if in two consecutive training blocks you experience a drop-off during the third week, you need to change up the exercises one week sooner. Likewise, if you consistently set a personal record the first week but experience a drop-off during the second week, you need to begin changing the exercises every week. The more advanced you become in training, the more often the exercises need to be changed.

What are appropriate exercises to perform for the maximal effort method? These exercises should be similar enough to improve the competitive lift but different enough to force new adaptations and continue high-level gains as illustrated in figure 7.1.

For the bench press, a short list of maximal effort exercises includes close-grip incline press, floor press, board press (one to five boards), rack press, reverse band press, band-resisted press, overhead press, overhead pin lockout press, towel press, carpet press, and foam press. With these exercises, you can make additional changes to the stimulus through the addition of chains, band resis-

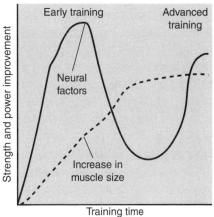

Figure 7.1 Improvements in strength and power over training time.

tance, and band assistance. Just from this short list, you essentially have over 40 maximal-effort exercises for bench press. You can also change the bars to change the stimulus. Using a fatter bar, a narrower bar, a stiffer bar, or a bamboo bar changes the stimulus and gives you additional exercises. If you simply have a fat bar as well as a normal bar, you double the number of simple exercises, taking the 40 exercises and changing them to 80.

For the squat, the list includes good morning, suspended good morning, arched-back good morning, box squat, a variety of bars to choose from, squats with the glutes going into foam, squats with the weight going into foam, good mornings with the weight going into foam, Zercher squats, front squats, Jefferson lifts, and Olympic squats. All these exercises are beneficial for the squat. Various bars such as the mastodon, safety squat bar, Texas power bar, deadlift bar, buffalo bar, and cambered bar change the exercise enough to be considered a new stimulus for the body to adapt to.

For deadlifts, there is the rack pull, deadlift off a block, deadlift against band resistance, or deadlift with band assistance. By changing the bar or adding bands or chains, you increase the number of exercises again. You can vary the height of the block you stand on or the height of the pins you are pulling off of to change the exercise again.

Developing Dynamic Strength

The dynamic method uses submaximal intensities moved at maximal velocities. This is to improve strength–speed, improve technique, and facilitate recovery. Use appropriate weight (30 to 70 percent of a 1RM) and appropriate volume (24 repetitions seems to work the best for squat and bench press, with 8 × 3 for bench press and 12 × 2 for squat; 8 to 12 × 1 for deadlift).

The improvement to strength–speed, which is having strength in relation to speed or learning to move heavy weights quickly, is a function of the SAID principle, or a specific adaptation to an imposed demand. The weight you push should allow you to perform 3 repetitions on bench in 3.5 seconds, 2 repetitions on squat in 3.5 seconds, and the deadlift as quickly as possible for each repetition. If you have a Tendo unit or a Myotest device to monitor bar speed, it should move between 0.7 and 1.0 meters per second. This ensures that you are moving an appropriate weight to increase strength–speed. You can train strength and speed appropriately and improve them both at the same time. People who use this method in training will notice that their maximal lifts start to go up quickly. This breaks down to simple physics, as it allows you to produce the most force. Force is a product of mass and acceleration ($F = ma$). If you can move a mass faster, you produce more force. A simpler way to think about it is, Imagine you are trying to break a board. How do you want to hit the board, fast or slow? If you hit it fast, the board is more likely to break; if you hit it slow, the board won't break. This is advantageous for you, the powerlifter; if you are able to accelerate the bar, you are less likely to have sticking points near the top because of the momentum you are able to produce throughout the duration of the entire lift.

The intensities used are approximately 30 to 60 percent of a geared 1RM, in which powerlifting gear such as a squat suit or bench shirt is used, or 50 to 70 percent of a raw 1RM, in which no powerlifting gear is used. The weight used must be heavy enough to cause a stimulus but light enough to move at an appropriate speed. To determine the best weight for you, use of a velocity measuring device, use a stopwatch, or train with an experienced lifter.

The first way to determine the best weight is to use a velocity measuring device. When you train specifically, you cause specific adaptations. To gain strength–speed, you need to train specifically for strength–speed. This is very simple when you realize that velocity dictates what specific strength is being developed. The Soviets used a velocity measurement similar to that of the Tendo unit and found that for developing strength–speed in the power lifts, the bar needed to be moving between 0.7 and 1.0 meters per second. If you train at this velocity, you will gain strength–speed. Now if you are using a weight that requires you to be below 0.7 meters per second, then you need to drop the weight to improve the velocity of the bar. If you are moving faster than 1.0 meters per second, you need to add weight to the bar to achieve appropriate bar speed. Remember, you are to move the bar at a maximal speed at all times. This is not a video game in which you are trying to keep the weight between those speeds. You must move the bar as fast as possible and allow the speed to dictate the weight. The upside of this method is the exactness of weight selection. The downside of this method is the expense and lack of access to this equipment. A Tendo unit costs more than $1,000 and a Myotest device is around $500.

The next method is to use a stopwatch. Most maximal lifts occur in 3.5 seconds from the start of the lift to the completion. You want to train yourself to be able to strain maximally for this amount of time. For the bench press, an appropriate weight allows you to get 3 repetitions in 3.5 seconds. For the squat, an appropriate weight allows you to get 2 repetitions in 3.5 seconds. (For deadlift only one repetition is done as quickly as possible.) This time does not include racking or unracking the bar; it is measured from the time of initial descent to final repetition completion. Pick your initial weight and see how you do. If you finish in less than 3.5 seconds, add 5 to 25 pounds (2.2-11.3 kg) and perform the next set. If you are right at 3.5 seconds, stay there. If you take more than 3.5 seconds, reduce the weight. While this is not as scientific as the Tendo, it's pretty good for the $10 that a stopwatch costs. The upside of this method is that it gives you a set protocol to follow that ensures you are using an appropriate weight. The downside of this method is user error. If you are a little bit off in your technique and need to reset your body or form between repetitions, you will cost yourself precious time and it will seem that you need to reduce your weight when in fact you are right on or could use even more weight.

The last method is to use an experienced training partner. If your partner has been using this method for some time, he not only knows intuitively what an appropriate weight feels like but also what it looks like. Simply watching you perform the exercise can help him recommend what weight you should use for subsequent sets and note any changes in form you should make. The advantages of this are that you use appropriate weights for the sets as well as get coached on form. The disadvantage is that finding someone who knows what to do simply by watching may not be the easiest thing to do.

The best way to improve form is to use submaximal weights. On the maximal effort day, you do not perform the competitive lifts, which you do on the dynamic effort day. Doing the competitive exercises on the dynamic effort day allows you to groove your technique and be able to perform properly on meet or test day. If you need to work on keeping your chest up or knees out on a squat, this is the day to do it. Likewise, if you have a tendency to keep your elbows flared the entire time on bench, this is a good time to learn how to tuck them in properly. It takes 10,000 repetitions to change a faulty motor pattern. When you focus on form during these repetitions, you can fix the faulty motor patterns and regroove them more quickly.

The dynamic effort method also aids in recovery. If you were to perform two heavy workouts in a week, the neuromuscular system would be heavily taxed and you might break down more quickly as a result. Jay Schroeder has said that velocity recovers everything. The strength continuum shows that the 40- to 60-percent range is the recovery zone. Also, the empirical rule of 60 percent basically says that a recovery workout needs to be in the 60-percent range of the first workout to allow proper recovery for the following workout. Between these three phenomena, you can see that the dynamic effort method can be very effective at improving recovery for the maximal effort day.

Developing Hypertrophy

The repetitive effort method is another submaximal weight method, but this time the lifter tries to do repetitions to the point of fatigue. This method is basically a method of bodybuilding in which the lifter tries to induce great amounts of hypertrophy through additional volume. This is the method to use when trying to gain weight. When trying to gain weight, you don't want just weight, you want to put on additional muscle. As stated in chapter 2, fat has no contractile components and does not add as much power behind the bar as added muscle. While adding fat may improve leverage, it does not improve actual strength in the ability to exert force. Many people refer to the old adage that mass pushes mass, but it may be more accurate to say that muscles push more mass than fat.

The repetitive effort method is essentially doing more than 6 repetitions per set. You really don't want to exceed 20 repetitions because it would not allow you to use enough weight to increase the strength of the muscle. Remember from chapter 1 that two types of hypertrophy exist, functional and nonfunctional. When you go over 20 repetitions, you have a high time under tension but low contractile strength improvement. Any gains in mass would be nonfunctional as the sarcomeres (the spaces between the contractile elements) increase in size, but the myofibrils (which do the contracting, the actual work of lifting) do not.

The *specific method* being used means the main exercise for the day. You don't want to be doing maximum effort for all of your supplemental exercises on a given day; for example, doing a maximum effort triceps extension will likely end in a torn triceps. All supplemental work is essentially repetitive effort, because you should stay over 6 repetitions but at 20 or below on the high end.

Workout Setup

How the workouts are set up and ordered throughout the week is very important. Ensure that you are getting enough rest between each workout to recover and prevent overtraining. Allow 48 hours between the maximum effort and the dynamic effort workouts, and 72 hours between the dynamic effort and the maximum effort workouts. For instance, if you do maximum effort bench on Sunday, do dynamic effort bench on Wednesday. If you do dynamic effort squat on Monday, do maximum effort squat on Friday. Table 7.4 shows a sample workout.

Supplemental Exercises

Use the supplemental exercises to develop the main lift of the day. If you are doing a maximum effort bench press workout, develop the muscles that do the bench press. Perform any volume press first, followed by a triceps exercise, a back exercise, a shoulder exercise, and some biceps just to maintain good elbow health. The volume exercise is used to increase muscle mass. If someone is trying to develop strength but not body weight, the volume exercise is not a good idea and should be left out.

For the lower body, after the main lift perform single-leg movements or box jumps to develop the posterior chain and abdominals.

TABLE 7.4 Sample Workout Using the Conjugate Method

MAXIMUM EFFORT BENCH PRESS				
	Week 1	Week 2	Week 3	Week 4
Board press (two boards)	Work up to 1RM	Work up to 1RM	Work up to 1RM	De-load to 225 for max reps
Board press (two boards; PR)	75% of 1RM	75% of 1RM	75% of 1RM	
Band pushdown	100 reps	100 reps	100 reps	100 reps
Pulldown	4 × 15	4 × 15	4 × 15	4 × 15
Face pull	4 × 15	4 × 15	4 × 15	4 × 15
Hammer curl	4 × 15	4 × 15	4 × 15	4 × 15
DYNAMIC EFFORT SQUAT				
	Week 1	Week 2	Week 3	Week 4
Bo squat	12 × 2	12 × 2	12 × 2	Sled pulls
Romanian deadlift (RDL)	4 × 6	4 × 6	4 × 6	4 × 6
Reverse hyper	4 × 8	4 × 8	4 × 8	4 × 8
Shrug	3 × 10	3 × 10	3 × 10	3 × 10
Spread-eagle sit-up	4 × 10	4 × 10	4 × 10	4 × 10
DYNAMIC EFFORT BENCH PRESS				
	Week 1	Week 2	Week 3	Week 4
Speed press	8 × 3	8 × 3	8 × 3	Suspended kettlebell bench 3 × 30
Rolling triceps extension (dumbbell)	4 × 8	4 × 8	4 × 8	4 × 8
Chest supported row	4 × 8	4 × 8	4 × 8	4 × 8
Bradford press	4 × 8	4 × 8	4 × 8	4 × 8
Leg curl	4 × 8	4 × 8	4 × 8	4 × 8
MAXIMUM EFFORT SQUAT				
	Week 1	Week 2	Week 3	Week 4
Good morning (cambered bar)	Work up to 1RM	Work up to 1RM	Work up to 1RM	Leg press 3 × 20
Pistol squat	3 × 12	3 × 12e	3 × 12e	3 × 12e
Glute-ham	4 × 8	4 × 8	4 × 8	4 × 8
Reverse hyper	4 × 8	4 × 8	4 × 8	4 × 8
Abdominals	3 × 30	3 × 30	3 × 30	3 × 30

Most people get the biggest benefit from supplemental exercises if one day is done with heavier weights and lower repetitions and the other day is done with lighter weights and higher repetitions. This seems to do the best job at increasing strength as well as maintaining health by pumping as much blood through the body as possible. The heavy weight increases the strength; the blood increases the health of the muscles, tendons, and ligaments. Many people have found it most beneficial to perform the light day with higher reps after the maximum effort exercise. Usually less time is allotted for this work on this day, and it is easier to superset and roll through the workout with light weight and high repetitions than it is for the heavier weights.

De-load

A de-load is crucial for the conjugate method. De-loading in intensity or volume, or both, every four weeks is recommended. For the conjugate method, it is basically doing high reps on both days and possibly adding in something different such as stability training through the use of suspended kettlebells. A lifter who does not perform a de-load regularly may go into overtraining. Remember, you can still make gains when you undertrain, but when you reach overtraining, you lose everything.

Summary

The goal of any powerlifting training program is to improve absolute strength. Each individual lifter should use the program he likes the best.

Undulating periodization rotates through different repetition maximum (RM) loads throughout the course of a cycle. The lifter performs whatever is on hand for the day on the squat, bench, or deadlift. The change in repetitions gives the body a new stimulus to adapt to.

The conjugate method of periodization has three ways to improve performance: the maximum effort method to develop maximal motor recruitment, the dynamic effort method to develop bar speed, and the repetitive effort method to develop hypertrophy. Focusing on two of these methods over the course of a week develops the core lift. The conjugate method also rotates exercises instead of keeping the same exercises and rotating RMs.

CHAPTER 8

Foundational Training

The most important part of any structure is the foundation. Without a good, solid foundation, skyscrapers would tumble to the ground from the wind or a very mild earthquake. In powerlifting, it takes a while to lay a good foundation, and honestly it's not very fun. But it has to be done in order to achieve the highest levels. Powerlifting meets are filled with many strong people. Some are really strong but have horrible form. You can't help but wonder what they would be able to lift if they had solid form and how long until they get hurt using the form they're using now.

Building a foundation in powerlifting is all about trying to build form, the supporting musculature, and work capacity. The neophyte powerlifter wants to jump under the bar and do as much weight as he can. Many of those powerlifters get hurt and walk out of the gym after the first few sessions and never return to the sport. This chapter helps you build the most solid foundation to have the tallest skyscraper possible in terms of the biggest total.

Work Capacity

Work capacity is basically the capacity to do work. It's the ability to get the workout done in a reasonable amount of time and recover between sets. A powerlifting coach once said that it's not the strongest powerlifter who wins the meet but the one who's in good enough shape to finish. You must have a good enough work capacity to recover between attempts, whether in a workout or in a competition. The stronger you are, the more weight you are moving, the tougher it is to recover between attempts.

Work capacity can be developed several ways: standing during breaks instead of sitting, dragging the sled, doing complexes, or supersetting. Instead of solely doing work capacity workouts, it is a good idea to incorporate them as a part of the workout and do them at the end. Work on form and develop strength at the beginning. Performing work capacity exercises at the end allows the technique and strength work to be done optimally and allow a little bit of fatigue to set in. Building work capacity at this point is optimal because you are already fatigued. You don't have to wait 10 minutes into the training session to start developing it; you are developing it immediately.

Form

Form must be perfected before weight is added to the bar. It doesn't matter what weight is on the bar; every rep must be performed exactly the same, whether lifting only the 45-pound bar or lifting 1,500 pounds. Every repetition is an opportunity to build or break down form. Whenever you are under a weight that is a new personal record, you want to have it grooved in and perfect, to where you don't even have to think about form. Refer back chapters 4, 5, and 6 for more specifics on technique for the three lifts. Here are some basic progressions.

Progressions are essential because not everyone knows how to do something the first time he performs it. A few lifters who are fantastic athletes can do it right the first time they pick up the bar. However, most of us have to work at it. Progressions eliminate some of the frustration from the learning curve. Many neophytes put a lot of pressure on themselves to do everything perfectly right off the bat. Changing the exercise away from the competitive exercise means the pressure is reduced and they are more free to feel what their body is doing and what it should be doing.

The question of when to progress from one level to the next is subjective. Stay with the current level until you get it, but don't spend any less than one week with one of the progression levels. It is even a good idea to do 1 set of one or two previous exercises as a warm-up to the current exercise. This allows the body to warm up but also to make sure that you still have the exercises down and are still proficient at them. If you show a gross deficiency during the warm-up, stay at that exercise for that day. You have time to compete in powerlifting, so take an extra day to do the exercise properly.

Foundational Exercises

Foundational exercises help build a stronger foundation to support all the heavy lifting you will be doing throughout your career. Also, they strengthen your stabilizer muscles, joints, and tendons. The stronger your foundation and stabilizing muscles, the more weight your body is able to handle. If you get out of the groove on a lift, you can recover to complete the lift. Finally, a strong foundation helps reduce the odds of injury and promote recovery.

Building to the Squat

Powerlifters have a great tendency to lean the chest over like a good morning to get depth and cave the knees in to push. Since that is a general trend, the progression is designed to teach the neophyte to not do this.

COUNTERBALANCE SQUAT

Powerlifting focus: Learn to keep the chest up, not forward, during the squat.

Muscle target: Quadriceps, tensor fasciae latae, fascia lata, iliotibial band, and hamstrings.

Starting position: Stand with both hands holding a 10- to 25-pound (4.5-11.3 kg) plate. Feet should be shoulder-width apart and the toes are pointed straight ahead or turned out slightly.

Execution: Push the hips back and squat down. During the descent, lift the weight to eye level to counterbalance your body weight, which keeps your chest up.

Coaching points: If at any point your chest, back, hips, and weight are in a single line (like an arms-extended good morning) realize that the chest needs to be held up more. Pay attention to the heels. If the heels are coming up, you either need to sit back harder or work on your ankle flexibility. Often lifters want to put plates on the floor and do the exercise like that. This is simply putting a bandage on the situation and not working to correct it. Stretches aid in ankle flexibility to allow the heels to stay flat during the exercise.

COUNTERBALANCE SINGLE-LEG SQUAT

Powerlifting focus: Learn to keep the chest up during the squat and recognize knee tracking.

Muscle target: Quadriceps, greater trochanter, tensor fasciae latae, fascia lata, and hamstrings.

Starting position: Stand on a box that is 18 inches (45 cm) high, with one foot on the box and one foot off the box. Hold a 10- to 25-pound (4.5-11.3 kg) plate in your hands.

Execution: Push the hips back and squat down. The foot that is off the box drops down. Raise it slightly in front of you with a straight leg. As you descend, raise the plate to chest level or slightly higher to counterbalance your body weight.

Coaching points: While ideally you would want to get your glutes all the way down until they make contact with your heel, this isn't realistic. Simply descend until it feels difficult to go any lower and then stand up. Pay attention to the knee position. The knee probably will be moving around wildly. Keep the knee from crashing around wildly and keep your heels flat. If the heels come up, you either need to sit back harder or work on your ankle flexibility.

FRONT SQUAT

Powerlifting focus: Keep the chest up and knees in line with the ankles during the squat.

Muscle target: Quadriceps, gluteus medius, gluteus maximus, fascia lata, greater trochanter, and hamstrings.

Starting position: Stand in an erect position, holding the bar in either a clean grip or with the arms crossed. Feet are shoulder-width apart and the toes are either pointed straight ahead or slightly turned out (figure 8.1a).

Execution: Push the hips back slightly and squat down (figure 8.1b). The chest should stay upright throughout the entire descent. Once the crease of the hips goes below the crest of the knee, return to starting position.

Coaching points: Keep the elbows high during this exercise. If not, the bar may slip out of position. The purpose of this exercise is to keep the chest tall and break or prevent the habit of leaning forward. It may also be beneficial to shrug the shoulders during the exercise; this creates more of a shelf for the bar to sit in. Again, pay special attention to the heels. At this point, they might be able to remain flat on the ground.

Figure 8.1 Front squat: *(a)* stand erect; *(b)* push hips back and squat down.

OVERHEAD SQUAT

Powerlifting focus: Keep the chest up when sinking to depth and lower.

Muscle target: Quadriceps, gluteus maximus, gluteus medius, fascia lata, greater trochanter, hamstrings, rectus abdominis, external obliques, and anterior and superior spina iliaca.

Starting position: Start with a wide grip on the bar overhead. The bar should be 6 to 10 inches (15.24 -25.4 cm) overhead. Feet are hip-width apart and the toes are pointed straight ahead or slightly out.

Execution: Squat as normal, making sure to keep the bar in the same position, directly over the shoulders. Once the crease of the hips goes below the crest of the knee, return to starting position.

Coaching points: Keep the chest high. If the chest falls to the knees, this may indicate a tight hip flexor, which needs to be addressed through stretching. This is a difficult exercise, but is crucial to learning how to keep the chest up during the squat.

BACK SQUAT WITH BANDS AROUND KNEES

Powerlifting focus: Keep the chest up and learn to push the knees out throughout the entire movement.

Muscle target: Quadriceps, gluteus maximus, gluteus medius, fascia lata, greater trochanter, and hamstrings.

Starting position: Start in the normal squat stance with a resistance band around your knees.

Execution: Start the squat by pushing the hips back slightly and driving the knees out to the sides. Drop down with the knees not going past the toes and stay in the same plane as the feet. Once the crease of the hips drops below the crest of the knees, return to starting position.

Coaching points: You very well may begin to cramp in your hips a little during this exercise. This is normal. It means that the muscles that have been dormant are now trying to fire.

BACK SQUAT

At this point, you have finished the progression and may begin squatting as described in chapter 4. See figure 8.2.

Figure 8.2 Back squat: *(a)* starting position; *(b)* squat.

Building to the Bench Press

The bench press is a very simple exercise. This progression ensures you have the strength and stability to start bench pressing without injury. If you can't do push-ups, you shouldn't start benching.

PUSH-UP

Powerlifting focus: Ensure the upper body is strong enough to begin bench press.

Muscle target: Pectorals, triceps, and deltoids.

Starting position: Lie facedown on the ground with the palms flat and placed directly underneath the shoulders. Hold your body tight and straight as a board from the back of the head to the heels.

Execution: Keeping the body rigid, inhale slowly as you bend the elbows until the nose touches the ground. Exhale as you return to starting position.

Coaching points: Watch the hips to make sure they don't sag during the press up or stay raised during the descent. Once you can perform 25 repetitions (male) or 15 repetitions (female), you are ready to move on.

INVERTED ROW

Powerlifting focus: Ensure the upper back is strong enough to begin bench press.

Muscle target: Latissimus dorsi and rhomboids.

Starting position: Lie on your back on the floor. Using an overhand grip, grasp a bar that is 4 feet (1.21 m) off the ground. Hands are shoulder-width apart. Start with your body rigid and in a straight line from the back of the head to the heels.

Execution: Keeping the body rigid, pull until the midline of the chest is in contact with the bar. Hold for 3 counts and then lower the body back to the starting position.

Coaching points: Make sure that the midline of the chest stays in contact with the bar for the 3 counts. Watch for the body to show slack in it, especially at the hips. Remember to stay rigid. If this is too easy, lower the bar or elevate the feet to make the exercise more difficult. This is a good supplemental exercise for the back.

DUMBBELL BENCH

Powerlifting focus: Experience the elbows moving in transition during the bench.

Muscle target: Pectorals, triceps, and deltoids.

Starting position: Lie on a weight bench. Hold two dumbbells so they are touching and at arms' length. The head, shoulders, and glutes should all be in contact with the bench. Feet should be in contact with the floor.

Execution: Bring the dumbbells down toward the chest in an arcing motion; the elbows are tucked into the lats during the descent. During the press, the elbows should flare at the sticking point and arc to the finish.

Coaching points: Get in the habit of tucking and flaring the dumbbells as you would during a competition lift. Many neophytes don't understand this concept, and this is a good exercise to learn.

BENCH PRESS

At this point, you have finished the progression and may begin performing the bench press as described in chapter 5. See figure 8.3.

Figure 8.3 Bench press: *(a)* starting position; *(b)* press.

Building to the Deadlift

To deadlift well, you need to have a strong back and good support muscles that are strong enough to handle the heavy load.

DIMEL DEADLIFT

Powerlifting focus: Experience pushing the glutes through at the top of the movement.

Muscle target: Gluteus maximus, gluteus medius, and hamstrings.

Starting position: Stand erect, holding the bar in either an overhand or alternating grip. (Figure 8.4a shows an overhand grip.) Feet are hip-width apart or slightly closer.

Execution: Drive the hips back until the bar hits the tops of the knees (figure 8.4b). Once the bar hits the tops of the knees, contract the glutes hard and drive back to the starting position.

Coaching points: Maintain control of the bar and do not let it get out in front of you. Keep the bar as close to the body as possible and do not relax at any point during the lift.

Figure 8.4 Dimel deadlift: *(a)* stand erect; *(b)* push hips back until bar hits tops of knees.

ROMANIAN DEADLIFT (RDL)

Powerlifitng focus: Experience driving with the hips and develop the hamstrings.

Muscle target: Gluteus maximus, gluteus medius, hamstrings, spinal erectors, biceps brachii, latissimus dorsi, and external obliques.

Starting position: Stand erect with your feet hip-width apart or slightly closer (figure 8.5a). Hold the bar in either an overhand or alternating grip.

Execution: Drive the hips back on the descent (figure 8.5b). Once you feel a good stretch in the hamstrings, lift the bar back to the starting position. Make sure that the back is held tight throughout the entire exercise.

Coaching points: You must push your hips back. The farther you push your hips back, the more the exercise shifts to the hamstrings. If you feel like your toes want to come off the floor, you are doing it right. Also, keep the upper back tight, pulling the shoulders back, and the lower back flat. A good cue is to arch like a cow and not like a camel.

Figure 8.5 Romanian deadlift (RDL): *(a)* starting position; *(b)* push hips back and lower barbell.

DEADLIFT OFF PLATES

Powerlifting focus: Experience driving with the quadriceps and learn to keep the chest up during the start of the movement.

Muscle target: Gluteus maximus, gluteus medius, hamstrings, spinal erectors, biceps brachii, latissimus dorsi, quadriceps.

Starting position: Stand on a 2- to 4-inch (5-10 cm) box with your feet hip-width apart or slightly closer. Squat down and grab the bar outside of the legs using an overhand or alternating grip.

Execution: Start driving the feet through the box and pulling your head back. When the bar hits the knees, drive the hips forward, snapping with the glutes as in the Dimel deadlift.

Coaching points: Throw the head back. Snap the hips through.

DEADLIFT

At this point, you have finished the progression and may begin performing the deadlift as described in chapter 6. See figure 8.6.

Figure 8.6 Deadlift: *(a)* starting position; *(b)* lift.

Programming

Often neophyte powerlifters start with no training. This would suggest that there is no way of knowing how strong they are or where they are when they start. After a lifter works through the progressions, a simple progressive overload program is best. The term *progressive overload* may sound familiar as it has been mentioned throughout this book. In this case, it simply means moving up in weight every week. Since no maximum has been done previously, there are no percentages for determining weights for sets and reps. This is one of the reasons you should use a simple progressive overload program.

While several types of progressive overload programs exist, we discuss two: the 5 × 5 and the autoregulating progressive resistance exercise (APRE).

The 5 × 5 program is an oldie but goodie. It hasn't changed over the years, but it hasn't needed to. It goes by the *if it ain't broke, don't fix it* rule. In this type of program, you simply warm up, pick a weight, and attempt to perform 5 sets of 5 repetitions. If you complete all 5 sets of 5 repetitions, the next workout you go up in weight by 5 to 15 pounds (2.26-6.8 kg). The bonus is that you naturally will hold back a little bit, which helps you learn form when tired. By the fourth and fifth sets, you deal with significant fatigue. If you learn to reproduce proper form when tired, you should be good to go on anything. The downside is how slowly strength progresses. Quite a bit of good coaching is required to stay interested.

APRE programming is a bit more complex. Before we go into the APRE itself, let's look at the history of the origin of programming. Back in the early 20th century, when someone in the military broke his femur (thigh bone), he was put into a cast. When the bone healed, the cast was cut off and the solider was presumed to be good to go. Army surgeon Captain Thomas DeLorme noticed that these soldiers really weren't ready to go. One leg was smaller than the other and the soldiers couldn't walk or run properly. He decided to try to strengthen the muscles the best way he could. The patient sat down and Captain DeLorme strapped weights onto his feet for leg extensions. He determined it was best to use 50 percent of the individual's 10RM for 10 repetitions, 75 percent of the individual's 10RM for 10 repetitions, and then go for a new 10RM. He saw great improvement in the size, strength, and functionality of the leg when the soldiers returned to active duty. Notice there are 3 sets of 10 repetitions in this protocol. Due to the success Captain DeLorme had, this became the standard for 3x10 in exercises today. DeLorme named this protocol the progressive resistance exercise (PRE) protocol. Many people still use DeLorme's PRE today. It has evolved to three protocols with a fourth set and is called autoregulating progressive resistance exercise, or APRE.

The APRE is simple. There are three protocols: APRE3, APRE6, and APRE10. Which one you use depends on what you are trying to develop. APRE3 is based off an estimated 3RM and is used for strength and power. APRE6 is based off an estimated 6RM and is used for strength and hypertrophy. APRE10 is based off an estimated 10RM and is used for hypertrophy. Tables 8.1 and 8.2 detail the routines.

As you can see from table 8.1, the setup is the same for each of the routines. There is a light set of 50 percent RM, a second set of 75 percent RM, a third set with repetitions to failure at the RM, and a fourth set that is adjusted off the third set to failure again, which sets the RM for the following week.

Let's use the 3RM routine for an example of an athlete with an estimated 3RM of 300 pounds on the bench press. He warms up to his first set, which is 150 pounds for 6 repetitions (150 pounds is 50 percent of 300). He then completes a set of 3 repetitions with 225 pounds (225 pounds is 75 percent of 300 pounds). He then completes a set to failure with 300 pounds, which is the estimated 3RM, and performs 7 repetitions easily. Now the adjustment chart, table 8.2, comes into play. Look under the 3RM routine in the left column to find the number of repetitions performed, which was 7. Look to the right to find that this lifter should increase the weight by 10 to 15 pounds. For the fourth set, he uses 315 pounds (300 pounds plus 15 pounds). The athlete performs 6 repetitions. Again referring to the adjustment table in table 8.2, notice that 6 repetitions indicates an increase of 5 to 10 pounds, which changes the estimated 3RM to a range of 320 to 325 pounds.

TABLE 8.1   Autoregulating Progressive Resistance Exercise (APRE) Routines

Set	3RM	6RM	10RM
0	Warm-up	Warm-up	Warm-up
1	6 reps at 50% 3RM	10 reps at 50% 6RM	12 reps at 50% 10RM
2	3 reps at 75% 3RM	6 reps at 75% 6RM	10 reps at 75% 10RM
3	Reps to failure at 3RM	Reps to failure at 6RM	Reps to failure at 10RM
4	Adjusted reps to failure	Adjusted reps to failure	Adjusted reps to failure

TABLE 8.2   Adjustment Table for APRE Routines

3RM ROUTINE		6RM ROUTINE		10RM ROUTINE	
Repetitions	Set 4	Repetitions	Set 4	Repetitions	Set 4
1-2	Decrease 5-10 lb (2.2-4.5 kg)	0-2	Decrease 5-10 lb (2.2-4.5 kg)	4-6	Decrease 5-10 lb.
3-4	Same	3-4	Decrease 0 -5 lb (0-2.2 kg)	7-8	Decrease 0-5 lb (0-2.2 kg)
5-6	Increase 5-10 lb (2.2-4.5 kg)	5-7	Same	9-11	Same
7+	Increase 10-15 lb (4.5-6.8 kg)	8-12	Increase 5-10 lb (2.2-4.5 kg)	12-16	Increase 5-10 lb (2.2-4.5 kg)
		13+	Increase 10-15 lb (4.5-6.8 kg)	17+	Increase 10-15 lb (4.5-6.8 kg)

Now, observe the progression in the next week. The lifter warms up to the first set, which technically is 162.5 pounds (50 percent of 325, the estimated 3RM), but he rounds up to 165 pounds. He lifts 165 pounds for 6 repetitions. The weight for the second set technically would be 243 pounds (75 percent of 325), but he rounds up to 245 pounds, which he lifts for 3 repetitions. For the third set, he lifts 325 pounds for repetitions performed until failure. This lifter is feeling strong and performs 7 repetitions. Look at the adjustment chart in table 8.2 again. Under the 3RM protocol, 7 repetitions leads to a recommendation to increase by 10 to 15 pounds (4.5-6.8 kg), so the lifter increases to 340 pounds for the fourth set. In the fourth set, which again is repetitions to failure, the lifter performs 4 repetitions at 340 pounds. According to table 8.2, the recommendation is to keep the weight the same. For the next week, the estimated 3RM is 340 pounds and the workout is set up off this estimate.

Any of the protocols are used in this way. Repetitions achieved in the third set determine the weight for the fourth set. Repetitions achieved in the fourth set determine the weight used in the third set of the workout next week.

Which protocol to begin with is determined by the needs of the lifter. If the lifter needs to get bigger and gain weight, the APRE10 protocol is the most appropriate. If the lifter needs to improve form, the APRE6 is a good place to start. The weights aren't as heavy in the APRE6 as they are in the APRE3, but the lifter can still learn how to push against weight. If the lifter already has good form and needs to focus on strength, the APRE3 is the most appropriate.

Technical Failure

Many powerlifters and bodybuilders know about training to failure, training until they can no longer perform the exercise successfully. This is a good way to fatigue the muscles and make sure that the lifter knows how to strain. For the neophyte, however, training to failure, especially on the core lifts, may not be a great idea. We have already talked about how important it is to develop good form. When fatigue sets in, what tends to happen? Form tends to get thrown out the window and all you want to do is push. This can lead to bad habits, so newbies should stop before achieving full failure. Instead, stop when you reach technical failure.

When the technique starts to falter, terminate the set. If the form is great for the first four repetitions but then turns bad during the fifth repetition, only four repetitions were achieved because only four successful repetitions were performed. Any bad repetition not only causes the termination of the set, it doesn't count. This helps take the thought process away from just trying to push as hard as possible to trying to push as hard as possible with good form. Understanding that any subpar work doesn't help in reaching the ultimate goal is a great mindset for the neophyte to achieve.

Using technical failure can be a great tool in helping shape and perfect form and strength. The better the form, the heavier the weight, the greater likelihood the lifter is of getting it, and the less the likelihood the lifter will get hurt while doing it. Strength and safety are paramount to a long and successful career in powerlifting.

Bar Body Elimination

It is easy to read the term *bar body* and think, *That must be the body developed with a barbell.* It may have been developed by a barbell, but the bar body is the exact opposite of what the powerlifter wants to develop. The bar body is what looks good in a tight polo shirt when someone is trying to meet people at the bar—big pecs and biceps.

The muscles most important aren't the ones you can see in the mirror. The ones that can't be seen make the difference. Although the pecs are most significantly developed by the bench press, the lats, deltoids, and triceps make the bench the strongest. While the quadriceps may get the biggest show in the mirror, it's actually the glutes, hamstrings, and lower back that do most of the lifting.

The majority of time and energy should not be spent on building bar muscles but on building the rest of the body. While the bar body gets initial results and attention, it lacks the ability to progress a lifter throughout a powerlifting career. Doing 60 repetitions of flys per workout may be able to increase bench press 10 pounds (4.5 kg) in 3 weeks, but 60 repetitions of pulldowns per workout may be able to increase bench press by 150 pounds (68 kg) in 2 years.

Developing the smaller muscles, especially at the beginning of a career, helps prevent injury later. Spend time working on the muscles of the rotator cuff and thoracic spine now to help prevent a mild kyphosis that leads to a shoulder injury later. If the muscles aren't trained at the beginning, they shut down and are harder to turn on and correct later. An ounce of prevention equals a pound of cure.

Get a Training Partner

To a neophyte powerlifter, a training partner is crucial. Form always needs to be checked, spotters are often needed, and, let's face it, there are going to be days when you need someone to motivate you. A good training partner is someone who won't let you down on any of those three things. He knows training well enough to know when you are doing something right or wrong. When you are doing something wrong, he can help you fix it. He needs to be strong enough to spot you or help spot you. Just because you bench 800 pounds doesn't mean that someone who only benches 315 pounds and deadlifts 365 pounds can't be your partner. He may not be able to hand off, but he can surely side spot. Also, you will experience days when you don't want to go to the gym. Knowing that you'd let someone else down by not showing up is a great motivator to make sure you show up.

You both must do your part to maintain a good training partnership. Your part is to show up, be ready to catch your partner's form, be a positive motivator to your group, show up for every workout, and be game for anything. The training partner relationship is a relationship, and it must be built. Show up every day and do what is required of you. Go above and beyond to try and help your training partners, as they will do the same for you. Just like a street, the training partnership goes both ways. Your partner must also show up, work hard, be your motivator and coach. If he isn't doing those things, it's time to break up and look for a new partner. That's not to say that sometimes people go through things and have little rough patches along the road. For example, someone may have a hard time being motivated to train the day he finds out that his parent has a terminal illness. You have to be understanding as well. But if the person has a history of no benefits as a training partner, the relationship needs to be cut off.

Select a Gym

When many people look for a gym, they look for the cleanest, brightest, shiniest place with the most cardio equipment. This place may look attractive, but it is the place where you most likely will be kicked out. Most gyms that have the brightest and shiniest equipment do not have a platform for deadlifting, do not allow chalk, the bars are not strong enough to hold more than 500 pounds (226 kg), and there is not enough weight to use to do any heavy lifting.

Look for a gym that has a few necessities. The first is a power rack. The power rack is essential because every exercise can be done with the greatest amount of safety. There are safety pins in case the weight is lost, and the versatility of setups for various heights and arm lengths is great. You don't have to try to squat out of an old two-tier rack, either standing on plates and stepping down to take the weight out or performing a full squat to take the weight out of the rack.

Next is plenty of free weights. If the gym only has three plates on each rack, bench, and weight tree, turn and walk away. If there are at least 5- to 45-pound (2.26 to 20.4 kg) plates on every rack, you are in the right place. The number of weights is placed in such a manner that the gym doesn't have to worry about too much weight being thrown on a cheap bar and bending it. If the gym is set up to have big weights accessible, that is a great sign. If it has 100-pound (45 kg) plates, you have reached commercial gym heaven.

Another factor to consider is if there are already powerlifters at the gym. If there are competitors there already, you should be pretty safe.

Is there a deadlift platform? Many gyms have lots of weights but do not allow deadlifting because the noise of the bar hitting the floor disturbs the other gym members. If you see a deadlift platform, you know that they are accommodating to you, and you should be OK.

Some gyms recently have made a special back room for powerlifters. It is separated by walls so the general population doesn't see the craziness that is powerlifting. This is the gold mine of commercial gyms for the powerlifter. These places cater to the competitor, and may charge an additional fee per month to use this room. They often come complete with monolifts, reverse hypers, glute-ham benches, and bumper plates.

There are only two things better than special back rooms, and those are garage gyms and barbell clubs. These two places have been opened because of powerlifting. The people who train here are powerlifters, and no one else populates these. There are no mirrors, and probably not even air conditioning. They may have homemade equipment and usually are not the cleanest or prettiest places. However, they do have one thing going for them—an intense atmosphere that drives lifters to get strong. These are tough places to find as they are not in the phone book.

What is the best way to find a place to train? Get on the Internet and search for *powerlifting* and your community and the surrounding area. You may find a few lifters in your area. Try to find a way to contact them via phone or e-mail to learn where they train and if they're looking for training partners. Extra pairs of hands are always useful.

Summary

Make sure you train with good form and technique to help build a stronger foundation. This will be your key to being successful in the sport of powerlifting. Regardless of which program you choose, once you make up your mind, stick with it no matter what.

CHAPTER 9

Experienced Training

As you gain experience and become stronger, it may take different methods to keep increasing strength. Instead of performing only the bench press, squat, and deadlift, you need to perform assistance work. Instead of a simple progressive overload, you need a longer plan of periodization. As you gain experience, things will change. Anything a beginner does will make him stronger because he is a beginner. The experienced lifter, on the other hand, may need to tweak and explore to reach his goals of becoming stronger.

Chapter 1 discussed progressive overload. For the experienced lifter who has only 6 weeks to get ready for a meet, this may be the way to go. However, if you have more time, say 12 to 16 weeks, periodization may be the proper choice. Planning on meets long in advance does several things for you. First, and maybe most important, you can book flights and hotels long in advance to save a lot of money. Second, it allows you to draw up a plan for your training.

Periodization is simply a plan of training. It isn't some mystical being that comes to make you stronger. It is just a plan of attack. At this point in the powerlifting career, failing to plan is planning to fail. Before it didn't matter what was done, you would still get stronger. Now, planning is necessary.

The experienced lifter never wants to take time off, so going back to a simple progressive overload is never going to happen, unless the lifter has a meet with only 6 weeks of preparation. That being said, if you do decide to take an off-season, training will be different than in-season training cycles. It is perfectly fine to go from one competition to the next, starting one 16-week cycle after taking a week off after the meet. However, if you do only one or two meets a year, then an off-season is necessary.

Off-Season Training

When the body starts breaking down due to all of the heavy weight training, it is necessary to back off. Notice the words *back off*, not *take time off*. Any layoff from training can turn from 2 weeks into 2 years before you know it, so it is not a good idea. Besides it will take time to get back up to any semblance of your old strength, and thus isn't a good idea.

Off-season training consists of lifting lighter weights for more repetitions. This isn't to say that performing 40 percent for sets of 20 repetitions is a good idea. The goal of the powerlifter is to get stronger, and a good way to develop strength is through submaximal loads of 65 to 80 percent. Training in these percentages ensures that the central nervous system and muscles get a break from maximal loads. This training should never be done to failure. At the end of the set, you should have at least 1 repetition left in the tank, preferably several. A good way to judge what volume to do is based on Prilepin's table (table 9.1). Alexander Prilepin developed the table to determine what volumes to do at what intensity to allow maximal gains in performance.

TABLE 9.1 Prilepin's Table

Work intensity (%)	Repetitions/set	Optimal volume	Volume range
55-69	3-6	24	18-30
70-79	3-6	18	12-24
80-89	2-4	15	10-20
90+	1-2	7	4-10

The work intensity listed in the left column is simply the percent of 1RM. Repetitions/set means how many repetitions are performed in each set. Optimal volume is considered the best total volume for that zone for a single workout, and the volume range is the range of repetitions performed for a single workout. For instance, using the chart and training at 70 percent for a given day, 3 × 6 (18 total repetitions) would fall right in the optimal zone. If you are beat and looking to de-load, then 4 × 3 (12 total repetitions) may be a better choice. If you are trying to gain base strength on that day, then 4 × 6 (24 total repetitions) may be the best option. For the same intensity, you can make three choices based on what you are trying to accomplish.

Random selection from the chart may be a bad idea as well, since you may end up getting too much volume and overtraining or too little volume and under-training. It is best to examine the training in a wave pattern if you are trying to get stronger; the highest volumes come on the heaviest days and the lightest volumes come on the lightest days. The three cycles shown in tables 9.2, 9.3, and 9.4 are great 8-week cycles for base training, off-season strength development, or recovery. They will all allow you to go back to your peaking cycle without missing a beat. Simply by manipulating the volume, you manipulate the goal even while keeping all of the intensities the same.

You can shorten or expand these cycles to fit your needs, but you should follow the basic premise behind it at all times.

TABLE 9.2   Eight-Week Off-Season Cycle for Base Training

Week	Sets	Repetitions	Intensity (%)
1	3	10	65
2	3	8	67.5
3	4	6	70
4	4	5	72.5
5	4	4	75
6	3	5	80
7	3	4	80
8	8	2	80

TABLE 9.3   Eight-Week Off-Season Cycle for Strength Improvement

Week	Sets	Repetitions	Intensity (%)
1	4	6	70
2	4	5	70
3	4	3	75
4	3	6	75
5	4	5	80
6	3	5	82.5
7	5	2	85
8	3	2	90

TABLE 9.4   Eight-Week Off-Season Cycle for Recovery

Week	Sets	Repetitions	Intensity (%)
1	3	10	55
2	5	6	55
3	4	6	60
4	6	3	60
5	4	4	65
6	3	6	70
7	4	3	70
8	4	6	70

In-Season Training

The goal of in-season programming is to bring maximal lifts to the platform on meet day. This is done by carefully planning training for 12 to 16 weeks. This is not to say that whenever a program begins it is written in stone. Life happens, injuries happen, and adjustments may be needed, but the basic plan is there. If you start out like wildfire training for a meet, then after 4 to 6 weeks you will burn out and not be in optimal condition when you reach the platform at 12 weeks.

Properly planned in-season training should be a great transition from the off-season and allow you to adapt to the various intensity zones and be prepared to perform on meet day. Jumping straight from 60 to 70 percent training to 90 to 95 percent training means you set up for failure by injury. You need a gradual transition. It is best to spend 3 weeks in an intensity zone before moving to the next zone. For instance, if you had been training in the 60-percent zone, you need to spend 3 weeks in the 70-percent zone before moving to the 80-percent zone, and 3 weeks in the 80-percent zone before moving to the 90-percent zone. You want to spend only 2 weeks in the 90-percent zone. Often 3 or more weeks above 90 percent causes the central nervous system to overreach, and you will not be able to perform at the competition. The heavier you go, the greater the motor recruitment that is required and the more motor units the body learns to recruit. So, while an increase in strength is seen in the use of submaximal percentages, you will not see improvements in motor unit recruitment until you use heavier loads (90 percent and above).

Table 9.5 is an example of a 14-week competition cycle.

TABLE 9.5   Fourteen-Week Competition Cycle

Week	Sets	Repetitions	Intensity (%)
1	3	8	70
2	4	6	70
3	4	3	75
4	3	6	75
5	4	4	75
6	3	4	80
7	5	4	80
8	3	5	80
9	10	2	85
10	5	3	85
11	2	5	85
12	5	2	90
13	4	2	90
14	3	2	90

Training With Gear

At some point during your training cycle you may decide to add lifting gear such as knee wraps, groove briefs, a power belt, power suit, bench shirt, and wrist wraps. This gear could be used only for training. As the meet gets closer, start to use the gear you plan to use in competition.

The debate about training with gear always arises, unless you are a raw lifter, in which case you never add gear. There is the school of thought that you want to train without gear to get as strong as possible so that when you add gear, you get a bigger total. The contrary school of thought says that you want to train in gear as much as possible so that you can learn the gear and get used to handling bigger weights. Neither is necessarily wrong. However, there is middle ground. You should get as strong as possible while lifting raw and you should learn the gear so you can be most effective with it.

Athletics arose from the ancient Greeks during times of peace. They gathered in Athens every few years to have the Olympics. Soldiers would train and get together to see who had the superior army. Games were held to see who could run the fastest and thus deliver the most damage on impact with the sprints, who could do the most damage from afar with war weapons such as a spear or heavy ball (shot) or a discus. There were competitions to see whose messengers could get great distances of 26.2 miles (42.16 km) the quickest. Fast-forwarding to modern track, two jumping events exist for height: the high jump and the pole vault. The pole vaulter jumps as high as possible by learning the timing and position of his equipment in addition to being able to run as fast as possible and jump as high as possible. If he were to worry only about jumping with the pole, he wouldn't be able to run as fast to gain momentum or jump as high by his own power to help transfer that momentum with the pole. Likewise, if the pole vaulter did all plyometric and speed work and nothing with the pole, he would not be able to perform on meet day because his timing would be thrown off. The pole vaulter does work with the pole, performs plyometrics without the pole, and executes simple running speed work drills.

Powerlifters need to perform gear work to understand how to use their gear, but they also need to get strong in general. They must do some gear work so they can perform on meet day, but must also improve raw strength at the same time. If one is done and not the other, the lifter will be out of balance and unable to perform come meet day. If both are achieved, the sky is the limit for growth potential and making personal records on meet day.

The question of what gear to add and when is tricky. Each federation has different gear rules. Every person has his own system. Basically add briefs first, knee wraps second, suit bottoms third, and throw the straps on the suit last. Essentially you increase in intensity with your gear as you would in training. In the days of single-ply lifting with groove briefs, lifters would commonly start adding briefs at 80 to 85 percent, knee wraps at 85 to 90 percent, suit bottoms at 90 percent, and full suit at 90 to 95 percent. One prevailing theory for the addition of gear was to hold off from using it as long as possible. That way when you add on the gear, the weight feels lighter.

The bench press and deadlift are both a little bit different than the squat, as there is much less gear. For the bench press, a shirt day is a shirt day. You throw the shirt on, get it set properly, and do the weights for that day. The only additional gear beyond the bench shirt is wrist wraps and a belt to hold the shirt down. Without a belt, the shirt is allowed to ride up higher onto the neck, allowing a lighter weight to touch. As more weight gets added, the shirt eventually needs to be held in place; this is when the belt is added. On the contrary, some lifters like to have the shirt seated and fit exactly as it would for every repetition. For those lifters, the belt comes on as soon as the shirt does, and the distance the bar travels is what varies from set to set. The more weight on the bar, the closer to the chest it comes.

The deadlift is like the bench press in that very little gear is involved. Some actually prefer to deadlift with a belt only if they can't find a suit that works properly for the deadlift. Obviously, if no gear is used, there is no worry about the addition of gear. If gear is used, it should be used only in a manner that allows the lifter to repeat his form. For instance, if a weight is too light and the lifter has to round his back or force his knees in an unusual direction when compared to other heavier weights, then he should not add the suit.

Experienced trainees are always trying to get into the tightest gear possible. The tighter the gear, the more assistance it gives, and the higher total you can expect. People who can stand tight gear and force their form throughout the movement will receive more assistance from their gear and receive the benefit of the higher total.

However, the flipside is, Can you stand the tightness of the gear? Does it keep the sport from being enjoyable? While the goal of powerlifting is to lift the biggest possible weights, you should have fun when you do it. If your main goal is to set a personal record and continually improve your own total, then a reliance on tight gear is unnecessary, especially if you don't like the feeling.

Over the years, you will have to deal with other powerlifters who try to get you to use smaller and tighter gear, attempting to sell you on the point that tighter gear could give your body an advantage on the platform. However, gear can be so tight that your focus is no longer on trying to be in the moment of making a successful lift. Instead, it is on the pain caused by the tight-fitting gear. When the gear becomes too tight, you can no longer focus on being right there. You have to focus on forcing your form and blocking out the pain. Using the tighter gear can cause you to lose your focus and actually cause your total to drop. Choose lifting gear that is not so loose you get nothing out of it but not so super tight that it alters your form and technique. Choose gear that is comfortable and will help you get the most out of your lifting.

Regardless of how tight the gear is, you must always force your form. Make sure that you are forcing the gear around your body and through your technique, not allowing a tight shirt to round your shoulders forward and cause your head to come up off the bench. If this happens, either you are not forcing your form or you are not strong enough for that shirt. Likewise, tight straps on a squat suit could force the shoulders to round forward and lose the form you have practiced in training. Forcing your form and forcing the gear to go where you want it ultimately will give you the most out of your gear. You will receive more rebound effect since you are stretching the gear more greatly.

You must be strong enough raw to handle tighter gear. A good way to know if gear is too tight is if you are not able to force your form. If after a few sessions you are not able to force your form, you must work on getting stronger raw. It may not be the strength of certain muscle groups that prevents using tighter gear. For instance, on the bench press, the pecs and the triceps may be strong enough to press the weight in the shirt, but the lats and the upper back are not strong enough to keep you in position; you roll forward in the shirt and are not able to maximize your strength. In a this situation, you may be better off in a bigger shirt because forcing the form will allow more rebound and more weight pressed out of the bottom. Remember the old adage that the chain is only as strong as its weakest link? It is especially true with equipment. You may have made some muscles so strong that you can lock out tremendous weights, but you can't get them to touch because you've neglected other muscle groups.

The great thing about powerlifting is that it is an individual sport. If you focus on bettering yourself both physically and mentally, it doesn't matter if you are getting more out of a tighter shirt. You are working to beat yourself.

The average career for an experienced powerlifter is 3 years. Often this is due to frustration about placing in meets. You'll never have Jason (Jay) Fry's bench press or Donnie Thompson's squat or Andy Bolton's deadlift, so why try? This is a wrong focus. The focus needs to be internal, to learn to push through your own plateaus and reach the highest peaks that you can. If you compare yourself to others, you always come up short. Look within to conquer your own struggles, both external and internal, and powerlifting can be a great focus to enable you to push yourself to greater heights.

Assistance Work and the Experienced Trainee

Assistance work becomes even more necessary with the experienced trainee. By now, form should be pretty well dialed in on all exercises. Now what determines if someone is achieving personal records often is what he does in assistance work.

Assistance work can be more specialized and more personalized at this point. For instance, two people are looking to improve bench press and know they need to improve back strength. One is doing pull-ups because he wants to improve back strength; the other picked a special exercise of heavy band tension band pull-aparts because he is trying to strengthen those muscles that pull apart against the shirt. Both lifters know they need to strengthen the lats, but the experience of the second lifter allows him to target what needs to be improved and choose an exercise that works on that.

Larry Pacifico once said that his assistance work for the deadlift was anything that made his deadlift go up. When you become a more experienced trainee, you note what assistance exercises bring up your lifts the most. For instance, a lifter's bench moves up very quickly when he does heavy T-bar rows and heavy Bradford presses. These exercises are specific to his weak points so, by performing them, he made his bench press go up significantly for quite some time. However, one day these exercises stopped improving his bench press. The weakest link on the chain had caught up, and it was time to find the next set of exercises.

It is easiest when you understand the exercises, the various sticking points, and ways to get through them. Where you stick is a sign of what part of the chain is the weakest. Selecting the appropriate exercises helps you make the weak link stronger, and thus improve your lift.

Summary

It is very important for the experienced lifter to understand his body and know what works and what doesn't. At no point should you wait until meet time to experiment with a new piece of equipment. You have an off-season during which you can try new things you learn during competition.

10

Advanced Training

After seeing great gains and gaining experience using the methods covered in the previous chapters, you need to add some twists and turns to keep the gains coming. As in a video game, you can't go to the next level until you've conquered the current one. Lifters should stay with their selected method for at least a year, sometimes longer, before trying the advanced methods. A good recommendation is to stay with the base method until results slow down. At that point, it is time to change up the routine. If you get anxious and change gears too soon, the gains may stop and never return.

Undulating Periodization

You can use two more advanced methods with undulating periodization, which was first discussed in chapter 7. The first method is to undulate exercises; the second method is to undulate velocity on the same exercise. Both methods have been scarcely used and are seldom discussed, but both are effective.

Undulating exercises simply means alternating among exercises. For bench press, you may have a day of bench press, a day of incline press, and a day of decline press. From this point, you can take it a few ways. You can perform workouts straight through with the same repetition maximum (RM), you can have the same RM on each lift but make it different for each lift, you can rotate through RM, or you can undulate RM for each week.

Same Repetition Max

Performing the same repetition max straight through for the lift is just as it sounds. You decide to build up your bench press and work with a 3RM on the bench press, close-grip bench press, and floor press. In every workout, you perform a

3RM but change the exercise you do. You can cycle through as many exercises as you desire, this example uses just these three. Understand that when keeping the RM the same, it is important to change the exercise more but repeat the exercises every 3 weeks to ensure that strength is improving. In the original undulating method, the change in repetition provided a different stimulus for the nervous system to adapt to. With this advanced method, changing the exercises also provides a different stimulus to adapt to. Because you never decrease in intensity, it may be necessary to plan a de-load every 4 to 6 weeks to prevent overtraining. As long as the RM keeps improving in at least every other to every third session, either by improving by a repetition or increasing poundage, you're making progress.

Tables 10.1, 10.2, and 10.3 illustrate sample schedules using this method.

TABLE 10.1 Sample Training Plan Using Undulating Periodization: One Session per Week, Same RM

Week	Exercise
1	Bench press 3RM
2	Close-grip bench press 3RM
3	Floor press 3RM
4	Bench press 3RM
5	Close-grip bench press 3RM
6	Floor press 3RM
7	Bench press 3RM
8	Close-grip bench press 3RM
9	Floor press 3RM

TABLE 10.2 Sample Training Plan Using Undulating Periodization: Two Sessions per Week, Same RM

Week	Session 1	Session 2
1	Bench press 3RM	Close-grip bench press 3RM
2	Floor press 3RM	Bench press 3RM
3	Close-grip bench press 3RM	Floor press 3RM
4	Bench press 3RM	Close-grip bench press 3RM
5	Floor press 3RM	Bench press 3RM
6	Close-grip bench press 3RM	Floor press 3RM
7	Bench press 3RM	Close-grip bench press 3RM
8	Floor press 3RM	Bench press 3RM
9	Close-grip bench press 3RM	Floor press 3RM

TABLE 10.3 Sample Training Plan Using Undulating Periodization: Three Sessions per Week, Same RM

Week	Session 1	Session 2	Session 3
1	Bench press 3RM	Close-grip bench press 3RM	Floor press 3RM
2	Bench press 3RM	Close-grip bench press 3RM	Floor press 3RM
3	Bench press 3RM	Close-grip bench press 3RM	Floor press 3RM
4	Bench press 3RM	Close-grip bench press 3RM	Floor press 3RM
5	Bench press 3RM	Close-grip bench press 3RM	Floor press 3RM
6	Bench press 3RM	Close-grip bench press 3RM	Floor press 3RM
7	Bench press 3RM	Close-grip bench press 3RM	Floor press 3RM
8	Bench press 3RM	Close-grip bench press 3RM	Floor press 3RM
9	Bench press 3RM	Close-grip bench press 3RM	Floor press 3RM

Varying Repetition Max With Each Exercise

For the next variation of this method, you continue with the same exercises of the bench press, the close-grip bench press, and the floor press. In this method, you change exercises each session. Each exercise has a set RM, but the RM is different for each exercise. This method is a better way to induce hypertrophy because it is best with higher repetitions. When you use repetitions lower than 5RM, overtraining tends to occur quickly. If you wish to use this method with lower repetitions, implement a de-load after every 2 or 3 weeks of training. If you don't, by the fourth week you likely will see a decrease in performance.

So, the goal is to get bigger and hopefully improve the 1RM strength of the bench press. Remember, this isn't a specific workout; plug in any exercises you want. Just make sure that you select appropriate exercises. For instance, don't plug in a leg curl to develop a bench press. Choose multijoint exercises as your main exercises. Save the single-joint exercises for the supplemental exercises.

Now that exercises have been selected, determine RM. You should use a higher RM, so let's go with 5RM, 8RM, and finally 12RM. In this example, the bench press uses the 5RM, the close-grip bench press uses the 8RM, and the floor press uses the 12RM. In tables 10.4, 10.5, and 10.6, you can see how the RM alternates within each workout.

Notice how the exercises repeat in the same order. This is a good idea, so the exercises are spaced out, allowing the body to recover from the exercise and repetition scheme. This permits the greatest amount of recovery as well as the greatest strength improvements.

TABLE 10.4 Sample Training Plan Using Undulating Periodization: One Session per Week, Varying RM per Exercise

Week	Session 1
1	Floor press 12RM
2	Close-grip bench press 8RM
3	Bench press 5RM
4	Floor press 12RM
5	Close-grip bench press 8RM
6	Bench press 5RM
7	Floor press 12RM
8	Close-grip bench press 8RM
9	Bench press 5RM

TABLE 10.5 Sample Training Plan Using Undulating Periodization: Two Sessions per Week, Varying RM per Exercise

Week	Session 1	Session 2
1	Floor press 12RM	Close-grip bench press 8RM
2	Bench press 5RM	Floor press 12RM
3	Close-grip bench press 8RM	Bench press 5RM
4	Floor press 12RM	Close-grip bench press 8RM
5	Bench press 5RM	Floor press 12RM
6	Close-grip bench press 8RM	Bench press 5RM
7	Floor press 12RM	Close-grip bench press 8RM
8	Bench press 5RM	Floor press 12RM
9	Close-grip bench press 8RM	Bench press 5RM

Varying Repetition Max Per Week

In this variation of the exercise-changing method in undulating periodization, the exercises stay the same but repetitions change globally from week to week. This means that if week 1 features 5RM, you do every exercise performed in week one at 5RM. Week 2 uses 8RM, so every exercise performed in week 2 is done at 8RM. RM depends on your goal, as we discussed in the basic method covered in chapter 7. If you want to improve size, go with a higher RM; if you want to increase strength, go with a lower RM. Tables 10.7, 10.8, and 10.9 illustrate sample programs using this method.

TABLE 10.6 Sample Training Plan Using Undulating Periodization: Three Sessions per Week, Varying RM per Exercise

Week	Session 1	Session 2	Session 3
1	Floor press 12RM	Close-grip bench press 8RM	Bench press 5RM
2	Floor press 12RM	Close-grip bench press 8RM	Bench press 5RM
3	Floor press 12RM	Close-grip bench press 8RM	Bench press 5RM
4	Floor press 12RM	Close-grip bench press 8RM	Bench press 5RM
5	Floor press 12RM	Close-grip bench press 8RM	Bench press 5RM
6	Floor press 12RM	Close-grip bench press 8RM	Bench press 5RM
7	Floor press 12RM	Close-grip bench press 8RM	Bench press 5RM
8	Floor press 12RM	Close-grip bench press 8RM	Bench press 5RM
9	Floor press 12RM	Close-grip bench press 8RM	Bench press 5RM

TABLE 10.7 Sample Training Plan Using Undulating Periodization: One Session per Week, Varying RM per Week

Week	Session 1
1	Floor press 12RM
2	Close-grip bench press 8RM
3	Bench press 5RM
4	Floor press 12RM
5	Close-grip bench press 9RM
6	Bench press 5RM
7	Floor press 12RM
8	Close-grip bench press 8RM
9	Bench press 5RM

Varying Velocity of Exercise

The final advanced method of undulating periodization is to vary the velocities of the exercises. This method hasn't been discussed much to this point because it requires special equipment to measure the velocity of the bar. Velocity measurement ensures that you are developing the intended trait. Every trait has a velocity, and if training is not meeting that velocity, the trait is not being trained. This goes back to the SAID principle. The body specifically adapts to the imposed demands placed on it. Remember the sledgehammer example in chapter 1? After the first 3 weeks, the imaginary worker could swing the hammer all day

TABLE 10.8 **Sample Training Plan Using Undulating Periodization, Two Sessions per Week, Varying RM per Week**

Week	Session 1	Session 2
1	Floor press 10RM	Close-grip bench press 10RM
2	Bench press 5RM	Floor press 5RM
3	Close-grip bench press 2RM	Bench press 2RM
4	Floor press 12RM	Close-grip bench press 12RM
5	Bench press 3RM	Floor press 3RM
6	Close-grip bench press 6RM	Bench press 6RM
7	Floor press 1RM	Close-grip bench press 1RM
8	Bench press 10RM	Floor press 10RM
9	Close-grip bench press 5RM	Bench press 5RM

TABLE 10.9 **Sample Training Plan Using Undulating Periodization: Three Sessions per Week, Varying RM Per Week**

Week	Session 1	Session 2	Session 3
1	Floor press 12RM	Close-grip bench press 12RM	Bench press 12RM
2	Floor press 2RM	Close-grip bench press 2RM	Bench press 2RM
3	Floor press 8RM	Close-grip bench press 8RM	Bench press 8RM
4	Floor press 4RM	Close-grip bench press 4RM	Bench press 4RM
5	Floor press 1RM	Close-grip bench press 1RM	Bench press 1RM
6	Floor press 10RM	Close-grip bench press 10RM	Bench press 10RM
7	Floor press 3RM	Close-grip bench press 3RM	Bench press 3RM
8	Floor press 6RM	Close-grip bench press 6RM	Bench press 6RM
9	Floor press 1RM	Close-grip bench press 1RM	Bench press 1RM

long, but when he first picked up a heavier hammer he was unable to move at the end of the day.

Velocity is the measure the determines specific strength. Following is a quick look at some velocities and what they improve: If you are training one of the competitive power lifts (bench press, squat, or deadlift) in the 0.1 to 0.4 meters per second range, you are developing absolute strength. At 0.6 to 0.8 meters per second, you are developing accelerative strength. In the 0.8 to 1.0 meters per second range, you are developing strength–speed. (The dynamic method is in this range.) At 1.1 to 1.5 meters per second you are developing speed strength. The difference between speed–strength and strength–speed is your priority. With strength–speed, strength is the number-one priority and speed is number two. You will be trying to move heavier weights moderately fast. With speed–strength, speed is the number-one priority and strength is number two. You will try to move lighter weights as fast as possible. Many other velocities and exercises and special strengths for specific sports exist, but these are the main ones to cover now. The other lifts and special strengths primarily deal with developing traits of other sports athletes.

You must perform every repetition with as fast a rate of force development (RFD) as possible and with sound technique. If technique is improper, the repetition doesn't count. If the proper speed is not achieved, the repetition doesn't count. If the speed of the bar is above the desired range for the set, you must add weight to the bar because the weight is too light to develop the desired trait. If the speed of the bar is below the desired range for the set, you must take weight off the bar because the weight is too heavy to develop the desired trait.

Now that you understand this main fact about how velocity determines the trait developed, you can use the same exercises from previous examples to develop several traits over the course of the week. You should develop up to two but no more than three traits at the same time, so perform a two- or three-session-per-week workout. You can use the same exercises for both sessions and change the velocity to develop the desired trait.

The addition of higher velocities aids in recovery since you use a lighter weight. Compare this to a light day of work, but instead of simply working to get some volume in and feel better with the light weight, you are develop a specific trait on that day.

Within these traits, you should work up to a 1RM for that trait for that day. This allows you to maintain strength and develop the traits as fully as possible. Tables 10.10 and 10.11 illustrate sample workouts using this method.

Conjugate Method

The advanced methods of the conjugate method discussed in this section are accommodating resistance (bands and chains), suspended kettlebells, band assistance, and circa max.

Accommodating Resistance

Essentially accommodating resistance means that when you are at the greatest mechanical advantage, the resistance is the greatest. Arthur Jones, inventor of the Nautilus machine, created programs that used various cams to increase the resistance as the lifter lifted the weights. This was a great concept, teaching people to continue to exert force throughout the range of motion. However, the machine was limited in that it couldn't be adjusted for different limb lengths. The current accommodating resistance modes, chains and bands, provide this flexibility.

Nearly any exercise can use chains or bands. Some exercises use them in addition to the weight, and some use bands or chains as the sole resistance.

TABLE 10.10 Sample Training Plan Using Undulating Periodization: Two Sessions per Week, Varying Velocity

Week	Session 1	Session 2
1	Bench press 0.1-0.4 m/s	Bench press 0.8-1.0 m/s
2	Bench press 0.6-0.8 m/s	Bench press 1.1-1.5 m/s
3	Bench press 0.1-0.4 m/s	Bench press 0.8-1.0 m/s
4	Bench press 0.6-0.8 m/s	Bench press 1.1-1.5 m/s
5	Bench press 0.1-0.4 m/s	Bench press 0.8-1.0 m/s
6	Bench press 0.6-0.8 m/s	Bench press 1.1-1.5 m/s
7	Bench press 0.1-0.4 m/s	Bench press 0.8-1.0 m/s
8	Bench press 0.6-0.8 m/s	Bench press 1.1-1.5 m/s
9	Bench press 0.8-1.0 m/s	Bench press 0.1-0.4 m/s

TABLE 10.11 Sample Training Plan Using Undulating Periodization: Three Sessions per Week, Varying Velocity

Week	Session 1	Session 2	Session 3
1	Bench press 0.1-0.4 m/s	Bench press 0.8-1.0 m/s	Bench press 1.1-1.4 m/s
2	Bench press 0.6-0.8 m/s	Bench press 1.1-1.4 m/s	Bench press 0.1-0.4 m/s
3	Bench press 0.8-1.0 m/s	Bench press 0.6-0.8 m/s	Bench press 1.1-1.4 m/s
4	Bench press 0.1-0.4 m/s	Bench press 0.8-1.0 m/s	Bench press 1.1-1.4 m/s
5	Bench press 0.6-0.8 m/s	Bench press 1.1-1.4 m/s	Bench press 0.1-0.4 m/s
6	Bench press 0.8-1.0 m/s	Bench press 0.6-0.8 m/s	Bench press 1.1-1.4 m/s
7	Bench press 0.1-0.4 m/s	Bench press 0.8-1.0 m/s	Bench press 1.1-1.4 m/s
8	Bench press 0.6-0.8 m/s	Bench press 1.1-1.4 m/s	Bench press 0.1-0.4 m/s
9	Bench press 0.8-1.0 m/s	Bench press 0.6-0.8 m/s	Bench press 1.1-1.4 m/s

For example, consider a good morning. Using a straight bar, you could perform straight weight good mornings; chain good mornings; chain and weight good mornings; band good mornings; band and bar weight good mornings; chain and band good mornings; and finally chain, band, and bar weight good mornings. Simply adding the accommodating resistance means one exercise has expanded to seven exercises you can use on max effort day. Changing the bar allows you to multiply that number. For instance, if you have a straight bar, a cambered bar, and a safety bar, you have 21 exercises. Changing foot placement—standard, close, and wide—results in 63 exercises. Your only limitation is your own creativity.

Chains

Chains weigh from 18 to 50 pounds (8.16-22.6 kg) each. They are connected to the bar by smaller feeder chains so that when the lifter is in the bottom portion of the lift, the chain weight is entirely de-loaded onto the floor and when the lifter is at the top portion of the lift, 80 to 90 percent of the chain is off the floor, adding resistance to the bar. This is very important to understand when using chains, ensuring that the weight properly loads and unloads. Today a device that is essentially a heavy chain on a collar allows you to lift the entire weight off the floor so very little is de-loaded. It does not elicit the desired response since there is no accommodation and the entire weight is on the bar. This is not to say that the chaotic swinging of the chains in the air doesn't have an added training effect. It does have an added effect; the constant change of direction of the resistance acts as a proprioception device. However, the desired effect of accommodation will not be reached. Also, more effective means of chaos training exist, which are discussed in the section on suspended kettlebell training.

What are the benefits of adding chains? Isn't this simply additional weight on the bar? Why not just throw another plate on the bar? When set up properly, chains allow you to accelerate through the movement. Christian Cantwell, 2008 USA Olympic silver medalist and three-time world champion in the shot put, relied on training with chains to learn to do just that. He thought that traditional weight training movements made him slow down at the top. Adding chains allowed him to accelerate throughout the entire range of the movement. He was able to improve strength and the RFD at the end of the movement so he could push the shot maximally all the way through the end of the movement and get the greatest distance possible. Without the use of the chains, he couldn't have trained his body to perform as it did, and the results may have been quite different.

Bands

Bands provide some of the same benefits as chains, but differences do exist. Bands allow much more tension to get onto the bar with less setup. Bands also have another effect on the body. Chains simply load and unload. Bands, on the other hand, accelerate the weight on the eccentric portion of the lift. Going back to Isaac Newton, we know that for every action exists an equal and opposite reaction. The faster you go down, the faster you come up. An example of this is a bouncing basketball. If you hold a basketball out at shoulder height and let go, the ball hits the ground and bounce up roughly halfway to the original starting height or around waist level. If you throw the ball down to the ground forcefully, it bounces up higher than the original starting position because of the additional force placed on it. Bands teach you to move faster.

For some reason, bands tend to be harder on the connective tissues of joints. When you start out using bands, use them for no more than 3 weeks at a time. After one wave, remove the bands from the bar. For the next 3 weeks, either use chains or no accommodating resistance at all. After that phase, it is OK to return to bands. Over time, the body will adapt to this resistance and you can use the bands week in and week out. However, do not try this until you go through several years of cycling with the bands.

The band's virtual forces have quite a profound effect on the strength development of many powerlifters. The amount of unloading and loading is amazing. It is quite easy for a lifter to stand with 700 pounds (317.5 kg) of force at the top of the squat and only 300 pounds (136 kg) of force in the hole of the squat.

Many debates exist about how much tension each band provides and how to calculate how much tension is on the bar. The issue is that for every setup exists a different amount of tension. So many variables go into this that it is impossible to determine a set tension. However, the one set variable in bands is that the band's tension is equal to its width. The order of band tensions is mini, light, average, strong, and monster.

When attaching bands to various implements to perform squats, good mornings, bench presses, or other exercises, make sure that the apparatus does not come up. You are standing with a massive amount of weight and band tension, so if the rack flips up, you will go flying. Obviously this is unsafe and unwanted in any gym. The costs in medical bills and repairs to the equipment and facility can be quite high. You can ensure that the rack or apparatus does not move in a couple of ways. The first and easiest is to bolt the rack or apparatus to the floor. If it is bolted to the floor, there is virtually no way the rack will tip up. The other way is to weigh down the rack until you have essentially a temporary bolting. Every rack is different, so it may take some time to figure out where to place plates or dumbbells, but it is essential to prevent damage and injury. When experimenting, try to have six people there: one to lift, one to back spot, two as side spots for the weight, and two to watch for the rack tipping. It may be tough to coordinate for one day, but it is the best way to do it.

Be sure you know how to attach the bands correctly. If the rack has band pegs (figure 10.1), use them. If the rack does not have band pegs, either attach the band to the bottom crossbar support or use dumbbells.

If you are attaching the band to the bottom crossbar, simply choke the band to the crossbar. If tension is not sufficient, add boards to the rail (figure 10.2) before choking the bands to stretch the bands and create more tension at the top. Choking the bands will lock the boards into place, if tight enough. If the choking is not tight enough, the boards can slide around and may come out, causing the tension to change and the bar to shift, which may lead to injury.

If you are using dumbbells, you need at least two heavy dumbbells per band (figure 10.3). Run the band around the first dumbbell and under the second. When possible, use the heaviest dumbbells available. The key is to make sure that the

Figure 10.1 Anchoring band on band pegs.

Figure 10.2 Adding boards to rail to create more tension.

Figure 10.3 Anchoring band with dumbbells.

weight of the dumbbells is heavier than the band tension on the bar. If not, the dumbbells will end up dangling from the end of the bar while you lift because they weren't heavy enough to anchor the band. Place plates on either side of the dumbbells to prevent the dumbbells from rolling out of place. Safety is a primary concern for lifting. Eliminate any possibility of an unsafe environment.

Suspended Kettlebell Training

Suspended kettlebell training is performed with the kettlebell hanging from the bar by a rope or a band. The thought behind suspended kettlebell training is to cause great amounts of chaos so you have to react to the subtle or not-so-subtle movements of the kettlebells on the bar. This requires a great amount of proprioception. The constant changes and speed at which things change cause a great contraction of the muscle. This has one other benefit, the carryover of the chaos training to sport. The kettlebells create a chaotic environment for training. The constant movement of the weights forces you to change your path and react quickly, without thinking. This is great for sports. A recent trend in strength training is unstable surface training; the thought is that the enhancements in proprioception carry over to sport. Often an increase in proprioception does occur, but usually it isn't sport specific. You see, the surface in sport is always stable; the environment causes the instability. Theoretically, if you can train in an unstable environment and gain proprioception from that, you have a gain in sport-specific proprioception.

To set up with the rope, it is important to have the kettlebells so that they will not touch the ground at any point. The key is to make sure they are allowed to swing freely. If they touch the ground, they stop swinging, which prevents the added benefits. The rope allows movement forward, backward, and laterally.

Use minibands for the band setup. Quadruple one individual band, run it halfway through the handle of the kettlebell, then place it on the bar. Bands allow movement forward, backward, and laterally and also add resistance up and down, causing a greater amount of proprioception adaptation.

An additional stimulus is an unstable bar. Two unstable bars have been used. The first is the bamboo bar, which is available through select dealers. This bar was developed specifically for the suspended kettlebell with bands. It has a great amount of flex as well as rings to place the hands, and the ends of the bar are specific to holding the kettlebell. The other bar is a simple long piece of PVC pipe. The PVC pipe can have some water in it, but no more than halfway full, to give a greater amount of instability. The thickness of the PVC pipe will dictate how much weight you can use. Use a pipe no less than 3 inches (7 cm) thick). The downside of the PVC pipe is that it can break, so it should be used with great caution.

Band Assistance

To use band assistance, the bands need to be hung from the top, so you must use a rack. The idea of band assistance is similar to band resistance in that the weight will be heavier at the top than at the bottom. For the equipped lifter, it seems to act more like gear when you're training raw. You can use bands to create momentum out of the hole and to power through the top of the lift.

Bands must be attached to the bar so that they will not slip. One way is to put the band between the weight and the inner collar. Another is to attach the band to the bar with carabiner clips. Use the large ones you would use for ab wings or rock climbing. Attach the bands to the bar evenly spaced, both between each other and in relation to the rest of the bar. If the bands are not evenly placed, one side will receive more assistance than the other and cause rotation, uneven extension, or both when you try to perform the exercise.

With band assistance, you do not receive the added benefit of the overspeed eccentric, so no overspeed capabilities are developed.

Another difference with band assistance, and an advantage of its use, is the increased confidence that comes with using it. When using the assistance, more weight is added to the bar. When you see the big weights and approach them successfully, you no longer get intimidated when you see the weights on the bar. Over time the fear of the big weights declines and you can achieve greater and greater personal records. It doesn't freak someone out when he goes up 100 or even 200 pounds (45 or 90 kg) on a competition lift because he already had that weight in his hands or on his back and felt it. Since he has already lifted it, confidence is not an issue. He knows what it will feel like. The band resistance uses the resistance of the bands, so the weights are not actually seen on the bar.

Which method is better? That's a question you'll have to answer for yourself. Try both and see which one helps you more. What makes the best results on meet day? That will be the best method for you.

Circa-Max Phase

The circa-max, or close to maximal, phase is done on squats before a meet. It uses a combination of heavy bar weight and heavy band resistance to enable the lifter to use his max or close to his maximal weights. Only very strong lifters should do this; it may be too much for the novice lifter to handle.

The body adapts over time and is able to use heavier and heavier weights over the course of a cycle. Trying to do a circa-max phase before you are strong enough may lead to overtraining or injury, and this is very detrimental considering that the circa max is the phase that leads in to the meet.

During the circa-max phase, maximal effort days typically are dropped and the circa max is performed on the dynamic day. It is advisable, however, to do supplemental work on the would-be maximal effort day as well as recovery and regeneration exercises such as foam rolling, active isolated stretching, or contrast baths.

The circa-max phase is a phase of training, not something that you can switch in and out like bands or chains. You must prepare for the circa-max phase with heavy bouts of maximal effort work. As you will find throughout your training, some maximal effort exercises, while still maximal effort, require much less load than others. These exercises are not appropriate when getting ready for the circa-max phase, as the body must be prepared to handle circa-max loads. If a weakness causes reduced loads, that weakness needs to be addressed with supplemental exercises as opposed to the maximal effort exercises.

The circa-max phase lasts 3 weeks, followed by a 1- to 3-week de-load. The de-load is required to realize a delayed transformation effect. This means that if you had the meet the week following the circa-max phase, you probably would not be lifting anywhere near your max. You might think you peaked early, when in reality you are in the delayed transformation effect time period. The stronger you are, the longer a de-load you need because of the amounts of stress that the consecutive weeks of training place on the body.

The delayed transformation effect simply means that you don't see the gains during the phase but several weeks after it. It is akin to when you overtrain slightly, take a de-load, and then supercompensation sets in. The training makes you stronger, but you have to back off to achieve or realize the results. If you keep training hard, you actually get weaker because you are not able to recover.

Only about six work lifts are done. Note that it doesn't say 6 sets. It can be anywhere from 6 singles to 3 sets of 2 repetitions. Most have achieved the best gains with 3 × 2. (Table 10.12 on page 172 is a sample circa-max cycle that uses 3 × 2.) Training with this method means a greater time under tension, which you may experience on meet day. The body becomes its function. If you train to strain for long periods of time, you will be able to do so on meet day. If you train to strain for only short periods of time, you will not be able to do so on meet day. On lifts that are missed from this type of training, people often say, "It didn't feel bad. I started pushing and then there was just nothing." This is simply because they weren't used to straining for that amount of time and the body decided it was done pushing.

For someone squatting in the 750- to 975-pound (340-442 kg) range, you should use a blue and a green (or strong and average) band. Someone squatting over 1,000 pounds (453 kg) should use two blue bands.

TABLE 10.12 Circa-Max Cycle

Week	Sets	Repetitions	Intensity (%)
1	3	2	55
2	3	2	60
3	3	2	65
3 (alternative)	1	1	55
	1	1	60
	2	2	65

After the cycle, you need to de-load. Here is how to do it: For the first 1 to 2 weeks following the de-load, use no chains or bands but achieve a single at 80 to 90 percent of your 1RM. Some lifters prefer to do only 1 week; others find that 2 weeks allow them to achieve their best results on meet day. Play with this to see what works best for you. If you perform 1 week of singles, the second week (or third week, if you perform 2 weeks of singles) will be 2 × 2 at 65 percent and that is it. The third or fourth week is the meet. During this de-load, make sure that you are performing high amounts of mobility work to keep, or make, your body feel good on meet day. If you do not do this, you may get tight and not be able to achieve depth on meet day. Try to get in two small meets, one after 1 week for singles on the de-load and one after 2 weeks of singles, to find what works best for you. It is best to make changes and experiment when getting ready for a state or regional meet. Big meets, such as the National or World Championships, are not the time to try this. (For more on meet preparation, see chapter 12.)

During the circa-max phase, you perform no additional dynamic effort or maximal effort work. The circa max is the main focus during this phase. However, be sure to continue doing supplemental work. If this is neglected, the results could be detrimental on meet day. The circa-max phase typically has been done on the day closest to the meet. For example, if you do dynamic lower on Tuesday and maximal effort day on Saturday, do your circa max on maximal effort day or Saturday if the meet is on a Saturday or Sunday.

Summary

Advanced training will keep you making gains throughout your career. Small changes to training after years of doing it other ways will allow you to make the biggest impact on your total. Undulating velocity, using accommodating resistances, suspended kettlebells, circa max, and so on will help take your total to the next level. However, you must have great amounts of foundational work in place for these advanced methods to be effective. If you try advanced methods too early in your career, you likely will experience suboptimal gains, burnout, and injury. Lifters should do advanced training only after they have been seriously training and competing for multiple years and have entered several meets.

CHAPTER 11

Powerlifting Mindset

Powerlifting is a very physical sport. It is based on muscle and sinew. Championships are won or lost by the amount of weight hoisted. Many people think powerlifting contains little mental skill. However, the mind is where lifts are made or missed and meets are won or lost. The mind, not the platform, is the true battlefield of powerlifting. If the body is strong but the mind is weak, all physical gains are lost.

How often has a competitor been tripped up by a roadblock, say a 600-pound (272 kg) squat? He performs attempts at 585 pounds (265 kg) that are a smoke show, yet stalls every time at 600 pounds (272 kg) and then misses. Once he finally hits this roadblock and breaks through, he quickly rises to 50 or 75 pounds (23 or 34 kg) above this. This is a mental block.

Another example is a powerlifter who hits tremendous weights in the gym and consistently beats his world-champion training partners, but on meet day has difficulty hitting an easy opener. The meet is lost on the battlefield of the mind.

Sport psychology is not voodoo. It is simply a tool for learning how to effectively use the mind in sport. It is learning to get beyond the roadblocks. It is learning how to be the best competitor your body will allow.

Before getting to the good stuff in sport psychology for powerlifters, you need to know some of the basics. One of these basic concepts is the inverted-U theory. Basically it is a chart with performance on the y-axis and arousal on the x-axis. Arousal levels rate how psyched up someone is for a lift. In powerlifting, arousal doesn't move up in a linear manner; an optimal level exists. Someone who is under- or overpsyched won't have optimal performance. Someone who is underaroused will not approach the bar with the necessary focus and won't be able to perform. Someone who is overaroused will find his mind moving way too fast for his body and will not be able to achieve optimal form.

This is not to say that every lifter has the same optimal arousal; in fact, it varies a lot. Even the same person may have different curves on different lifts. Even the lifts may change from raw to geared. In the case of the author Bryan Mann, the raw bench press is best achieved with a high level of arousal, a near foaming-at-the-mouth rage. However, for a bench press with a shirt, he must approach it calmly. This is because of the added complexity of the powerlifting equipment. The technique with equipment is different from raw lifting, and thus arousal must be managed to meet the technical demands. If he approaches the competition bench press with a shirt overly psyched, foaming at the mouth, ready to kill, Mann typically throws the bar off the chest quickly and presses back toward the face and loses the bar halfway up. However, if he approaches it with a lower level of arousal, he can maintain technique and complete a successful lift. This is because of the relationship between mastery and complexity. The lower the complexity, the more quickly the athlete can master the skill. The greater mastery achieved, the higher level of arousal he can use. This is why competitors often change their approach over their careers. A lifter may start out very calm but once he learns to harness his energy and direct it appropriately, he is able to improve his lift by increasing his level of arousal.

When using powerlifting equipment, ranges of motion and strength grooves change. It takes time to learn these grooves. It is best to remain calm when trying to learn these grooves, to get a feel for the suit or shirt. If you approach the geared lift over aroused, you will miss the lift and may get hurt as you are not pushing or pulling or keeping tight what needs to be kept tight. Any time a new shirt or suit is used, the learning curve starts over. This is not to say that someone who has mastered a shirt will take just as long to master a new shirt. But he will have to calm down from his earlier optimal arousal level to learn the shirt before moving it back up.

It is best to sit down with your training partners and discuss when you do your best on which lift. How psyched up do you need to be for a big squat, deadlift, and bench press? Your training partners must know you and know how to get you where you need to be, to calm you down if you go overboard. In Mann's case, his training partner Keith Caton has physically grabbed him and pulled him away from the platform in order to calm him back down to the appropriate level.

Relaxation

Relaxing may be the furthest thing from a powerlifter's mind, but it will do him good. All stress affects the body the same way. Stress from home or work will drain the ability to train. One way to combat this is through relaxation.

Another benefit is that relaxation will help you keep calm on meet day. Often lifters get nervous about the meet, and their nerves get the best of them. Some lifters may be able to do 100 to 200 more pounds (45-90 kg) on their total in the gym than they can on meet day because of their nerves. Relaxation is a way to combat nerves and prevail on the platform.

Two main relaxation methods exist: physical relaxation and guided relaxation. During physical relaxation, you contract and relax the muscles so you can feel the difference. You perform guided relaxation with either a CD or other recording or with a psychologist who leads the listener to relax.

Physical Relaxation

To perform physical relaxation, fully contract a muscle, hold the contraction for a few seconds, and release. When you release the contraction, feel the relaxation based on your knowledge of what a contracted muscle feels like and what a relaxed muscle feels like. Often physical relaxation is coupled with a verbal cue, usually said in the head. Typically a physical relaxation begins with the left foot and moves through every muscle group up the leg (left foot to left calf to left thigh), followed by the right leg in the same order. Then move to the left arm, moving through the hand, forearm, and upper arm, followed by the right arm. Move into the trunk, chest, and neck. Just before the relaxation, think or say a verbal cue, usually something simple such as "relax." Follow with other words to facilitate the relaxation. Coordinate your breathing. Typically inhale deeply then perform the contraction, exhaling as you relax the muscle.

For example, let's go through the physical relaxation for the left leg. Start with the left foot and contract it maximally. Hold the contraction for 10 seconds. Mentally say, "Relax" as you relax the muscle. Once the muscle is relaxed, think or say softly, "My left foot feels warm and heavy. I am relaxed." To involve another sense, imagine the tension leaving your foot like the heat coming off an asphalt road in August. Say to yourself one or two more times, "My left foot feels warm and heavy. I am relaxed." Next, contract the left calf maximally and hold for 10 seconds. Mentally say, "Relax" as you begin to relax the muscle. Once the muscle is relaxed, think or say softly, "My left calf feels warm and heavy. I am relaxed." Imagine the tension leaving your left calf like the heat coming off a road. Next, contract the left thigh maximally for 10 seconds. Mentally say, "Relax" as you begin to relax your thigh muscles. Once relaxed, think or say softly, "My left thigh feels warm and heavy. I am relaxed." Imagine the tension leaving your left thigh like heat coming off a road.

If you do this sort of relaxation technique repeatedly, the word *relax* will elicit a conditioned response. Just think *relax* and you will lose tension and feel relaxation setting in. This will come in handy on meet day when nerves are starting to build. If this conditioned response is already ingrained, simply saying those key words can invoke a relaxed state.

Guided Relaxation

In guided relaxation, you either listen to a person guiding your relaxation or to a recording. Many excellent guided relaxations are available, and it is as easy as buying a CD. The benefit of guided relaxation is it features many cues to help you relax. Here is an example of a script for a guided relaxation taken from *Coaching Mental Excellence* by Ralph Vernaccia, Rick McGuire, and David Cook:

> Use your imagination to visualize yourself as you relax. As you relax, observe yourself as though you were watching yourself through a camera mounted on the ceiling or from a chair across the room. Observe the features of your face. Start at the top of your head as you relax all the muscles of your body. Spend a few moments visualizing each muscle group and allowing those muscles to respond to your images and affirmations of relaxation. Visualize the muscles of your scalp and your forehead, allowing the muscles in your temples, over the top of your head, and down the back of your neck to become loose and warm and relaxed.

Observe that your breathing automatically and spontaneously becomes slower and deeper, enabling you to slow down every process of your physical body to a state of deep relaxation. Allow the muscles way down deep in the sockets of your eyes to relax. Be sure that your jaw is hanging loose and relaxed with your teeth unclenched. As you visualize your muscles becoming loose and relaxed, experience a corresponding feeling of relaxation and a sensation of warmth as the tissues relax and allow your heart to pump that warm, rich, nourishing liquid to every cell and every fiber and every strand and piece of flesh in your body.

Allow the muscles across the tops of your shoulders, neck, and chest to relax. Relax the muscles down your arms to the tips of your fingers. Recognize that as you relax, you maintain awareness. Any outside sounds become like music in your ears. If an emergency situation external to your reality occurs, you are able to open your eyes and respond to that emergency normally. Otherwise, sounds are blending in and assisting you in your relaxation.

Feel the muscles in the small of your back and in your stomach. Relax the muscles in your hips and lower abdomen, the muscles of your pelvis, the muscles of your arms all the way down to the tips of your fingers. It doesn't matter which hand gets warm and heavy and numb first. Avoid trying to control body sensations. Simply experience them, observe them, and feel your body as it relaxes naturally, reducing tension, fatigue, and stress. As you exhale, exhale the residues of fatigue and tension. As you inhale, inhale pure, fresh oxygen.

Feel the muscles in your hips, thighs, and pelvis, and down each leg to your knees and into your calves. Relax your ankles and the tops and bottoms of your feet, all the way down to the tips of your toes. Every muscle, every fiber, every strand and piece of flesh in your body hangs loose and limp and relaxed.

Repeat simple affirmations to yourself as you relax. Repeat, "It is easy for me to relax. I enjoy taking the time each day to relax." Feel how the muscles are loose and warm and heavy and relaxed. Your breathing pattern is easy, comfortable, and deep. Warmth flows through every muscle, every strand and piece of flesh in your body. As your physical body becomes more deeply and completely relaxed, enjoy discovering that you are able to visualize more clearly, even colors and shapes. Your ability to maintain these colorful images and shapes in the form of meaningful figures, images, and situations is improving as you relax more deeply.

With every breath you exhale, simply repeat, "It is easy for me to relax. I enjoy taking the time each day to relax." To deepen your relaxation, imagine a stairway with five steps. Each step is numbered from 5 to 1. As I count from 5 to 1, allow yourself to enjoy the sensation of stepping down one step per count. Allow yourself to become 20 percent more deeply relaxed with each step so that by the time you reach the bottom of the stairs, you'll be twice as comfortable, twice as relaxed as you are now.

Five. As you step down, imagine the stairway leads to a quiet scene that will be your communication center.

Four. Step down another step and allow yourself to gently drift into deeper levels of relaxation. Keep the images of the stairway clear and distinct in your mind's eye. Imagine a pleasing environment that helps you relax.

Three. With each breath and with each step, feel yourself becoming more deeply, more completely relaxed. Your perception is improving and you are experiencing perception with greater clarity, both through sight and hearing.

Two. Step down another step, deeply and completely relaxed.

One. You are close to the bottom of the stairs. Approach the door that leads to your communication center.

Zero. Step off the last step and walk through a doorway into a beautiful, pleasing scene that is appealing to you. Imagine plants and fresh air. See the sky, blue and clear with a few clouds rolling by. Hear a stream or river running nearby. As your relax in that scene for a few moments, take time to communicate to yourself images and affirmations that provide your inner mind with understanding of your desired goals, your desired realities and achievements in life.

Spend a few moments mentally rehearsing and communicating with your inner self. See yourself each day, all aspects of your life, each day more free from the self-limiting, distressful reactions that can interfere with and inhibit anybody's quest for excellence. Mentally rehearse effectively using these skills to set your mind for success. Use these skills during the day for momentary rest and refreshment. Whether 5 seconds or 5 minutes, at strategic times during the day, quiet and clear your mind to reduce tension and stress and relax. Clear your mind and enjoy your free time.

Communicate these goals, these ideas, these successes to your unconscious mind in your own way, using images and affirmations while deeply relaxed.

Now, it's time to practice visualization skills.

In a few moments, count from 1 to 3. When you reach 3, open your eyes fully. Find yourself completely returned to the state of waking awareness, able to fully understand and appreciate the effectiveness of using these skills daily at the beginning, during, and at the end of each day. Give yourself silent, quiet, and deep relaxation time for a few moments once or twice each day to mentally rehearse, to provide your unconscious mind with the images and communication of your needs and goals. Effectively use these tools to increase time efficiency, increase stamina, and maintain consistency and high quality performance in all aspects of your life.

One. Feel yourself beginning to come up, deeply and completely relaxed, yet refreshed as though you've enjoyed a 3-hour nap.

Two. Alert, relaxed, revitalized, refreshed, you have enjoyed yourself thoroughly. You have a song in your heart and a smile on your face, having enjoyed exploring your own inner space.

Three. Fully and completely return to awakened awareness, rested, refreshed, relaxed.

Adapted, by permission, from R. Vernaccia, R. McGuire, and D. Cook, 1996, *Coaching mental excellence: It does matter whether you win or lose* (Portola Valley, CA: Warde), 180-184.

Affirmations

You converse more with yourself than with any other person. Therefore, the things you say to yourself are very important. People unnecessarily let what others say, or what they tell themselves, get to them. Negative thoughts creep into the head and linger, changing the mentality. If a lifter hears over and over, "Don't worry about him. He never gets his opener," it is planted in his head and he never will be able to get his opener.

These thoughts do not have to trap the powerlifter in a prison of helplessness. It is difficult to change these thoughts, but it can be done. Affirmations are a great way to do this. Affirmations are essentially affirming what you know to be true. Even if it isn't true at this moment, it is true for what the change needs to be. It is a way to train the brain on positive thoughts rather than let negative thoughts dominate the performance.

It is easy to institute the use of affirmations by following a few rules. First, put it on an index card that you carry around with you and review at least three times a day. Review it with emotion. Believe it is true now. People cannot lie to themselves; what they say and believe will become true. It is also good to put up signs around the house or in the car where you will see them and be reminded of the affirmation.

Second, write the affirmation positively and in the present. For example, write, *I always make my opener. I love starting out the meet in a dominating fashion, and I set the tone with my opener,* instead of *I never miss my opener. That's something I don't do.* If you use negative words, your mind focuses on the negative instead of the positive. Also, write the affirmation as it is now and not in the future. Procrastination is easy, so make sure it is written as if the change has already occurred.

Here are some more examples of affirmations:

- I always lift my best in front of a crowd. The crowd invigorates me to new levels. I love lifting in front of a room full of people.
- I always sit back during my squat. I forcefully push my glutes to the rear and allow the hamstrings to do their job.
- I always bench press perfectly in my groove.
- I am a very confident, focused competitor. I know what my goals are, and I do what it takes to achieve them.
- I always lock out every deadlift. My body knows the groove and goes hard all the way to completion.

Thought Stoppage

Like affirmations, thought stoppage is a way to harvest the power of the thought. Thought stoppage is simply stopping negative thoughts. The competitor must approach the bar with only one thought in mind, and it must be a positive one.

There is a saying that you must take out the trash from time to time if you want to keep a clear mind. Anything that is not going toward the task at hand, which is getting a good lift, is trash. It must be taken out of the competitor's mind and not allowed to return until an appropriate time. You always have power over your thoughts. You can choose whether or not to allow them to remain in your head. Realize that a negative thought is trashing your mind, stop the thought, and take out the trash. A clear mind is the mirror of the opponent. A clear mind allows you to react and not think, to be completely in the moment. There are no thoughts of *what will happen if this lift doesn't happen.* There is no thought that *if I miss this lift, what do I have to pull to beat him?* or *if I make this squat, I only have to bench 20 pounds (9 kg) less than normal to win.* There is only *right here, right now, in this moment.* There is no *tomorrow,* there is no *next meet.* There is *now, on this platform, at this time,* and *I will complete this lift in this moment.*

Any time a negative thought enters the mind, the athlete has the power to stop the thought and replace it with a positive one. When an athlete is approaching the platform, he should be completely confident that he will achieve the lift. If there negative thoughts about the lift enter the mind, the lift is over before it has begun. Thought stoppage is a simple yet effective tool for making a positive mentality.

Goal Setting

Goal setting may be the most used part of sport psychology in powerlifting. Goal setting is determining what your goals are but that is only half the story. Two types of goals exist: product goals and process goals. Product goals are the end product of a series of goals. Product goals are the finish line, the 600-pound (272 kg) bench goal, the 2,000-pound (907 kg) total goal, and many others like it. The product goal is the destination.

Process goals are the ones along the way. They make up the road map to the destination. For the product goal of a 600-pound (272 kg) bench press, the first process goal may be to use 100-pound (45 kg) dumbbells on triceps extensions, if the triceps seems to be a limiting factor, or increase the number of pull-ups performed to bring up the lats, or be able to do bent-over rows with 405 pounds (183.7 kg) to improve the ability to tuck the lats on the bench or the ability to arch higher, or to improve leg drive. It could be one, two, or all of these. While you should have one main product goal, the process goals are numerous. Process goals are something to focus on while achieving the main goal. You will have many process goals to assist the main product goal.

Product and process goals go hand in hand. They are likened to a destination and a map. For example, the goal *Get to a stadium* is nonspecific. A goal must be specific, such as *go to an NFL stadium.* That is more specific, but 32 NFL teams exist, so an even more specific goal is *Go to Soldier Field in Chicago.* You need to know where you are and how to get there. Someone traveling from Los Angeles will take a different route to Soldier Field than someone in Evanston, Illinois, and they'll have a different number of stops.

This illustrates that the main goal, the product goal, must be precise. Saying you want to get a big bench is like saying you want to go to a stadium. What stadium, and where? How big of a bench? Is a 400-pound bench big? It may be, but a 500-pound (226 kg) bench is bigger, and a 600-pound (272 kg) bench is even bigger than that. Saying that the goal is to bench press 660 pounds (300 kg), is like determining you want to go to Soldier Field. It is very specific. There is only one 660 pounds (300 kg), on bench press. The process is how to get there, the set of smaller goals that take you on many roads.

Process and product goals must be aligned. If the goal is to obtain a 660-pound (300 kg) bench press, all process goals must go toward that. When selecting process goals, a goal of increasing the ability to do deadlifts is not in line with the main goal of the bench press. Process goals must be specific. Improving technique is like saying that the goal is to go to an NFL stadium. What stadium, what city? Be specific. Improvement in tucking the elbows into the sides during the descent of the bar is specific to technique. Improving the changeover point so you flair the elbows out is specific. Improving the use of pulling down the collar of the bench shirt is a specific process goal. If you want to get to Soldier Field, be sure the entire map is of Chicago, and not half Chicago and half New York City.

Here is another example of a product goal and process goals.

Product goal: Squat 1,000 pounds, up from current 750 pounds.

Process goals: Squat 800, 850, 900, and 950 pounds. Improve the ability to sit back in the hole. Improve the use of the suit. Increase the Romanian deadlift (RDL) by 150 pounds for sets of 8. Increase the intensity of the glute-ham raise by being able to do them with a 25-pound plate behind the head for 4 × 8. Improve technique by raising the head and chest first out of the hole.

For this product goal, improving the use of the suit is an invalid process goal. It is too vague. How will you know if you have improved? A more appropriate goal is to keep the head and chest up in the hole when using the suit, if you have issues with dropping the head and chest or raising the hips before the head and chest. Goals must be specific. A vague goal will never be achieved. The product goal is long term; the process goals are small mile markers on the road to achieve the product goals.

Product goals don't change until they are achieved. You can add or take away process goals as often as needed on the road to the main goal. For instance, maybe you are doing great at leading with the head and chest out of the bottom of the hole so now it is instinctive. However, when the weight gets heavy, the knees cave in (go valgus). The process goal changes to keeping the knees out over the feet during the ascent of the squat. Or the 150-pound increase on the RDL becomes a 200- or 250-pound increase, the glute-ham raise moves up to 45 pounds. Process goals keep you busy focusing on the journey of improving and moving toward the main goal. Process goals need to be continually updated until the main goal is reached.

Visualization

Powerlifters stand to make the greatest gains with the use of sport psychology. Only one person is involved, and the activity is known. This makes it easy to use tools from sport psychology to improve technique and strength, decrease fear and anxiety, and help you on your way to becoming a warrior.

Visualization occurs when you get into a relaxed state and then go over the performance in your mind. It's that simple, yet it's not. It's not simply a process of thinking about the performance or seeing it in a movie. It's getting fully engaged in the moment. Later this chapter covers how to perform visualization, but firs, here are some examples. Draw from them what you can to help yourself as a lifter.

Major James Nesmeth, who liked to golf, was a POW for seven years during the Vietnam War. To maintain his sanity while imprisoned, Major Nesmeth played every course in his mind every day. He felt the club in his hand and the impact it made on the ball. He felt the wind on his face, heard the birds and fellow golfers, and felt the green underneath his feet. Once he got back to the United States, one of the first things he did was play golf. Previously his best game was a very respectable 90. On the first hole of his first game back, he hit a hole in one. For the game, he hit a 74, a 16-stroke personal record.

Next, consider the example of the great U.S. shot putter Brian Oldfield. In his later years as a competitor, Oldfield was broken down but he still competed at a high international level through his regimen of 1,000 throws a day. He said he took 1,000 throws a day, every day, no matter what the weather or how he was feeling. However, most of his throws were in his mind while he was reclined in a chair. He was able to maintain a high level of sportsmanship through the use of his mind.

When you think about an activity, an electrical impulse is sent to the muscles in the pattern required for the activity. For instance, if you think about doing a bench press right now, the muscles are receiving an electrical impulse to do it. This is a way to help groove or perfect form on a lift.

Following are some steps to get the most out of visualization. The better the visualization, the better the effect it will have on sporting form.

First, get into a quiet and relaxing place. Next, see the event in your head, and see yourself performing it perfectly. This is your visualization and you control if you get the lift or not, so be positive and get it. Once you see that visualization, get deeper into it, like James Nesmeth did. Feel the weight on your back for a squat, the knurling digging into your upper back; hear the sound of the monolift when you unrack the weight, the feel of your hips going back and down; feel the suit and how it pulls on your body; feel the knee wraps as you get lower and lower; hear your training partner yell "up" as you start the ascent with perfect form and finish the lift by standing up easily and in control of the weight. Taste the victory, and smell the ammonia and liniment in the air. Get fully engaged.

Visualization is especially great for a lifter who has a technique flaw. When doing the visualization, feel yourself doing it right, how it should be done. The next training session, don't be surprised if you do it right automatically. This is because you've done it several times correctly.

To make visualization even more effective, see the warm-ups and see yourself putting on the gear properly.

Visualization helps to improve form and reduce anxiety. Because you've been there before and done it before, you don't get anxious for a weight that you try every week in training or anxious before a training session with your partners. Visualization gives you the ability to perform thousands of reps with whatever weight and expend no energy.

Do you get nervous in front of crowds? Visualize the crowd, feel their energy, hear the cheers, feel the heat in the room, and feel yourself there and performing the big lift successfully. Anxiety often occurs due to the new stimulus of the crowd. There are no crowds in the gym.

Visualization for the Squat

You start your preparation for the squat. Your knees are being wrapped to the perfect tension, and they are in the perfect position. You feel their tightness and rebound as you are helped up from the chair. Your suit straps are pulled up into perfect position and the suit quickly set. You feel it is in the perfect spot to be able to use your technique. You feel yourself approaching the platform confidently and aggressively as you chalk your hands and your partner chalks your back. Stepping onto the platform, there is no doubt in your mind that the lift is yours. You step under the bar and slide it into the groove on your back where you like it. When you stand up with the bar and move into position to squat, it feels perfect. From the moment the bar was on your back, it felt light. You push your hips back and start the descent. The suit is working with you to achieve depth as it is perfectly set. Once depth is achieved, the bar is reversed and rocketed back to the finish. As you wait for the judge's "rack" command, you hear the roar of the crowd. You see the judge commence the "rack" command. You turn to see the judges' board, and it shows three white lights.

Visualization for the Bench Press

When you hear your name, you and your training partners begin setting your shirt. It gets set perfectly, and the belt is set. You go around your wrists with the wrist wraps to the perfect tightness for the lift. You know exactly how to alter your equipment for each attempt and it is perfect for this weight. You are on deck and approach the platform, getting the chalk for your hands and back.

You approach the bar as it is loaded. You set up, perfectly. Your arch is set and you know that your body will not move or shift on the bench, so you are free to press without fear of the shift. You set your grip on the bar after setting up. The bar feels powerful in your hands, even before you unrack it. You know that this moment is yours for the taking. You give your normal commands—1, 2, 3—and the bar is handed to you. The bar becomes unracked and it feels light in your hands. You descend perfectly in the groove. The bar gets ever closer to your chest and touches without effort, no pulling down or wavering with the bar, as your gear was set perfectly. You get the command to press and drive your heels to the ground while pressing. The bar flies off your chest as if it is weightless and rams into lock out. You maintain control and show your mastery over the weight as the crowd roars. The rack command is given and you place the bar in the rack and stand up to see three white lights for your bench press.

Visualization for the Deadlift

You have been sitting in your seat, focusing yourself after a fantastic warm-up and fantastic meet. You know what you need to lift to achieve this and have selected the perfect weight. You hear your name called and stand up. You get adjusted and your gear feels perfect. You are on deck and move to the chalk bucket to improve your grip. You are up and approach the platform. There is no fear, only confidence. You trust in your training to this point, and know that it has prepared you for this. You set your feet, and you know that your base is rock solid. You prepare and reach down to grab the bar. The bar feels small in your hands, as if your hands have grown larger. Grip will not be a problem today. You start the pull, and it is coming up smoothly, as if weightless. The bar hits your knees and you transition smoothly to driving the hips through and you snap into the lockout. You stand there, effortlessly holding on to the bar and waiting on the "down" command. After getting the command, you lower the bar softly to the platform, rise to look at the light board, and see three white lights.

Visualization and Technique

When training, only so many repetitions can be performed. If a technique is flawed, it must be fixed through repetitions performed correctly. The body wears down quickly, but the mind will wear down slowly. You can take an infinite number of repetitions in your mind to improve technique. Here is how to do it:

Relax. Like a movie playing in the mind, see yourself performing the perfect technique. Notice all of the small, intricate movements. Be very perceptive to the timing, when different muscle groups are used and joints moved. Next, step into the movie. Feel what it is like to do each of the small movements and do it correctly. Feel the weight, feel the feet, and smell the air. Sense what it tastes like when done properly, the feel of the bar in the hands. Feel it all, get to know it all. After stepping into the movie and doing it several times, make sure belief is evident. Make sure that the weight is something conquerable and the technique will be perfect when the weight is achieved. The final step is to achieve it. For the next set or workout, simply do the movement with the perfect technique you have practiced through visualization. This method is also called Cook's model (see chapter 1). See it, feel it, trust it, believe it, achieve it.

The Right Mentality

The right mentality is everything. When you step on the platform, you should know your goal and be in the proper place to achieve that goal. Step on the platform and know that you will do this weight. Whole-heartedly believe you own the lift, and now is the easiest part of the entire lift. You will be able to overcome whatever chaos may ensue during the lift.

The lifter who approaches the platform with fear and apprehension, concerned because he has never done that weight before, his gear isn't exactly right, or the audience is staring, will never make the lift. He has already decided that isn't his day.

The right mentality is to accept responsibility for actions instead of looking for someone or somewhere to blame. If you miss a squat, why did you miss it? It wasn't because of the judge, it wasn't because of the bar, it wasn't because of someone talking or taking a picture. You missed the lift. Winners look to fix it, losers look for blame.

Circle of Concern, Circle of Influence

In powerlifting, many things will bother someone. From Hans Selye's work on stress, it is evident that all things, whether eustress (good stress such as a birthday, birth of a child, promotion, or vacation) and distress (bad stress such as the death of a family member, job loss, or relationship problems), affect the body the same way. Think about how many times people say they are more tired when they return from vacation than they were before they went on vacation. The positive stress and enjoyment of being on vacation drained the person of energy until he needed a vacation from his vacation.

Many things concern people, including family issues, relationship issues, work issues, training, competition, food, shelter, academics, world issues, and the economy—the list of concerns is infinite. When people worry about the things they can't control, it takes time and energy away from the things that they can do something about. Constant worrying draws attention away from areas that can be controlled and turns toward areas in which no influence is possible. Nothing can be done by worrying about these things, so there is no point in worrying about them.

Focus on what you *can* influence, within the circle of influence. You always can influence your attitude and effort. No one can control what a judge red-lights, but he can control how he responds to the red light. He can control how to approach the next lift after the red light. Focusing on what can be controlled empowers the individual. Focusing on what can't be controlled leads to apprehension, fear, and tension.

One of the best examples of focusing on the circle of influence comes from Stephen Covey's book *The Seven Habits of Highly Effective People* (2004, Free Press). In this book, Covey speaks of Viktor Frankl's experience in a concentration camp during World War II. Frankl was held in Auschwitz. Every day his Nazi captors told him that this would be the day he died. They would taunt him and the other people in the camp. They would try to make their lives a living nightmare. Frankl realized that he could not control what the Nazi guards said or did to them. He could, however, control his own thoughts. He could choose not to let the guards get to him. He could choose not to let the beatings bring him down. He could choose to be free in his mind while his body was imprisoned.

For instance, many people have jobs that prevent them from training as they wish. Instead of focusing on the fact that they can't train when or how they desire, which would only drain them, they can focus on getting the most out of their training in every session. They can't control their work situation since it pays the bills. However they, can alter their training sessions and their attitudes to be able to get the most out of training while at their current jobs.

Sometimes people feel that their training is not going anywhere and they are not making gains. The key is to not feel hopeless but do what can be done. Figure out what is wrong by analyzing training (is it technique, the program?) and work to correct it. This may be a difficult task and may require the help of others, but it can be done. You are in control if you put forth the effort to change your training. You are in control of your positive attitude throughout the change. You are in control when you pick up a phone and call someone who can help or get on a forum and ask questions.

Many situations seem hopeless because the wrong things are the focus. When working within the circle of influence, what once were mountainous problems often seem like mildly annoying hills.

Coming Back

At some point in a lifter's career, for whatever reason, he will bomb. It happens. The next time the individual competes, he either will fear the bomb out again, and then can't be effective because of that fear, or will forget about the bomb.

Remember the circles of influence and concern. You have no influence on something in the past, thus you should waste no energy on it. It happened, it's over, and nothing done today can change the fact that it happened. Nothing can be done to change the fact that the bomb occurred. However, you can learn from the bomb and prevent it from happening again. Was it too drastic a weight cut, or perhaps improper training? Did something change on meet day? Was it improper form? Figure out what it was and fix it. Beyond this, what can be done? Make a choice: Do not dwell on the bomb-out. If you do start thinking about the bomb-out, use thought stoppage to trash the thought and replace it with a positive one. All it takes to come back is a simple decision. Decide not to dwell on the bomb-out.

Summary

Thoughts are powerful, and they often are the difference between a good lift or a bad lift, a win or a loss, success or failure. You have control over what goes in your head. Your thoughts can become tangible and can be used for good. Control your thoughts, harvest them, and use them for your own good to better your lifting.

CHAPTER **12**

Meet Preparation

When powerlifting first started back in the 1960s, only one organization, the Amateur Athletic Union (AAU), held competitions and the rules were pretty simple. Today we have more than 30 organizations, each adding their own touch to create their own rules. Regardless of which organization you choose to participate in, it is vital that you acquire a rule booklet from each organization so that you can learn, understand, refer to, and abide by that organization's rules.

Once you decide you are ready to enter your first powerlifting meet, sit down with your training partner, coach, or handle to map out a game plan for mentally and physically preparing. Consider these questions:

- How many weeks to you have to train for the meet?
- What weight percentages, sets, and repetitions will you use as you train?
- Which organization is sponsoring the meet?
- Is the meet sanctioned?
- Is it an equipped or raw meet?
- What materials (entry form, membership card) do you need to complete? Is there a fee you need to pay?
- What time is weigh-in? Is there an early weight in?
- Where is the meet and how will you get there?
- Is all your equipment ready and legal?

Without doubt, one of the best ways to prepare for a powerlifting meet is to observe a powerlifting meet. Take a pen or pencil and note pad so you can write down things that are important to you such as the chief referee's commands for the squat, bench press, and deadlift. Write down how the judges are judging, why the side judge has his hand up, what name brand each athlete is wearing, how the athletes handle a good or bad lift, and any additional information you think can benefit you. Keep this information with you and refer to it as you prepare for your first competition. Once you have found a powerlifting meet you want to enter, get a copy of the entry form so that you and your handler or coach can review the details of the form: where the meet is being held, when weigh-in is, what kind of equipment check they do, how many lifters are expected, who (raw or equipped) the competition is open to, what time the meet starts, and when the rule briefing is. Find out if the meet is sanctioned and if you can purchase a card at the meet. At the midpoint of your training, you or your coach should call the meet director to confirm that the meet is still on and ask if the weights being used in the meet are in kilograms or pounds. It is very important to know this. If you are training in pounds and the meet is in kilograms and you planned to open your squat at 395 pounds (179 kg), you have to decide if you will open at 391 pounds (177.5 kilograms) or 396 pounds (180 kg). Then you have to adjust all of your second and third attempts. Contacting the meet director also gives you the opportunity to get a kilogram chart and learn the conversions. At one meet, a young lifter who weighed 132 pounds and did not know the meet was in kilograms listed his opening squat at 345 kilograms, thinking it was pounds. Actually, 345 kilograms is 760 pounds, as was his other opener listed in kilograms. This mistake was caught early enough to save this young lifter before the meet started, and he had time to change his opener to the weight he wanted.

Leading up to the Meet

Two weeks before the meet, perform your deadlift with just a belt, no suit, for 3 to 5 repetitions. When you are a week out from your competition and are scheduled to lift Saturday morning, plan your week. On Monday, do your opener squat with briefs and belt for 3 to 5 repetitions and light leg work. On Tuesday, do bench press with or without your bench shirt. Do your opener for 1 to 3 repetitions.

The two days after Tuesday, rest, recover, heal, and stretch to help prepare your body for the competition. You should not change your schedule and just sit around doing nothing. Yes, you should stay off your feet as much as possible, but keep going to work or school. On Wednesday and Thursday, keep your mind occupied and use your time wisely. When you ordinarily would do your lifting, check your body weight to see if you need to lose weight in the steam room or sauna. If your weight is good, spend the time in the hot or cold tub, use a foam roller, or get a massage. You can never get enough stretching or ab work.

One of the biggest mistakes a lifter can make is to sit around doing nothing for a day or two, thinking he is resting up for the competition. This type of behavior will drive a person insane, so do not change your daily routine. After your Tuesday workout, sit down with your handler or coach and write down your three attempts for each lift on an index card and note if you need to pull this weight to place or to win.

Use your time wisely. Get away from everyone and have some me time. Study the numbers on your index card. Use visualization and mediation to picture yourself performing each lift successfully with perfect form and technique. Refer to the notes you took at the meet you observed. As you visualize yourself performing each lift, hear the judge's voice commanding you on the squat ("squat," "rack"), bench press ("start," "press," "rack"), and deadlift ("down").

Repetition is a key to success. The more you do something, the more it becomes a habit and you give yourself a better chance to be successful. Remember, although powerlifting is a sport of strength, the strongest lifter is not always the one who wins. Sometimes the one who makes the most attempts wins. Mentally study the numbers on your index card. Finally, use this time to study the rules of the organization running the meet.

Traveling and Weighing In

Once you know the location of the meet, determine if it is close enough to your home so that you can sleep in your own nice bed. If the meet is out of town, travel on the day before the meet. Give yourself plenty of time to get there just in case. Make reservations ahead of time to make sure you have a place to stay.

After checking into your room, locate the scale. Check your weight to make sure things are looking good. Locate the warm-up area and check out the platform. Get a good feel for the place. Get something to eat and then rest. If the meet has an early weigh-in on Friday, skip check-in and go straight to weigh-in. Have your handler or coach check in your equipment. Refer to your index card when you put down your opener. After making weight, have a good meal then go to your room to relax.

If you are weighing in on Saturday morning, get up 90 minutes before weigh-in. Take a hot shower to help you wake up and to loosen up your body. Get to weigh-in early; you may move up if other lifters are not there when their lot numbers are called.

Weigh-in is your first opportunity to check out your competition. Some guys will look bigger than the weight class and some will look smaller. You cannot gauge how strong an individual is by looking at him even if he is in your class. You have control over only one person—you. If you pay too much attention to your opponents, your mind will start playing tricks on you. You will began to question why you are here. Being nervous is part of lifting. If you are not feeling tense, nervous, and excited, if your adrenaline isn't flowing, this is not the sport for you.

The rule briefing is a must-attend event. Ask questions if you do not understand something or want a clearer interpretation of a rule. Other lifters will have the same questions. Remember, there is no such thing as a dumb question.

Lifting in an Equipped Meet

A raw, or nonequipped meet, is exactly as it sounds—no equipment except belts, knee sleeves, wrist wraps, and singlets. If you are training for a raw meet, there is no equipment to add to weekly training. You can train with equipment, if you choose, but on meet day, the equipment has to go.

If you are lifting in a equipped meet, use all the supportive equipment allowed by that organization during training. Start slowly and add a piece of supportive gear every 2 weeks until you are wearing the full gear. Here is an example of when to add equipment to the squat based on an 8-week training cycle with the meet on week 9.

Week 1: Briefs and power belt

Week 2: Briefs, knee wraps, and power belt

Weeks 3 and 4: Briefs, knee wraps, meet suit with straps down, power belt

Weeks 5 and 6: Briefs, knee wraps, meet suit with straps up, power belt

Weeks 7 and 8: Briefs, knee wraps, meet suit with straps up, power belt

Week 9: Meet week; hit opener with briefs and power belt

Your handler or coach should be someone you trust who knows your training cycle. The handler or coach will check to see where you are when it is time to squat. Use the same warm-up you and your coach noted on your index card. If you are in the first flight, start your warm-up and put on your lifting gear right after the rule briefing. For example, let's imagine you are in the first flight and fall between lifters 1 and 5 starting the squat. The meet opener starts in 30 minutes. You want to finish four or five warm-up exercises. Time your warm-ups so you are doing one every 5 minutes, giving yourself plenty of time to get to the platform and rest before your opening squat.

If you fall in the second flight, you will have some time to settle down, ease your nerves, and relax. Once the lifters in the first flight start their first attempts, begin your warm-up. Do a warm-up exercise every 3 to 5 minutes. When the lifters in the first flight are on their third squat attempts, finish your last warm-up fully geared. Follow the same procedure for the bench press and deadlift.

When getting ready for that first squat attempt, start wrapping your knees when you are in the hole (the third lifter up). When you are on deck (the second lifter out), pull up your straps, put your belt on, and chalk your hands and back.

At your first powerlifting meet, it is normal to be nervous. To make things easier, for your first squat attempt pick a weight you can do for 5 repetitions. Regardless of the situation, you will be able to get it even if you do not have the right lifting suit or are feeling sick. You spent the past week mentally preparing yourself and the last 8 weeks physically getting ready. Let your ego take over. The one sure way you can compete in a meet is if you make one attempt of each lift to get a total. Stick to the numbers you and your coach put together. The more attempts you make, the more confidence you build. Your ultimate goal is to total in the meet, go 9 for 9 for each successful lift. This is a personal record. If the opportunity is there, you want to place and receive a trophy or medal for your hard work over the last 9 weeks.

After the Meet

Once the meet is over, you cannot wait to get something to eat and talk about what took place before, during, and after the meet. Discuss what you wish you had done. More than anything, you will be glad the meet is over. Ask when the next meet is.

How many meets should a beginner lift in a year? This question easily could be answered by looking at how many weeks you train for a meet. If you train 10 weeks or longer, you may be able to enter only two or three meets in a year. If your training cycle is 10 weeks or less, you may be able to lift in three or four meets a year. Because you need experience, exposure, and confidence, you should lift in three meets your first year. This will give you valuable experience and lessons in nutrition, goal setting (short-, mid-, long-range), dedication, hard work, patience, rest and recovery, preparation, sacrifice, overcoming adversity, and never giving up. As a beginning powerlifter, understand you cannot lift in every powerlifting meet even as you dream of becoming the best. The ultimate goal is to go to a meet and lift as much as possible at your peak, increasing your individual and total poundage each time you compete.

After you have competed in a few powerlifting meets if your total has not increased or increased just a little, take some time off to focus on strengthening your weaker muscles, making your strong muscles stronger, moving past your sticking points, strengthening your stabilizers, and building a stronger foundation. If you are competing all the time, you will never have the opportunity to develop these areas. Use your offseason wisely. If you lift weights correctly, you will get stronger faster and you will become the champion you know you are.

Selecting Equipment

When you start out in powerlifting, make yourself aware of all the equipment available and the pieces allowed by the organizations that run the meets. Today's equipment changes frequently for the better to advance the sport of powerlifting. However, there is a limit on how far you can go with a piece of equipment. Consider today's race cars. A driver can do several things to make his car faster, but it has to be legal and pass inspection. Following is a summary of some of today's additional equipment and their purposes.

Squat Suit

How much does a squat suit help your squat? A lot, especially if you use the suit the way it was intended and to your advantage. Go through your training cycle. At the end of your cycle, go as heavy as you can without your suit. Then add your suit and see how much you can do in it.

In the 1970s, George Zangas introduced the supersuit. It was a single-ply, cream-colored suit. Later he drastically improved the stitching, cutting the sides lower so the lats were exposed and cutting the front lower to show more chest. Both cuts enhanced the experience for lifters because they felt they could breathe easier. He also made the straps wider and provided different colors. As George continued improving his supersuit, other companies began to make their own squat suits. By the 1980s, the squat suit was very popular both in the United States and internationally. Lifters such as Fred "Dr. Squat" Hatfield, the late Dave Passanella, Dave Waddington, and Kirk Karwoski were squatting 1,000 pounds (453.6 kg) or more. The first man to squat this weight at a national meet was Lee Moran at the 1984 Men's Nationals in Dayton, Ohio. This will go down as one of the greatest squats ever. When Lee approached the 1,000-pound squat weight and attempted to unrack it, the collar on one side came off and the weight followed, then the other side. Lee just stood there as the spotters scattered everywhere. They reloaded the weight and with the collars secured and spotters in place, Lee went down and back up and the lift was good. The crowd went wild and so did Lee. This was done in a single-ply suit.

In the 1980s and 1990s, few powerlifters attempted, tried, or had done 1,000 pounds (453.6 kg) or more. Since the turn of the new millennium, due to advances in training, nutrition, and equipment, powerlifters have been squatting 1,000 pounds or more and there is no stopping. Lifters today are squatting 1,200 pounds (544.3 kg) the way lifters in the 1970s and 1980s were squatting 800 pounds (363.8 kg). Likely past lifters who squatted mid-800 pounds would be 1,000-pound squatters today. Perhaps Ed Coan would have squatted 1,000 pounds at 181 (82.1) or 198 pounds (89.9 kg). How much would Bill Kazmaier, Kirk Karwoski, Gene Bell, Fred Hatfield, Doug Furnas, John Gamble, and all the other great squatters have been able to squat?

The new squat suit gives lifters the ultimate restriction in the hips and glutes and provides support by distributing the body weight and stress as evenly as possible throughout the squat movement. The new squat suit holds up a lot better because it is made with heavier and thicker material. To fit better, you can have a squat suit tailored to your body, whether you use a wide or a close stance. Suits are designed to provide more power, speed, and explosion out of the bottom of the squat. Perhaps the biggest change to the squat suit has been the two-ply squat suit or the canvas hybrid. This suit weighs close to 6 pounds (2.7 kg) with two thick layers of canvas. It has hook-and-loop straps that give you the choice to wear them tight or loose. What suit you wear depends on the organization running the meet. Whatever suit you choose, you are guaranteed to increase your squat by at least 50 pounds (22.6 kg).

Bench Shirt

The bench shirt was invented by John Inzer in the early 1980s. Before the bench shirt, powerlifters wore T-shirts or no shirt. There were a lot of good bench pressers before the bench shirt. Pat Casey was the first to bench 600 (272.2 kg) pounds. Jim Williams was the first powerlifter to bench more than 600 pounds in competition; he benched 675 pounds (306.2 kg) in 1972 without a bench shirt. Bill Kazmaier benched 661 pounds (299.8 kg) in 1981, and Sam Samaniego benched 655 pounds (297.1 kg) in 1988. The next step was the exclusive 700-pound (317.5 kg) club. It was reported that Jim Williams did 700 pounds, but it has never been confirmed. The man who set the bench press standard was Ted Arcidi, who was the first powerlifter to officially bench more than 700 pounds in 1985. He benched 705 pounds (319.8 kg.) Many powerlifters in the 181-pound (82.1 kg) and up weight class, powerlifters such as Mike Bridges, Larry Pacifico, and Mike McDonald (who was hailed as the king of the bench press after he set records in several weight classes), were benching more than 500 pounds (226.8 kg).

When the bench shirt first came out, many lifters avoided it. They did not want to deal with the hassle of putting on a shirt. Their answer was to use a tight T-shirt. The one key ingredient missing was the material (cotton versus polyester). Lifters got smart and started using the bench shirt. As lifters had success while wearing the bench shirt and bench records were falling, manufacturers of bench shirts improved the quality of the shirts and designed them differently.

The purpose of the bench shirt is to help keep everything tight and support the bench press throughout the full range of movement, help start the initial drive off the chest, and protect your shoulders whether or not they are already injured.

Today's bench shirts are much more advanced than the early ones. Learn to make the shirt work with you to your advantage and your bench press will increase in poundage. Some lifters can get more than 200 pounds (90.7 kg) out of their bench shirts.

At almost every big powerlifting meet, you will see a lifter open up with or attempt a personal, state, meet, or world record. Even at local powerlifting meets, you will see the majority of lifters opening with some type of record.

For the beginner powerlifter, the goal is to find the shirt he is the most comfortable in and that is allowed by the organization running the meet. Not all bench shirts are the same. There are single-ply shirts with 90-degree sleeve angles, shirts with a stretch back that allows you to arch, shirts that are thicker with necks cut high or low. Some bench shirts are double- or triple-ply to give the lifter even more power to drive the weight off the chest. Then there are denim shirts with hook-and-loop closures, and some with open backs.

Regardless of which bench shirt you use, once you learn the technique in a single-ply you will put 30 pounds (13.6 kg) or more on your bench. If you use a bench shirt that is double-ply or made from another material, your bench press number is unlimited in how much you gain.

Deadlift Suit

The deadlift suit is designed to keep the body tight, increase pulling power at the initial start of the pull, keep the back erect, and provide power to help straighten the legs during the lift. The deadlift will test your grip and overall strength. In the deadlift, you either have it or you don't. Lamar Gant had it; pound for pound he was the greatest deadlifter of all-time having pulled 639 pounds (289.8 kg) at 123 pounds (55.8 kg) of body weight and 683 pounds (309.8 kg) at 132 pounds (59.8 kg) of body weight. Up until the millennium, only three powerlifters had deadlifted more than 900 pounds (408.2 kg): Ed Coan lifted 901 pounds (408.6 kg) at 220 pounds (99.7 kg) of body weight, Doyle Kenady lifted 903 pounds (409.5 kg), and Gary Heisey lifted 925 pounds (419.6 kg), which at the time was the most weight deadlifted ever. Gary's deadlift was the highest until Andy Bolton of the UK deadlifted 1,003 pounds (457.5 kg) recently.

In the past, squat suits often doubled as deadlift suits. Today manufacturers have designed a deadlift suit that can be tailored to fit your body and improve your deadlift whether you are a sumo or conventional deadlifter. Because deadlift suits are tailor made, they give you more explosion from the initial pull and a stronger lockout at the top. The increased seams in the crotch and hips make lifters feel tighter and more powerful. You are able to get your straps loose, tight, or with hook-and-loop closures to adjust the fit to your liking. There are suits on the market for lifters who use a lot of back during the deadlift. Today powerlifters can deadlift 1,000 pounds (453.6 kg) or more. The right deadlift suit is sure to add weight to your deadlift.

Powerlifting Belt

The belt has improved from the leather belt of the past that had a wide back and was small in the front. Today's improved power belts come in suede on both sides or just one side, come with one or two prongs for a quicker fit, or have a lever belt that just snaps on. They are legal in all federations.

The power belt is designed to protect the back during heavy squats and deadlifts and to give the abdomen something to push against. Beginners should use one-prong or lever belts as these are the easiest and quickest to put on.

Knee Wraps

The purpose of knee wraps is to give the lifter the greatest rebound, explosive start, more power, and more protection when coming out of the bottom of the squat with heavy weight. Past knee wraps were very thin, did not stretch well, and wore out quickly. New, advanced knee wraps are more comfortable, stretch more, and hold together longer. They are thicker, which keeps the knees warm for more protection. Be sure to get the most out of your knee wraps.

There are several ways to wrap your knees. For beginners, start at the top or bottom of the knee and make a circular motion, wrapping the knee from top to bottom or bottom to top. If you want to get a little more aggressive, start with a wrap around the knee, then crisscross the wrap to make a figure 8. Finish with a circular wrap at the top of the knee. Wrap the knees as tight as possible to get the most out of them. Also know how high and low you can wrap them. Wraps that are too low will cause you to cramp in your calf.

Briefs

The purpose of briefs is to provide additional support in the hips and glutes in the squat and deadlift. Make sure the briefs fit you comfortably under your squat suit. This is the illusion of wearing a two-ply suit except you don't have to worry about the straps. When used correctly, briefs will add 50 pounds (22.6 kg) or more to the squat and provide support for locking out in the deadlift.

Wrist Wraps

Wrist wraps of the past were very thin or cut from old knee wraps and did not stretch well. New wrist wraps are a shorter version of knee wraps made of the same material. They are more comfortable, are thicker, stretch better, and hold together longer. They have a loop for the thumb that allows the lifter to wrap them as tightly as he wants. At the end of the wrist wrap a hook-and-loop closure helps to keep the wrap in place. The new wrist wraps help to stabilize the wrist during squats, bench presses, and deadlifts.

Squat Shoes

Lifting shoes have improved greatly from the past. No longer do lifters have to use their walk-around shoes for squatting. The squat shoe provides stabilization, support, comfort, angle, and drive. Shoes have rubberized bottoms and high tops. They provide room for the feet and have heels. You can lace them to your liking. Whatever shoes you decide to use, make sure it does not turn on its side if you are a wide stance squatter and the shoes fit you.

Deadlift Shoes

In the past, Lifters wore the same shoes for deadlifting they wore for squatting: tennis shoes with an elevated heel. Today lifters can choose what kind of shoes to wear when deadlifting. Today lifters are able to get a variety of shoes such as wrestling shoes, tennis shoes, and slippers. All shoes have rubber bottoms and no heel elevation. Most powerlifters choose one of these shoe types because they are lower to the floor, which cuts down the distance of the pull of the deadlift to lockout.

Summary

Regardless which organization or federation you decide to lift in, you want to make sure that you are aware of the rules and regulations and understand what pieces of equipment you can use for that organization.

CHAPTER 13

Meet Day

You have trained for months, put in hours of sweat equity, planned your training carefully, paid attention to nutrition, and perfected the use of your gear. Now it is time for the competition. What you do on meet day and the day before can make or break the performance.

Meet Checklist

It is good idea to have a simple meet checklist to make sure you have everything you need for the meet. There is no worse feeling than showing up on meet day and realizing that the shoes you used in every training session are still at the house. While most powerlifters are great people and will help you out, small changes like this can make a huge difference at the meet.

Make sure you have everything you need and backups, if possible. If a piece of equipment fails during an attempt, usually it is not possible to find a suitable replacement before the next attempt. Also, it is common to open up in a loose shirt on bench press and switch to a tighter one on successive attempts. If a lifter forgets the tight shirt, his attempts must be more conservative. If a lifter forgets the loose shirt, the opener will have to be far higher than he is accustomed to. Also, having several knee wraps is a good idea. Many competitors like to have their knee wraps rolled very tightly before they are put on. If a handler drops the wrap, it cannot be re-rolled tightly and thus will feel different on the knee. Having several pairs of knee wraps ensures that you have the knees wrapped the same way in spite of the malfunction.

Each lifter will have his own variations of what he wants, but table 13.1 on page 196 shows a basic checklist of what to bring to each meet.

TABLE 13.1 **Meet Checklist**

Item	How many?	Colors?
Squat suit		
Bench shirt		
Deadlift suit		
Squat shoes		
Deadlift shoes		
T-shirt		
Belt		
Knee wrap		
Wrist wrap		
Socks		
Chalk		
Baby powder		
Ammonia cap		
Membership card		

Pre-Meet Checklist

Before the meet, make sure your travel plans are in order. Find flight numbers and times or travel directions several days before the meet. Next, know if you have an early weigh-in and what time it is. Knowing this information ensures that you won't underestimate how long it will take to get to the site. If you plan to arrive after the early weigh-in, you may need to alter your diet plan for 1 day instead of 2 days. However if you arrive a day or two before the meet, find the meet scale and check your weight. If the meet scale shows you are two pounds or more heavier than your home scale, change your diet to make sure you make weight.

Next, locate a hotel near the meet. It is best to find one at the meet site to eliminate travel time, but also locate any in the area that may be more affordable. Read hotel reviews and make sure that the hotel is acceptable. If the hotel is only $19 per night but you can't sleep because the air conditioner doesn't work or the bed is uncomfortable, it will be detrimental to your lifting.

Also, check for local restaurants. It is best to eat at places you know. This is very easy with the high number of chain restaurants. Stay with familiar dishes. When compounded with the nerves of a meet, new dishes may upset your stomach. Diarrhea is not optimal for a prime meet day performance. No one wants to be sprinting from the squats on the platform to the bathroom in full gear. When in doubt, bring your own food in a cooler. Many lifters bring their own food because they know what their bodies like and are used to. Another option is to plan to buy food at a grocery store if you aren't sure about the restaurants near the meet.

Plan ahead where you will stay, where you will eat, and any attractions you want to see. Bring maps or print them from a website. You have enough to worry about when lifting; minimize other stressors such as how to get to the restaurant from the hotel. A GPS system it is a great way to eliminate the need for finding maps. Just make sure the GPS is up to date.

Handler

A handler is someone you have trained with who knows how you like your equipment and how to get it there. Also, he is familiar enough with your lifting to help select attempts and get you up for each attempt. The lifter's job on meet day is to lift, not to worry about anything else. The handler's job on meet day is the anything else. The handler keeps track of wraps, belts, flight information, and what it will take to break a record or win the meet. The handler's job is much more stressful than the lifter's job, but a good handler will help to make a champion.

The handler should expect to be just as tired, if not more tired, than the lifter. The handler will be loading the weights, wrapping the knees, pulling up straps, tightening belts, putting on bench shirts, setting bench shirts for attempts, setting bench belts, pulling up straps on deadlift suits, applying powder, providing emotional support between each lift, watching for technique, giving up calls, and trying to remain a good friend to the stressed-out lifter. The handler helps psych you up before each attempt by feeding you positive reinforcement. He knows what buttons to push to get you fired up, including slapping the face, back, and head.

Backup Gear

The worst thing that can happen to a lifter on meet day is for a shirt or suit to blow out. It is inevitable though, if you compete long enough, to have this happen to you. It is not advisable to buy a new shirt or suit from a vendor or even to borrow gear from another competitor. Each piece of gear has its own unique groove, and if you're not used to it, you could possibly get hurt if you throw it on for your next attempt. The best thing to do is keep some of your old equipment over the course of your career. You already have trained in it and know its groove. Never completely wear out a shirt or suit. This way, if you have one or two extra, you never have to worry about it when you have a blowout.

Over the course of your training cycle, every few weeks take a repetition or two in the old shirt, just to keep the feel of it. Also, if you change gear, it's always good to keep some of the old stuff in case you end up not liking the new.

Some people will bring all of their backups just in case their normal equipment doesn't fit right on meet day. Some people who cut weight and rehydrate notice that their weight doesn't distribute back to where it normally does. Because of this, they bring in all of the gear they have so they can change into something that fits better. Nothing is worse than bombing because your shirt got too tight. The backup gear also gives you the added security of not having to worry if anything happens.

Gear Organization

Over the course of a full meet, a lot of gear is used—different shoes for each lift, wraps for each lift, shoes, slippers, chalk, and powder. This can get very jumbled in a gym bag, leading you to not see gear in the bag or spend extra time digging. A good idea is to separate the gear for each lift into separate small bags and then place the small bags into a larger duffle bag. Place gear used for multiple lifts in the bigger bag. This way, you grab your bag for bench or squat and don't have to worry about digging for anything.

Keep chalk in a plastic container that seals well so it does not get all over the bag. Keep powder inside a zip-top bag. You don't want to get powder all over your gear because something heavy got placed on the bag and it forced open the powder container.

Inside the pockets of the bag, place membership cards, ammonia caps, nose tork, and so on. Important things you need to find quickly will be in the pockets. It also is a good idea to keep some small bills in the pocket so you can buy a sports drink if you run out.

Warm-Up on Meet Day

Start by doing the light stretching you do on any normal workout day. If a muscle feels tight, stretch it. There is no sense in altering form with tight muscles that you could simply stretch.

Next, get the blood pumping but not with a vigorous workout. Try some lunges, body-weight squats, or lying trunk twists. Simply move blood through the body and loosen the joints. When you step up to the bar for the first actual warm-up set, minor aches and pains should have worked themselves out. Restrictive gear is hard on the muscles, and increasing the core temperature of the muscles is key in preventing muscular injury.

Finally, approach the warm-up for the lift itself. Start warming up in the previous flight. For instance, a competitor who is lifting in the fourth flight should start warming up during the third. You do not want to rush your warm-up, but you also want to get it in. At large meets, everything runs quickly with no time between flights, so it is important to time your warm-up. To gain an idea of what the flight times will be for that given day, have a handler time a round of a flight and multiply that time by 3 to get a ballpark estimate of how long you have to warm up.

Squat Warm-Up

After the general warm up, the warm-up for the squat begins. Most people choose to start out going raw. When starting out raw, make sure that the maximal depth possible is achieved. Make sure to squat well below parallel to make sure the muscles will be able to achieve the depth when gear is put on.

Most people start out at 135 pounds (61 kg) and do 3 to 10 repetitions. The key with the warm-ups is to make sure that the nervous system is ready to handle the load, but the weight is still small enough not to fatigue the lifter. Remember, the weights that matter are those on the platform, not those in the warm-up room. A good guideline is to jump up by at least 40 pounds (18.14 kg) per set, but no more than 150 pounds (68 kg). This will ensure that the repetitions and weights are appropriate.

When starting out raw, add gear in gradually. Don't add in everything at one time, as the additional support will make heavier weights feel lighter, which will give the feeling of greater strength on the platform.

Table 13.2 shows some sample warm-ups for various opening weights.

Bench Press Warm-Up

After the squat, the shoulders often will be tight, and they must be loosened back up. An exercise such as arm circles or a dowel rod for flexibility work is good. Start by making big circles with the arms forward and backward. The posterior capsule stretch is also excellent to loosen the shoulders after the squat. To perform the posterior capsule stretch, lie on your right side with the right arm directly out in front of the body and bent at the elbow so the hand points toward the ceiling. Using the left hand, take the right hand down toward the floor until you feel a good stretch in the right shoulder. Hold for 30 seconds. Change sides.

TABLE 13.2   Sample Warm-Ups for Various Opening Weights for the Squat

Opening weight	Pounds and repetitions
400 pounds (181.4 kg)	135 × 5 185 × 3 225 × 1 (add suit, straps down) 275 × 1 (add knee wraps) 315 × 1 365 × 1 (optional, with full gear)
600 pounds (272 kg)	135 × 5 225 × 3 315 × 1 (add briefs) 365 × 1 (add suit bottom) 405 × 1 (add knee wraps) 455 × 1 495 × 1 (full gear)
800 pounds (362.8 kg)	135 × 5 225 × 5 315 × 3 (add briefs) 405 × 1 (add suit bottom) 495 × 1 545 × 1 (add knee wraps) 585 × 1 635 to 675 × 1 (full gear)

Also, back cramping often occurs on the bench press after squatting. It is a good idea to stretch out the back after squats to prevent the mid-repetition cramp that can cost the lift. An exercise such as the cat–camel stretch is great to loosen the back between the squat and the bench press. For the cat–camel, start on your hands and knees in crawling position. Carefully arch your back and hold for 3 to 5 seconds. Your back should resemble a camel's hump. Next, gently let your back sag and hold for 3 to 5 seconds. You will look like a cat. Repeat 5 to 7 times.

Although most federations prohibit the use of elbow sleeves in competition, they are good to use during the warm-up. The additional heat and support provided by the sleeves help ease tendinitis. Wear elbow sleeves only for the first few sets before putting on the shirt. Elbow sleeves slightly alter the groove, and since they can't be worn on the platform, you want the groove in the warm-up room to most closely resemble the groove on the platform.

After stretching, begin warming up for the competition. As with the squat warm-up, warm up for the bench press during the previous flight. Make sure you know how long previous flights are taking so you know how long you have to warm up. Table 13.3 shows a sample warm-up for various opening weights with a shirt.

Some people have a set way that they warm up in the gym every time. It is best to warm up like that. For instance, some people like to hit sets of 5 all the way up. Some people like to warm up in a loose shirt and then switch to a tighter one to open with. Stay with your normal routine. Comfort is key on meet day, and you want to have as few worries as possible. Keep a close eye on all of your gear as wrist wraps often look similar and may end up walking away. It is often a good idea to let your handler take care of the wraps.

Deadlift Warm-Up

As the last lift of the day, the deadlift is the one for which people feel most beat up. (That is why a foam rolling program shown in table 13.4 is beneficial.) Some people even like to take a short nap before they begin the warm-up.

Comfort is key on the deadlift. After the bench, a lot of people have low-back pain, glute pain, and hip pain from the stress of the other two lifts. Often the muscles are in spasm from the contraction and the dehydration. Before deadlifting, rehydrate with an electrolyte drink or mix. The electrolytes will prevent cramping. You can use drinks such as pickle juice and Gatorlytes, but these are often hard to obtain. Gatorade does a great job, as does Pedialyte, which is marketed for use in children with gastrointestinal issues and contains electrolytes.

Massage also can help relieve spasms. At some large meets, a masseuse is on hand to help loosen tight muscles. There is no greater tool of recovery between lifts than a masseuse. Your muscles will be pliable and be able to fire properly. However, not all meets include a masseuse, and often money is an issue. A less expensive solution is the foam roller, a self-massage tool that loosens the muscles. To use a foam roller, simply place it on the ground and roll it back and forth over the muscle. If you feel pain at any point, it means there is a knot or adhesion. The pain is caused by the knot or adhesion breaking apart. In many situations, pain will guide you away from the activity. In foam rolling, the opposite is true. If it hurts, keep doing it until it doesn't hurt anymore. One session will not fix long-standing adhesions, but will help make the muscle more pliable and ease joint pain.

TABLE 13.3 Sample Warm-Ups for Various Opening Weights for the Bench Press With Shirt

Opening weight	Pounds and repetitions	Opening weight	Pounds and repetitions
300 pounds (136 kg)	bar × 5 95 × 5 135 × 5 (add wrist wraps) 185 × 3 225 × 1 (add shirt) 250 × 1	600 pounds (272.4 kg)	bar × 10 to 15 135 × 5 185 × 3 225 × 3 275 × 1 315 × 1 (add wrist wraps) 365 × 1 405 × 1 (add shirt) 455 × 1 495 × 1
400 pounds (181.4 kg)	bar × 10 to 15 135 × 5 185 × 3 225 × 3 275 × 1 (add wrist wraps) 315 × 1 (add shirt) 350 to 365 × 1	700 pounds (317.8 kg)	bar × 10 to 15 135 × 5 185 × 3 225 × 3 275 × 3 315 × 1 365 × 1 (add wrist wraps) 405 × 1 455 × 1 (add shirt) 495 × 1 545 × 1 600 × 1 650 × 1
500 pounds (226.7 kg)	bar × 10 to 15 135 × 5 185 × 3 225 × 3 275 × 1 315 × 1 (add wrist wraps) 365 × 1 405 × 1 (add shirt) 455 × 1		

TABLE 13.4 Foam Rolling Program

	Exercise	Repetitions
1	Foam hamstring	10
2	Foam quad	10
3	Foam glute	10
4	Foam back	10
5	Foam thoracic	10
6	Foam lat	10
7	Foam calf	10
8	Foam IT band	10

Usually joint pain is a sign of something going on at a different point in the muscle and not necessarily in the joint. For instance, pain in the knees and back typically is due to the iliotibial (IT) bands, hip flexors, or hamstrings. Pain in the shoulders is due to the pecs or lats. After rolling out the appropriate muscles, the joint pain often disappears. This will help you get through the meet and let you know what needs to be worked out before the next competition.

Table 13.4 shows a comprehensive foam-rolling program. If you use this program before the meet and work on it consistently, you may be able to prevent issues with spasm and cramping on meet day.

Attempt Selection

There is a theory for attempt selection and how it varies. One theory is for big meets and one is for small meets. Big meets are regional championships, national championships, and world championships. Smaller meets are small local meets.

Opener Selection

For a beginning lifter, the simplest way to determine what the opener should be is to use the heaviest weight you can lift for a solid triple. On meet day, you will face many factors that you can never account for in training, such as the judging and the crowd. Often the first-time competition experiences a rude awakening in factors such as what real squat depth is or how long a pause is at a meet. Often training doesn't account for the fatigue you will experience on meet day for the bench press and the deadlift. In training, usually you have a squat day, a bench day, and a deadlift day, not all three lifts on one day. This is why, for the meet, you want to open with what you can triple on each lift. This way you can be sure to overcome whatever technical difficulties or problems you may have with your lifting or the judging. Set yourself up for success and not failure. In subsequent lifts, you can play around with making larger jumps but make them realistic. Increasing by 100 pounds (45.35 kg) between attempts is all right for the advanced lifter, but for the beginner, make it more reasonable. After all, if it is your first meet, anything you come away with will be a personal record.

Most advanced lifters already have their openers set. They open with the same weight every meet. You should open up heavy enough to have good technique but still light enough that so you experience no anxiety or question yourself. In geared training, if the bar has insufficient weight to achieve depth on the squat or touch the chest on the bench, a competitor will force it to happen. This occurs when the lifter changes body angles and leverages. Some lifters cave in the knees or round the back to create slack in the gear to be able to hit depth, or some round the shoulders. On the bench, some people drop the bar further toward the belly than optimal or round the shoulders to create more slack in the shirt. While this may make it possible to achieve legal depth or to touch, it creates an unsafe environment for the body when it is under strain, and thus it greatly increases the incidence of injury. So, you should have enough weight on the bar to be able to achieve the lift with good form. You also should have no doubts going in to your opener that you will get it. If you need to open with a personal record or higher weight to be able to achieve form, it may be time to get bigger gear. Some people open up in a loose shirt and switch to the tight one. This allows the opener to still be light enough for them to not cause anxiety about the lift. Then, once they are already in the meet, they switch to tighter gear and make a large jump to be able to achieve proper depth. In powerlifting, it isn't necessarily the strongest lifter who wins the meet; it's the smartest lifter, the one who understands and knows how to use his gear.

Big Meets

At big meets, no one cares about your personal records. They ask you how you did, and you want to have placed as highly as possible. To do this, go for the biggest possible total, and the biggest possible total comes with weights that were properly selected that allow you to go 9 for 9. Remember, what you miss does not count toward your total. When you are conservative with your attempts, you ensure that the most possible weight will go to total. For instance, if a lifter jumps from 600 to 650 but and 650 was 10 pounds too heavy, then only 600 will go to his total. However, if he goes 600, 625, and 640 and makes all three, he will have 40 pounds to put toward his total. What you miss isn't noted in the record books; only what you made is recorded. Meets are a game of chess, not checkers. Put a great consideration into your attempts.

The next thing to do is know what your competitors' strengths and weaknesses are. Are they huge squatters but poor benchers and deadlifters? Are they poor squatters and benchers but have a sick deadlift? When you know their strengths and weaknesses and compare them to yours, you can most effectively select your attempts and force the ball into their court. Know their personal records and how often they have achieved these lifts. If someone has pulled a 700-pound deadlift 15 times in his career, you can bet he will pull a 700-pound deadlift that day. However, if someone pulled 700 pounds once 3 years ago but hasn't gone over 675 since then, you know he is more likely to be around 675. You cannot control everything in your competition. You can control your attempts and how they go. You cannot control your competitor, but you can do your best to make him sweat. Select your attempts conservatively so that you can get everything you can and make the competitor worry. Most of the time, if you are conservative and build up the highest subtotal possible, you can force your competitor's hand and may cause some anxiety, which may cause him to miss a lift.

Another idea is to have your handler track your competitors' lifts on meet day. If you know their tendencies and where they are now, you will have a good idea what they need to pull to beat you or for you to beat them, depending on who is ahead at subtotal. Being conservative will help you gather the greatest possible subtotal. You simply can pull what it takes to win, which will hopefully be below your personal record.

Small Meets

The small meets are the meets you attend to set personal records. Plainly and simply, this is where you should perform the biggest lifts. This is the time and place to try different attempt selections for huge personal records. Go to the big meets to win because no one cares how you lifted, they only want to know where you placed. Go to the small meets to lift big because there is less competition and if you botch something, it's not a big deal. Small meets are where you often find out the most about your technique and equipment because you can afford to take the time to play around with it. The small meets are where you hone your strategies for the larger meets.

Small meets are also the best meets to compete in when a rule change occurs. For instance, in 2009 the United States Powerlifting Federation (USPF) changed where the bar can land on the chest in the bench press. For many competitors, the national championships was the first time they competed with this new rule (possibly the national meet was the first meet at which the rule was implemented), and they were unable to get a bench in because of the rule change. However, if they had been able to compete in a smaller meet to try out the new rule, the results of the national championships may have been very different.

Single or Multiple Federations

The debate continues about what is the right thing to do as far as competition with multiple federations. Essentially the debate boils down to this: Do you compete in all of the meets, or are you as true to a federation as to your spouse?

When people do whatever is available, often it is because they have a limited schedule and limited funds. Whatever federation is putting on a meet within a few-hours' drive and is scheduled for an available day, that is the meet you do. You enjoy competing and don't get very many chances, so you take advantage of every opportunity. It is OK with you that the rules are slightly different; you just want to be on the platform. Besides, when competing with different federations, you get to find out which one you like the best and who lifts at what meets.

The other argument is for the people to be loyal to a federation. Lifters love everything about the federation, are comfortable with the rules, and want to support the federation. They try to bring all their friends to it and would never consider giving money to any other federation. Why would they want to do a meet in another setting? This place is perfect and they want to help it move up to the next level.

It seems that both groups are passionate about why they choose to do the meets that they do. Sometimes mud-slinging occurs when they don't stop to look at each other's side. Maybe someone really likes a certain federation, but that federation is never around during a slow time at work, so the lifter has to do a different meet. The point is, each person does what they do for a reason. If you love a certain federation and have the time and money to travel to its meets and do its meets exclusively, that is outstanding; continue to be exclusive with their meets. If you don't have the time to travel, then by all means do whatever is in your area. Many meet directors talk about how loyalty to the federation is needed, and this is true for them to keep doing what they do. However, if you can't do their meets, you shouldn't stop competing because of your loyalty.

Cramping

Typically cramping results from overly tight muscles, dehydration, or lack of electrolytes. Each of these phenomena is easy to take care of.

For overly tight muscles, static stretching, active isolated stretching, and foam rolling does the trick. Static stretching is more traditional stretching in which you get into a position and hold it. In active isolated stretching, you go through a

Bill Clark, Founding Father of Powerlifting

Every year in mid July in sleepy Columbia, Missouri, a push–pull meet is put on as a part of the annual Show-Me State Games, a statewide sporting competition encompassing every sport imaginable. The meet is held in a junior high school multipurpose room. To start the meet, a gray-headed gentleman of at least 70 years hobbles to the door. The man walks as if every joint has been replaced, which is nearly true, but still with the power and bulk of a man that you know you don't want to mess with. His growl of a voice and his demeanor reinforce that this is not a man to be messed with. The rules meeting starts the same way every year: "I don't care what federation you've lifted in and what their rules are. This is the way you're doing it today, and if you do it this way, you won't have any problems."

Some people are offended or turned off by this. They think, "Well, who is this guy and why is he telling me what to do? I've been competing in this sport for 5 years now." This man is Bill Clark, and he is the last remaining member of the committee that started the sport of powerlifting.

During an interview at a truck stop cafe, Mr. Clark shared the origins of powerlifting and his involvement in it. Mr. Clark talked for several hours, discussing powerlifting, Olympic weightlifting, running, birding, and living life in general.

In the beginning, there was Olympic weightlifting. It was the strength sport sponsored and regulated by the Amateur Athletic Union (AAU), which before 1981 was in charge of virtually every sport. Olympic weightlifting had more than 10,000 participants in various levels of local to international competitors in the United States. Then in 1960, another strength sport popped up. Back then, everyone who trained for Olympic weightlifting performed squats and deadlifts to supplement their training. Because competitors are competitors, people were coming together to have unsanctioned meets centered around these two exercises to find out who could lift the most. Initially the squat and deadlift were joined with the jerk from the rack and often strict curls. (Although the first three exercises were directly related to improving the Olympic lifts, the last was included mostly because everyone loves to do curls. Times haven't changed much.) Bill remembered, "The Olympic lifters didn't ever do bench press much because they didn't want to get tight in the shoulders. Everyone else was doing it though, so the bench press found its way into odd-lift meets pretty quickly." Once odd-lift meets became standardized, they included the bench, squat, deadlift, jerk from the rack, and the competition lifts. Shortly they changed from the jerk from the rack to the curl.

In 1963, Clark and some of the other revolutionaries decided to approach the AAU to petition for subcommittee status. In the eyes of the AAU, this would make powerlifting an offshoot of Olympic lifting. The AAU would sanction championships and validate records. The Olympic weightlifting committee emphatically said no. Some harsh words were exchanged but the vote stayed no. In 1963 the first national meet for powerlifting was held, although it was not sanctioned. It was called a national tournament rather than championship since it could not be defined as a championship due to the AAU's overreaching governance. Remember, at this time the AAU controlled everything in every sport in the United States.

(continued)

The national tournament for powerlifting was held in Bill Clark's home town of Columbia, Missouri.

In 1964, there was a second attempt made to make powerlifting a sanctioned sport. This time, however, the differences of opinion were within the Olympic lifting community. Many people have heard of the legendary York Barbell in York, Pennsylvania, run by Bob Hoffmann. York Barbell was a mecca for all things strength, from newsletters to supplements to equipment to Olympic weightlifting. Bob Hoffmann was the most respected and revered man in Olympic lifting at this time, and Bill Clark got to be friends with Mr. Hoffmann while running his teenage and junior Olympic lifting national championships. This friendship blossomed as a result of Clark's assistance in running both of these meets. When Clark proposed the vote, this time it narrowly passed, and the sport was approved under AAU national chairman Dave Mattland. To coronate this new sport, a national championship was set. Only two locations were up for vote: York, Pennsylvania and Columbia, Missouri. York got the go-ahead to host the national championship at York Barbell by one vote.

Clark's influence has affected more than just the inception of the sport. Clark did quite a bit of work with the prison system and its weightlifting community. In 1962 at Leavenworth Penitentiary in Leavenworth, Kansas, Clark started Olympic weightlifting competitions for the prisoners. In 1964 or '65, Clark expanded the competition to include powerlifting as well. There were many strong lifters in prison. Although many people were concerned that weightlifting in prisons produced bigger, stronger criminals, Clark thought that it taught the prisoners discipline and gave them something to look forward to each day. It burned the nervous energy they once used to get into trouble and actually lead to more peaceful prisoners. Clark said that the guards often told him that they loved when he and his guys came in and did a meet with the prisoners. A prisoner would get beaten and then want to train so hard. He became so focused on that goal of outlifting his opponent that he would transfer that discipline elsewhere in his life. Clark had several prison lifters change their lives around through lifting; they went on to be very productive, law-abiding citizens. Clark started the Prison Postal National Championships. Obviously a prisoner could not travel to compete in a meet outside the walls of his own prison. To compensate for this, over the course of a 2-week period, each prison would have its own meet, with judges brought in to watch the lifters. The results of each meet would be sent in to Clark from all over the country and as soon as the results were in, they were compiled and ranked, and champions were named accordingly. This grew to have more than 50 prisons involved in the Prison National Postal Championships.

Clark also was instrumental in creating women's powerlifting and had the first All Women's meet in 1976. It required some creative wording on his part to get the AAU to approve it, and after it was over and people realized what was done, some were very upset. This meet actually was the first for the legendary Judy Glenn, beginning her path to being an influential woman in the sport of powerlifting as a lifter and individual in general.

Clark's journey into powerlifting was a very winding road. It started in 1951 when he entered the Army and saw what some people were doing in the weight room. In 1953, he was sent to Korea, but got sidetracked in Japan. In Korea and Japan, he saw small people lifting amazingly large weights and was completely enthralled. However, because he lacked consistent access to weights at the time, he put his interests on the back burner.

In 1958, after he returned to the United States, Clark started a boxing club for the troubled youth of Columbia. After the end of boxing season in 1959, Clark's disciples decided they wanted to have something to do in the offseason and thought lifting weights would be a good idea. By happenstance, Clark ran into Don Wickle in Fulton, Missouri. Don was the 1940 state champion for Olympic weightlifting in his age bracket and happened to have an old weight set in his house. Clark's boxers became offseason weightlifters. Clark's weightlifters grew extremely strong under his guidance and thought they were strong enough to enter a weightlifting meet. There were none in the state of Missouri, so Clark contacted the state chairman, Dr. Joseph Van Nuye, to host it. This could have been disastrous as Clark had never even seen a meet, let alone run one. Fortunately, one of the entries happened to be a former national champion whose coach stepped up and took the lead at the meet and taught them how to run a meet on the fly.

Clark is definitely a purist, as would be expected of someone who had a hand in developing every rule of the sport. He cares nothing for shirts, belts, wraps, high squats, short pauses, or any other deviation from the letter and spirit of the original. Clark's involvement in all strength sports has been reduced to what goes on in his Clark's Gym, be it daily workouts or the occasional odd-lift meet, and the powerlifting portion of the Show-Me State Games.

Clark has seen it all and done it all, from baseball scouting in every country in North America to powerlifting and masters weightlifting to founding the Heart of America Marathon, considered the second toughest marathon in the United States. He is a man to be respected and revered by any athlete or fan for his contributions to many sports. It has been an honor getting to know the man whose contributions have so greatly influenced the sport.

range of motion, hold the stretch for 1 or 2 seconds at the maximum range of motion, and then go through the range of motion again. Active isolated stretching is detailed in the books *Active Isolated Stretching: The Mattes Method* (Aaron L. Mattes, 2000) and *The Whartons' Stretch Book* (Jim Wharton and Phil Wharton, 1996). These books go into how to stretch each muscle by changing the exercise and joint angle. The claim of active isolated stretching is that it increases the range of motion of the exercise without reducing the power producing capability of the muscle. Essentially, you are getting the benefit of stretching without the detrimental side effect of a decreased production of power.

The foam roller, covered earlier in the section on warming up for the deadlift, is a long, cylindrical piece of foam that is very dense. Foam rollers are available at most exercise and fitness stores and online. To use the foam roller, place it on the floor and roll back and forth across it until you find the hot spots as indicated by pain. When the hot spot is worked out, the muscle typically becomes much looser.

Dehydration and lack of electrolytes are related. When you are dehydrated, it is best to drink plain water. Water absorbs quickly and doesn't have the sugar in sports drinks. A good way to know how dehydrated you are is to weigh yourself. However much weight (in pounds) you are down from normal, you should multiply that number by 24 and drink that many ounces of water. For example, if a lifter is down 3 pounds, he should drink 72 ounces of water (3 × 24 = 72). This will ensure hydration. Remember to use the color of urine as a guide.

Electrolytes are salts in the body that are lost through sweat. If someone is a salty sweater, these salts may need to be replaced during the meet. You know if you're a salty sweater when you wear a black T-shirt that turns white when you exercise. For the salty sweater, Gatorade is an option. However, it may not be enough to prevent cramping. Electrolyte mixes and salt tablets are available in pharmacies. For some people, this much salt upsets their stomachs. Another recommendation is Pedialyte, a drink used to rehydrate children after illness. It tastes pretty good and has a high level of electrolytes. Other options are Gator-lytes and pickle juice if you can find them. Both of these beverages are excellent sources for getting in electrolytes.

Meet-Day Nutrition

On meet day, do not eat anything you haven't eaten before. That's not to say that you can't have a hamburger from a restaurant that is not your usual restaurant; it means you shouldn't eat the onion jalapeno burn-your-face-off burger when you usually don't eat spicy food. Beyond that, you may want to restrict your fiber intake for the day and stay with primarily liquid foods. The last thing you need on meet day is to have to take your suit off to defecate. Protein shakes and Gatorade do not affect the stomach adversely, provided you can usually take those in.

It's a good idea to bring a cooler with you that has Gatorade, sandwich meat, bread, and other small food items. It's not a good idea to bring things such as milk or condiments that could spoil.

Also, be sure to eat small meals. For digestion, blood is required in the stomach area. When you are doing physical activity, it is pulled away from the stomach. Any food is left sitting there and won't digest. When the body starts to work at maximum capacity, such as during lift attempts, the body attempts to rid itself of the food in the stomach. Either nausea or vomiting occurs. Neither are good for the lifter. Vomiting on the platform delays the meet and would probably earn you quite a nickname for awhile.

If you have a food allergy, it is crucial that you bring all of your own food for meet day. The risk of cross-contamination combined with the adrenaline pumping from the competition can spell dire consequences.

Meet-Day Mentality

On meet day, no matter how nervous you are, always be approachable. You want to put off a confident air about yourself but not be aloof. You should *be* very confident in yourself. You have trained for this meet for several weeks. You have poured your heart out into making sure that you were perfect in your form. You have done everything you could in your nutrition to make sure you were ready to go. You have planned all of your openers and subsequent attempts perfectly. You have mastered your gear. You know your strengths and weaknesses. You know what you will do in any situation. You have already visualized yourself at this meet and been successful numerous times. You are not doing this meet for the first time, you are doing it for the ten thousandth time. You are confident because you could not walk into a meet more prepared.

Always approach the platform knowing that you are going to successfully perform the lift. As the old saying goes, *Whether you think you can or you can't, you're right.* This statement can never be more true than it is in powerlifting. If a lifter approaches the platform with a bit of doubt in his mind about his ability to lift the weight, the lift is condemned from the start. If the lifter approaches the lift knowing that he owns it, he will achieve the lift. A successful powerlifter must have a great combination of swagger and humility. Men who have been around the sport for decades and excelled have shown this. Look at Mike Bridges, Bill Gillespie, Dan Austin, and Louie Simmons. They have great swagger about them and in their weightlifting techniques. However, you never hear them boast of their own lifting ability. They sit down with anyone to talk for hours about training and give advice. Several people have been afraid to approach Louie Simmons because of the Westside Barbell aura, what he has done and advocated. But everyone who has approached Louie has walked away amazed at how open he was about training, how he invited them to come to the gym sometime and spent two hours talking to them.

Making Weight

Making weight is one of the most important things for meet day or the days leading up to the meet. There are several methods listed here, and all of them involve getting rid of water.

The way most athletes try to lose weight is with nutrition. This method has the least impact on strength on meet day. It is very gradual and requires no extra work so it won't cause fatigue on meet day. Some athletes choose to go on a low-carbohydrate diet for several days to a couple of weeks before the meet. Carbohydrates hold onto water in a 1 gram to 3 gram ratio, as opposed to protein and fat, which hold on to water in a 1 gram to 1 gram ratio. The elimination of carbohydrates means a decrease in body weight due to water. A small amount of lipolysis (fat burning) may occur, but the majority of the weight is water weight.

Some athletes like to restrict sodium to lose several pounds. Salt is part of an osmotic gradient, which is part of the body's natural process. Biology teaches that water will cross a barrier from higher concentrations to lower concentrations of salt. If you decrease the amount of salt in the body, more water will leave the body because it is not being held there by an osmotic gradient. The more water that leaves the body, the lighter the athlete will be on the scale.

Many lifters use saunas or heat suits to sweat out weight. They sit in the sauna and lose 5 to 10 percent of their body weight immediately before weigh-in. This method can be dangerous because an increased core temperature mixed with a decrease of fluid has been linked to many health issues. If you need to lose 1 to 2 pounds (0.45-0.9 kg), this may be very effective for making weight. However, if you are trying to lose 10 to 15 pounds (4.5-6.8 kg), it will adversely affect strength and overall health.

Other methods to making weight exist, but these are the most common. All of the methods eliminate water and electrolytes from the body, both of which must be replaced. After weighing in, it is extremely important to rehydrate properly. Gatorade is an excellent means to rehydrate after making weight. It has the electrolytes and glucose that make the water hold into the muscle cell. If you try to rehydrate from a water weight loss with water alone, the body may not hold on to as much because there is no glucose to hold the water or sodium to restore the osmotic balance. After the weigh-in, most people like to drink a gallon of Gatorade. The use of nonsteroidal anti-inflammatory medications such as ibuprofen have anecdotally shown to have a positive benefit on rehydration as they cause the body to hold water as well. After they drink the Gatorade, they eat. If the body doesn't have enough water, it will not digest the food properly. From dinner on in, it is a race to get as much food and liquid back into the body as possible.

Another means that people use to rehydrate is the use of intravenous (IV) fluids. This is obviously difficult to do; one needs to obtain the IV and someone to be able to administer it. Some have tried this without someone who knows how to administer the IV and they have experienced dismal results of collapsed veins and inability to lift at the meet.

On meet day, the best results are achieved by people who come in and lift what they weigh. Those who pay attention to their weight year-round do not have to experience drastic weight loss and regain. Often people who drastically reduce and regain weight for weigh-in have issues with their equipment not fitting properly, and they say they got their weight back, but it's not in the right places. This change in fit causes gear problems and has been the cause of numerous bomb-outs. Sometimes people overshoot their body weight and end up walking into the meet looking bloated. With such a drastic weight regain, the gear cannot fit correctly, and if the lifter doesn't have backup equipment for this weight, often he can't get a lift in.

Those who come in and lift what they weigh know how their gear will fit and they can lift what they have planned. Those who have cut and regained the weight have one other issue to fight. All stress affects the body in the same manner, so weight loss and regain is another stress to act on the body in addition to the stress of the meet.

Summary

Most lifters do a great job of planning their training. However, some falter on meet day. Many falters occur for lack of planning for the actual meet itself. Many lifters forget something as important as a belt or squat suit. Some may get to the competition without a suitable place to stay or eat. Some may get to the competition without their supplements. Some may even get to the meet way over or under weight for lack of planning or consideration to their body weight. Any of these things can be detrimental come meet day. Lt. Colonel James Palmer Mann was a logistics officer in the U.S. Army. He gave many lectures and most of them revolved around his six Ps. Here is an adapted version of his six Ps statement:

Proper planning prevents pathetically poor performance.

Be sure to properly plan out your meet day with various checklists and prior thought. Make lifting, not trying to find suitable food or ibuprofen, the most important thing on meet day.

About the Authors

Dan Austin is the assistant head strength coach at the University of South Carolina. He has been at the university since 2003, working with the football and men's soccer teams. Before joining South Carolina, he was the head strength coach at Oklahoma State University, Mississippi State University, UNLV, Tennessee State University, and Austin Peay State University. While at Oklahoma State, he was voted the Big 12 Conference's Strength and Conditioning Coach of the Year.

A native of Greenville, South Carolina, Austin earned his bachelor's degree in health physical education from Newberry College and a master's degree from Austin Peay State University. He has been a strength and conditioning coach for more than 20 years.

Austin is certified by USA Weightlifting, the International Sport Sciences Association, the National Association of Speed and Explosion, and the Collegiate Strength and Conditioning Coaches Association. He is also a level II specialist in sport conditioning. He is a masters collegiate strength and conditioning coach, which is the highest certification a strength coach can achieve.

Austin has been powerlifting for 30 years and was voted into the Powerlifting Hall of Fame in 2011. Throughout his career he has won 9 world powerlifting championships and 15 national championships while holding several world records in the deadlift and combined total weight. He was voted the greatest 148-pound powerlifter of all time and was the first lifter under 148 pounds to deadlift over 700 pounds.

Bryan Mann has been involved in the sport of powerlifting since 1996. Since then, he has set numerous records as a high school, teen, and junior athlete. Throughout high school and college, Mann was a four-time national and two-time world champion in powerlifting for the Natural Athlete Strength Association and was considered among the top 20 athletes in the world for his age.

As an assistant director of strength and conditioning at the University of Missouri, Mann is responsible for assisting with the player development program for football and baseball as well as for Missouri's women's basketball and soccer teams. In addition to these team duties, he is the director of research and development. While at Southwest Missouri State, Mann worked with great athletes such as Philadelphia Phillies first baseman and league MVP Ryan Howard, Texas Rangers pitcher John Rheinecker, Toronto Blue Jays pitcher Shaun Marcum, and NCAA basketball's all-time scoring leader Jackie Stiles.

Mann received his degree in health promotion from Missouri State University in 2003, a graduate certificate in sports management in 2004, a master's degree in health education and promotion in 2006, and his PhD in 2011. Mann is recognized as a certified strength and conditioning specialist (CSCS) through the National Strength and Conditioning Association (NSCA) and is certified as a strength and conditioning coach (SCCC) from the Collegiate Strength and Conditioning Coaches Association.